# The 1812 *Doctrine of Right* and Other Late Political Writings of J. G. Fichte

SUNY series in Contemporary Continental Philosophy

*Dennis J. Schmidt, editor*

# The 1812 *Doctrine of Right* and Other Late Political Writings of J. G. Fichte

Edited by Jeffrey Church and Benjamin Hofmann

**SUNY PRESS**

Published by State University of New York Press, Albany
© 2026 State University of New York
All rights reserved
Printed in the United States of America

No part of this book may be used or reproduced in any manner whatsoever without written permission. No part of this book may be stored in a retrieval system or transmitted in any form or by any means including electronic, electrostatic, magnetic tape, mechanical, photocopying, recording, or otherwise without the prior permission in writing of the publisher.

Links to third-party websites are provided as a convenience and for informational purposes only. They do not constitute an endorsement or an approval of any of the products, services, or opinions of the organization, companies, or individuals. SUNY Press bears no responsibility for the accuracy, legality, or content of a URL, the external website, or for that of subsequent websites.

EU GPSR Authorised Representative:
Logos Europe, 9 rue Nicolas Poussin, 17000, La Rochelle, France
contact@logoseurope.eu

For information, contact State University of New York Press, Albany, NY
www.sunypress.edu

Library of Congress Cataloging-in-Publication Data

Names: Church, Jeffrey, editor. | Hofmann, Benjamin, editor.
Title: The 1812 Doctrine of Right and other late political writings of J. G. Fichte / Jeffrey Church and Benjamin Hofmann, editors.
Description: Albany : State University of New York Press, [2026]. | Includes bibliographical references and index.
Identifiers: ISBN 9798855805444 (hardcover : alk. paper) | ISBN 9798855806991(epub) | ISBN 9798855805468 (PDF)

# Contents

Introduction
    *Jeffrey Church and Benjamin Hofmann*    *1*

1. The Application of Eloquence to the Present War (1806)
    *Translated by Anne C. Reitz*    *15*

2. Patriotism and Its Opposite: Patriotic Dialogues (1806–1807)
    *Translated by Anne C. Reitz*    *19*

3. The Republic of the Germans (1807)
    *Translated by Benjamin Hofmann*    *55*

4. Lectures on the Vocation of the Scholar (1811)
    *Translated by Anne C. Reitz*    *89*

5. The Doctrine of Right (1812)
    *Translated by Jeffrey Church and Benjamin Hofmann*    *129*

*Glossary*    *225*
*Index*    *229*

# Introduction

*Jeffrey Church and Benjamin Hofmann*

Johann Gottlieb Fichte is one of the great political thinkers of the post-Kantian idealist tradition. He began his career in Jena as an ardent defender of the French Revolution, and then drew on his distinctive philosophical system, the *Wissenschaftslehre* or Science of Knowledge, to ground a vision of liberal socialism in his *Foundations of Natural Right* (FNR 1797–1798). A radical thinker in religion as well as in politics, Fichte then became embroiled in controversy and lost his position at the University of Jena over concerns that he was an atheist. Fichte left Jena for Berlin in 1800 where he spent the remainder of his career. His most famous text from this period is the *Addresses to the German Nation* (AGN 1807–1808), one of the most significant early works of modern nationalism. After an itinerant few years teaching at various German universities, Fichte finally settled at the newly founded University of Berlin until his death in January 1814.

Readers of J. G. Fichte's political philosophy are confronted with a puzzle while comparing the two main works of his Jena and Berlin periods, the FNR and AGN. How can the philosophy of the FNR, with its liberal commitments to intersubjective recognition, universal rights, and the social contract, be reconciled with the theories in the AGN, with their nationalist views of German linguistic superiority, a state educational program, and cultural (and perhaps ethnic) chauvinism? Scholars have attempted to resolve this puzzle in different ways, either by arguing that Fichte changed his views — gradually becoming more authoritarian and less liberal over time — or that his liberal socialism and nationalism are compatible — in that, for example, his nationalism and educational program are necessary political conditions for the establishment of his liberal socialist vision.[1]

This puzzle is a difficult one for English-language readers because of the focus on these two texts in particular, which are readily available in English translation.[2] Very little of Fichte's Berlin period political writings have been translated, giving readers the mistaken impression that the philosopher abruptly shifted course.[3] This volume affords readers a fuller picture of Fichte's political thinking and it can help readers understand his development more completely. We have included three unpublished texts of 1806–1807 that precede the AGN and provide some helpful context in understanding it — Fichte's "Application of Eloquence" essay, his dialogues *Patriotism and Its Opposite*, and his fragment *The Republic of the Germans*. We have also included two lectures from his University of Berlin tenure that show the ongoing development of recurring themes in his philosophy — the lectures on *The Vocation of the Scholar* of 1811 and the lectures on *The Doctrine of Right* of 1812.

These works have not previously been translated in their entirety into English.[4] With the publication of this volume, English-language readers of Fichte can now have complete access to Fichte's late political philosophy.

## Texts Prior to *The Addresses to the German Nation*

Like many thinkers of his era, Fichte was influenced by the tumultuous political period he was living through. His 1793 work *Contribution to the Correction of the Public's Judgment on the French Revolution* launched a powerful defense of the Revolution even in its most radical Jacobin phase.[5] As revolution gave way to empire in France at the turn of the century, and Napoleon began to threaten the self-determination of the German people, Fichte shifted the target of his concern. In his Berlin period, Fichte feared the rise of Napoleon and the danger he posed to European moral and political progress. In his "Application of Eloquence," he states that the war will decide "whether what humankind has achieved since its beginning . . . shall persist and grow according to the laws of human development; or whether everything the poets have sung, the wise have thought, and the heroes have consummated shall be swallowed up by the bottomless maw of an arbitrary will" (16). For Fichte, though Napoleon claimed to represent the principles of the Revolution, his rejection of the rule of law, coupled with his universal ambition and his tyranny, amounted to the subversion of freedom and equality everywhere.

In 1805–1806, Emperor Napoleon Bonaparte won a series of decisive victories against Austria and the German states. The last ruler of the millennium-old Holy Roman Empire abdicated in August 1806. Napoleon proceeded to conquer and occupy Jena and Berlin, turning the German states into enforced allies in his war.

In the summer of 1806, Fichte, alarmed by Napoleon's campaign, offered to the Prussian authorities to help the war cause in his own distinctive way: by becoming a kind of secular army chaplain and rousing the troops with his speeches. He submitted to his contact in the Prussian government, Minister Carl Friedrich von Beyme, a kind of sketch and precis of his speech, "The Application of Eloquence to the Present War." Von Beyme kindly responded to Fichte, denying the request, writing, "Dear Fichte, your ideas honor you. The king thanks you for your offer. Perhaps we can make use of it in the future. But first the king must speak to his troops through his deeds. Thereafter can eloquence expand the advantages of victory" (GA III/5.367).

The "Application of Eloquence" argues that any rhetoric rousing the troops must be delivered with an understanding of the significance of this historical moment. On Fichte's view, Prussia is facing a world-historical enemy and must face up to its responsibility. Fichte provides his own credentials as a philosopher trained as a theological orator. Yet he concludes the proposal with some advice for the government. In order for this war to succeed, the government must carefully articulate the ethical ends of this war and conduct the war with ethical means. On Fichte's view, it is a war of the spirit for the meaning of the future of humanity, not just a war of the flesh.

This proposal offers some useful context for reading the AGN. Fichte argues that the struggle between France and Germany is not a narrow national struggle, but a war for the fate of humanity. In his AGN and his 1806 work, the *Characteristics of the Present Age*, Fichte develops a philosophy of history, describing humanity as proceeding through five moral stages. Humanity currently is in an egoistic stage — the third stage — and in his AGN Fichte develops a plan to move Germany to a moral stage — the fourth stage — that would represent a transformation of humanity. The "Application of Eloquence" similarly draws on his philosophy of history to understand the end and conduct of war not just for Germany's future but also for humanity's. This proposal helps underscore the universal or cosmopolitan scope of Fichte's political thinking.

That cosmopolitan nationalism continues in Fichte's next political work of this period, *Patriotism and Its Opposite*. Fichte wrote this work in two installments. The first dialogue was composed prior to Napoleon's conquest of German territory in mid-1806. Fichte sought publication for the first dialogue, but ultimately decided against it, possibly out of a fear of censorship (the dialogues were not published during his lifetime). Fichte penned the second dialogue under much different, wartime circumstances a year later. As Napoleon's forces occupied Berlin in November 1806, the Prussian king and his court fled Berlin for Königsberg. Fichte accompanied them, leaving his wife and child behind. He would remain in exile for nearly a year, lecturing at the University of Königsberg, immersing himself in the educational philosophy of Johann Heinrich Pestalozzi, whose theories would play an important role in his second dialogue, as well as in the AGN. During this time, Fichte also intensively read Dante and Machiavelli, and published an essay on Machiavelli.

*Patriotism and Its Opposite* situates AGN's nationalism in the right context precisely because the former work aims to critique narrow, chauvinistic patriotism. In the first dialogue, the speaker "A" represents a composite and caricature of the mainstream form of Prussian patriotism, which Fichte found expressed in the *Preußischer Hausfreund*,[6] a Berlin journal of the time — a "Patriotic Newspaper for Educated Readers of Every Class" — that published uncritical, obsequious praises of the Prussian authorities. As such, at the beginning of the dialogue, we find A engaged in "patriotism exercises" and blindly expressing loyalty to his community. By contrast, Fichte advocates for a more reflective and cosmopolitan nationalism through speaker "B." B points out that the purpose of patriotism is not the good of one nation, but the good of humanity as a whole. That good can only be advanced when citizens adopt a self-critical and philosophically informed perspective on public affairs. Published just two years after this first dialogue, AGN could not advocate for a narrow or close-minded form of nationalism.

These dialogues also clarify more fully than AGN does the place of Fichte's philosophical system, the *Wissenschaftslehre*, in his political thought. In both the first and second dialogues, Fichte argues that the most significant feature of modern life is that human beings are emerging from a condition of guidance based on their instincts to a condition of being guided by their own "insight" (*Einsicht*). We have not yet fully made that transition, however, which accounts for much of our selfishness and errors. The *Wissenschaftslehre*, on Fichte's view, represents that philosophical system that can help the modern mind come to maturity, independence, and equality. In the second dialogue, a new interlocutor comes on the stage — "C" — and pushes B particularly on this point. Now that Napoleon is rampaging across Europe, is it really the time for the *Wissenschaftslehre*? B insists that it is, because philosophical thinking can help inform "art" (*Kunst*), that is, practical activity broadly understood, including the art of war. Only through a developed scientific understanding — and respect for science throughout the populace — can Germany hope to emerge victorious from this war. As in the AGN, the vehicle for the education to this philosophical maturity will come through Pestalozzi's educational theory.[7] What is different here, however, is Fichte's emphasis on the *Wissenschaftslehre* specifically as the content of that education, as well as Fichte's frequently expressed frustration over the widespread misunderstanding of his work

During his exile in Königsberg, likely in the spring of 1807, Fichte sketched notes and fragments for an intended work entitled *The Republic of the Germans at the Beginning of the 22nd Century Under the Fifth Magistrate*. As in his previous dialogic work, Fichte is experimenting with expository style. Here, he speculates on the political conditions of Germany in the distant future. The first part of the work was intended to give an account of Germany's downfall, particularly as a result of the pusillanimity and selfishness of the upper classes who, Fichte predicts, will sell out the German states to the highest bidder. The second part then discusses the new constitution of a republican Germany that will emerge from the ashes of Germany's downfall. The aim of this constitution will be nothing less than the moral and scientific education of humanity generally. The subsequent parts discuss the features of this constitution. The third part describes the religious confessions of Germany's future, particularly the modern, universalist Enlightenment form of Protestant Christianity that Fichte defends. This religious faith would form the basis of the fourth part's discussion of education, which Fichte did not write before he abandoned the project. Finally, in the fifth part, he would discuss the main institutions of politics and society, the structure of government and the rituals of the civil religion.

*The Republic of the Germans* is the most fragmentary of the texts we include here, mostly consisting of preparatory drafts and notes for each of these parts. Indeed, Fichte did not arrange these drafts in the intended order sketched above. The older complete works of Fichte edited by Fichte's son reconstructed this work, seeking to structure it according to Fichte's plan.[8] We have instead followed the editors of the modern critical edition of Fichte's *Gesamtausgabe* and maintained the fragmentary character of the text as Fichte left it.

Despite its fragmentary character it sheds important light on the AGN. One of the recurring questions readers have about the AGN is whether and to what extent Fichte thought that government should enforce the nationalism he defended, or whether he thought that nationalism should develop organically.⁹ Much of the analysis in this text suggests the former interpretation. Fichte holds that the constitutional order as a whole has as its goal the moral progress of humanity, so the design of the coercive institutions of government would serve that end. Near the end of the text, for example, there is a memorable discussion of the civil religion Fichte imagines will characterize future German society. In that discussion, Fichte gives several examples of coercive features of his civic nationalism — compulsory military service, religious confession, burial practices, and baptismal and funeral rites.

At the same time, this text also challenges a strongly authoritarian reading of Fichte's republican politics. Throughout his analysis of government offices, Fichte is insistent that there be an important role for the deliberation of small councils (Senates) and large councils (representative bodies). These bodies ultimately remain advisory to the sovereign on Fichte's view, but their presence does suggest that Fichte involves more democratic participation than previously understood.[10]

None of these writings saw the light of day in Fichte's lifetime, unlike his very public lectures, the AGN, and their publication shortly thereafter. Nevertheless, these texts show the breadth and creativity of Fichte's writing style and give us greater scope for appreciating and understanding his nationalism and constitutionalism in the Berlin period.

## The Third Lecture Series on the Scholar

With the end of the French occupation of Berlin in 1809, the king of Prussia returned from exile. One of his early decisions was to revisit and approve the founding of a new university in Berlin. Fichte had in fact submitted a plan for the design and curriculum of the University of Berlin in 1807, which reflected his own educational aim of moral and scientific progress along the principles of the *Wissenschaftslehre*. Wilhelm von Humboldt's plan was selected instead to guide the creation of the new university. Although Fichte's plan was not chosen, Fichte himself was selected to be one of the first faculty members; he also served as university rector for a short time.

From his first course in autumn 1809 through his death in 1814, Fichte had a stable university post, a regular teaching schedule, and tremendous discretion over what he taught. This period represented a remarkable flourishing of Fichte's late philosophical system. He developed a series of courses that would gradually introduce students to the *Wissenschaftslehre*. In addition to his speculative philosophy, he also lectured on the vocation of the scholar, and the philosophy of ethics, right, and the state. Very little of this material has been translated into English.[11]

At the University of Berlin, Fichte had the opportunity to revisit important topics he had been exploring throughout his career. In particular, Fichte harbored a long-standing interest in the nature and role or "vocation" (*Bestimmung*) of the philosopher in society. For most of human history, it was the inspired religious leader who occupied a central place in society. Fichte sought to restore the place of the philosopher or "scholar" (*Gelehrten*) to its rightful central place, a kind of modernizing of Plato's philosopher-king. Reason should guide the political community, not be governed by it. At the same time, Fichte set out to respond to the critique of reason and science in society leveled by Rousseau in the eighteenth century, whom he cites in his Jena lectures on this topic. Rousseau argued that scientists and philosophers corrupted society with their airy bloviating. Fichte endeavored to show they could have a significant moral role in reforming society. Reason is and should become practical reason. In this way, Fichte anticipates Marx's famous dictum that "philosophers have hitherto interpreted the world . . . the point, however, is to change it."[12]

Fichte lectured on this topic first in Jena in 1794 as he was conceiving of and writing his *Wissenschaftslehre*. In "Some Lectures on the Vocation of the Scholar," Fichte argued that the vocation of humanity as a whole can be derived from the nature and aim of our free subjectivity, which enjoins us to create, maintain, and transmit a moral and spiritual community over time, which he calls a "culture" (*Kultur*). Each member of society has a distinctive role to play in realizing human culture, and the scholar in particular has the role of comprehending the purpose of human history and communicating that end to others. In these lectures, Fichte is concerned with the problem of inequality among the various roles in this community and redressing them.

In 1805, Fichte returned to this topic in *On the Nature of the Scholar and Its Manifestations*. Many similar themes remain, especially about the vocation of the scholar to identify the end of humanity and to share it with others. Yet the presentation of these ideas has a different focus and motivation. Fichte is less interested in the "vocation" of the scholar than its "nature," and, as he puts it in the first lecture, how we can become a scholar. This change of focus is motivated in part by Fichte's effort to distinguish his view from the rival Romantic view popular at that time in intellectual circles. Philosophers such as Schelling extolled the role of the genius in expressing the deepest longings of nature to rejuvenate human society. Fichte argued that the scholar instead must channel the "idea," that is, the moral-spiritual nature of humanity, rather than nature more generally. And it should be the scholar, not the genius, who leads society, who can lead humanity to reason rather than blind emotion.

Fichte's third and final set of lectures on the scholar, translated here, was delivered at the University of Berlin in 1811. The first two lectures of this series were published in the journal *Die Musen* in 1812–1813. *Lectures on the Vocation of the Scholar* represents a synthesis of Fichte's first two efforts on the topic. We find in these lectures his Berlin emphasis on the scholar as the conduit of the idea. Indeed, the announcement for these lectures stated that they would be based on his 1805 book.[13] We also find in these lectures his Jena emphasis on the social vocation of the scholar to communicate learned ideas to the public in what Fichte here calls the "Mittelwelt" or "middle world" between the idea and our sensuous nature (105).

At the same time, he incorporates these prior efforts within his new articulation of the *Wissenschaftslehre*. Very broadly speaking, Fichte's Jena *Wissenschaftslehre* represented a kind of subjective idealism, according to which truth and knowledge rested on the nature and structure of our subjectivity. Fichte came to appreciate the limitation of this subjective idealism and turned in the first half of his Berlin period — which his 1805 lectures represented — to argue that truth exceeded the ego, that knowledge synthesizes our reflective perspective and the given world as such. Knowledge is the appearance of the "absolute."[14] Finally, in his mature *Wissenschaftslehre* of 1809 and after, Fichte explored more deeply the nature of this knowledge, and held that it is more intimately implicated with our subjectivity than he thought in the first half of his Berlin work. In this way, Fichte sets out to synthesize his Jena and Berlin *Wissenschaftslehren*. As such, in his 1811 lectures on the scholar, Fichte argues that knowledge appears to us in various forms, in morality, politics, and religion, and that we could "see" (*sehen*) or have "insight" (*Einsicht*) about the true "ideas" (*Gesicht*). Fichte's term for idea, *Gesicht,* literally means "that which is seen," capturing the essential character of appearance or perspective in Fichte's mature *Wissenschaftslehre*. Though we can use our cognitive and sensuous vision to grasp appearances of the truth, the truth itself always exceeds our grasp as we are finite, subjective creatures.

In the 1811 lectures on the scholar, Fichte invests the philosopher with the power of sight to see what can be seen, the appearance of the truth that has no correspondence in the empirical world. The vocation of the scholar, then, is to set about to make what is merely an appearance into a reality by helping reform the empirical world according to the idea that she has witnessed. Whereas the 1805 lecture series envisioned a quasi-mystical role for the scholar, these 1811 lectures bring the speculative insight down to earth with an intensely practical role for the scholar, a role that retrieves some of the spirit of Fichte's 1794 lectures.

# Continuity or Break in Fichte's Philosophy of Right?

In addition to the scholar, another abiding concern for Fichte throughout his career was the nature, basis, and conditions for a system of "right" (*Recht*). *Recht* is a difficult term to translate into English, as it refers to a just or rightful system of law governing a political community. We translate *Recht* as "right" in line with standard translations of texts on this topic from the period, such as Kant's *Doctrine of Right* (*Rechtslehre*), Fichte's *Foundations of Natural Right* (*Grundlage des Naturrechts*), and Hegel's *Elements of the Philosophy of Right* (*Grundlinien der Philosophie des Rechts*). Yet readers should not understand "right" as equivalent to Anglo-American discussions of natural or human "rights." In the German context to which Fichte is contributing, the guiding question is not how to protect individual rights, but rather how to construct a system of law that enables and coordinates the often conflicting freedoms that individuals have. A system of right — and ultimately a lawful or just state (*Rechtsstaat*) — is one that structures individual relations under law by conferring rights, privileges, and duties on each member of the system.

As scholars have shown, Fichte's philosophy of right changed over the course of his career. In his early writings, especially his 1793 work on the French Revolution, he drew on Kant's moral philosophy to defend a kind of radicalized natural rights philosophy in the tradition of John Locke. On this view, human beings have certain moral rights that precede government, and government can and should be assessed with reference to this prepolitical standard. If it fails to live up to this standard, citizens can permissibly dissolve government.

By the time he revisits these matters in his 1797–1798 Foundations of Natural Right (FNR) Fichte changes his views markedly. What he now calls "original right," the prepolitical freedoms of all individuals, no longer serves as a standard for evaluating positive law but as a justification for creating the political community. The prepolitical condition, what theorists including Fichte call the "state of nature," is one in which rights are indeterminate and so in fundamental conflict with one another. Human beings thereby require a sovereign authority to make right determinate by expressing and codifying it in positive law. Only within a political community and through a sovereign's law does right become determinate and effective. In this work, Fichte turns from a radicalized Locke to a moderate Rousseau, for whom the "general will" represents the system of right manifested in a political community.

In his late work on right, according to some scholars, Fichte gradually drifts away from his early liberal and republican commitments and defends a form of authoritarianism — from Locke and Rousseau, Fichte finally embraces Hobbes. According to this reading, the early glimpses of this authoritarianism can be seen in Fichte's 1800 *Closed Commercial State* with its comprehensive state planning. Then, in his 1806 *Characteristics of the Present Age*, Fichte expands the scope of state power beyond its role in coordinating the external freedoms of individuals to develop and educate individuals' inner character. In the 1812 *Doctrine of Right*, Fichte abandons his institutional checks-and-balances scheme that he had put into place in his 1797–1798 work to restrict state power. In 1812, he declares his earlier theory of the "ephorate" — a system of magistrates that would be the judge of conflicts between government and the people — as unworkable, and instead places even fewer restrictions on state sovereignty. Finally, in the 1813 *Doctrine of the State*, Fichte envisions an important role for an "overlord" (*Zwingherr*) in founding new states by coercing individuals into submission.

The translation of the 1812 *Doctrine of Right* in this volume provides English-language readers an opportunity to evaluate this account. Fichte lectured on the doctrine of right from April to June 1812 as part of the development of his Berlin philosophical system, which shares some similarities but also important differences with his earlier Jena system. Nevertheless, in his 1812 lectures, Fichte used his own 1797–1798 work FNR as the textbook for the course, citing from it extensively at various points in the course. Our translation indicates the relevant portions that Fichte read from. At a very basic level of presentation, then, Fichte himself considered there to be some continuity between his early work and late work, or else he would not have used his *Foundations* as a textbook.

Consider three other substantive continuities between his 1797–1798 work and his 1812 lectures.

*Distinction Between Morality and Right*: One of Fichte's signal contributions in his 1797–1798 work was to make a sharp distinction between the nature, basis, and aims of morality and right. Kant would himself proceed to make a similar sharp distinction in his own 1797 *Metaphysics of Morals*. Broadly stated, right governs and guides the external relationships among human beings, while morality governs and guides our inner moral character. As such, the state can prevent us from violating one another's liberty, but it cannot force us to be morally good. It is sometimes claimed that Fichte abandons this distinction and argues that the state takes on increased moral authority in his late work. However, this distinction between morality and right reappears in the 1812 work, sharply delineating the rightful scope of state power. For example, the proper moral action for the state might be to take from the rich and give to the poor, but Fichte argues that right demands that property rights be respected. "The state is no moral person," Fichte claims. "Rightfulness is its morality. The state has to protect my property to the death" (216n168).

*Contractual Basis of Government*: In his Jena works of 1793 and 1797–1798, Fichte argues that for governments to be legitimate, they must be popularly authorized. The main theoretical mechanism for conceiving of state legitimacy is the idea of the social contract, that citizens can be understood to have consented to certain agreements that ground their rights and duties in society. Fichte envisions several forms of the social contract in his 1797–1798 FNR. Despite the claims of Fichte's growing authoritarianism, however, he remains a contractualist in his 1812 work. Citizens enter into contracts with one another to protect and promote a system of right through "property contracts" (137), an agreement to respect the rights of others, as well as a "positive performance contract" (141), an agreement actively to provide support to others to defend their freedoms. Finally, citizens contract with one another to create a government to uphold right, what Fichte calls the "civil contract" (184). If government fails to guarantee right, it violates its popular authorization and becomes tyrannical force. In this way, Fichte's view of sovereignty is not absolute as for Hobbes but limited by the contractual requirement to realize public right.

*Property and Political Economy*: In his FNR, Fichte leaves room for private property in what he calls "absolute property," above all our home and what is contained within it, which cannot be invaded by the state without meeting a very high standard of justification. At the same time, even in that work, Fichte envisioned a large role for the state in redistributing our "relative property," that which we might possess but would be put to better use for those who have greater claims of need. His 1812 lectures continue to reserve a space for absolute property, as well as a considerable role for the state in redistributing resources.

Nevertheless, there are important revisions to Fichte's philosophy of right. Consider three revisions from the three major parts of the 1812 lectures: the basis of right, the nature of economic right, and the nature of civil or constitutional right.

*The Basis of Right*: In his 1797–1798 work, Fichte offers a seminal discussion of "recognition" (*Anerkennung*) as the basis not only of right but also of individual self-consciousness generally. Scholars have argued that Fichte's discussion influenced Hegel's account of recognition in the celebrated "master-slave dialectic" in the *Phenomenology of Spirit*. In the 1812 work, there is no discussion of mutual recognition at all, no account of the intersubjective grounding of right. Instead, we begin with the "concept" of right as given to this part of the system, derived from the Berlin *Wissenschaftslehre*. As many scholars have pointed out, Fichte displaces the I from its central role in his philosophy, replacing it with impersonal norms and concepts of "knowledge" and the "absolute." The antisubjectivism of Fichte's late work appears here, in his abstraction from any intersubjective basis for right. Nevertheless, on Fichte's view, the concept of right does not precede human interaction, but only emerges through community, through the agreements that citizens make about which rights and duties they are to possess. In this way, the intersubjectivity of Fichte's FNR returns in his philosophy of right at a different place. This synthesis of impersonal and intersubjective forms of authority is characteristic of Fichte's mature *Wissenschaftslehre* system.

*Economic Right*: Fichte analyzes the just distribution of state resources with great care in his 1797–1798 work and in his 1800 *Closed Commercial State*. In his 1812 lectures, he maintains much of the same account as his earlier work. However, his late lectures do place a much greater emphasis on the importance of the value of leisure for human life. In fact, Fichte conceives of leisure as a resolution of an antinomy in his political economy: the purpose of a division of labor is to liberate human beings, but it turns out that we must contribute to a system of social cooperation through necessary work, and we are often subject to state redistributive taxation. The resolution to this antinomy is that the ultimate result of our cooperation is the realization of leisure for all members of society in which we can truly enjoy our freedom (150).

*Civil or Constitutional Right*: In his FNR, Fichte argues that state power should be sovereign. Yet, he asks, what happens if government exceeds its rightful authority or acts contrary to right? He argues that the people should appeal to a constitutionally legitimated body, the "ephorate," and raise grievances to it. The ephorate would thereby serve as the judge. In his 1812 work, Fichte rejects the idea of the ephorate, since the latter endangers the notion of sovereignty. If the government can be challenged by another body, then it is not legitimate after all (196). However, Fichte does not in this sense reject the idea of constitutional checks and balances. What he rejects is the unwise idea of a power outside of government that could rival it, in particular a power that appeals to the undifferentiated power of the people to resolve the disagreement. On Fichte's view, the assembled people is a mob without reason, "because human beings as a whole are far too bad" (197). It is better at this historical juncture to invest power in the "wise." Fichte's view here is compatible with the idea that institutions representing the people within government can check the executive, assemblies Fichte described in the "Republic of the Germans." In addition, Fichte also envisions a time when the people can be educated and could take up this role of adjudicator of the government's actions. Yet "until they improve on the whole," we should be skeptical of unlimited democracy (197).

Unlike Fichte's 1811 lectures on the scholar, we do not have a polished version of Fichte's 1812 lectures. Instead, we have his lecture notes, which are at times polished but at other times elliptical and fragmentary. Since these lecture notes are difficult to follow, we have followed the recent German paperback edition of the 1812 lectures that draws on student lecture notes to smooth out the rough edges of the text. In addition, we have translated some relevant portions of the 1812 student lecture notes in the footnotes when they further illustrate and amplify Fichte's own notes.

Our hope in translating these works is to provide English-language readers and scholars with a broader perspective on Fichte's late political philosophy beyond the AGN. In our view, this late thought reveals important developments and continuities with his more familiar Jena work. Unfortunately, few English-language readers have ventured to discuss Fichte's late political philosophy outside of the AGN. We hope this volume can help change that.

## Notes

1. For the former view, see, for example, Zöller (2009, 61–62; 2015, 71–77; 2020), Beck (2008, chapters 4–5), Siep (2017), Verweyen (1975, part 5). For the latter view, see, for example, James (2015, 2011), Fuchs (2010), Kinlaw (2006), and Leon (1927, vol. 2, part 2, chapter 2).
2. For the FNR, see Fichte (2000); for the AGN, see Fichte (2013) and (2009).
3. Other political texts of Fichte's Berlin period that have been translated include *The Closed Commercial State* (Fichte 2012), "On Machiavelli" (Fichte 2016), and *The Doctrine of the State* (Fichte 2025).
4. A partial translation of the Patriotism dialogues appeared in Turnbull (1926, 160–69).
5. For an English translation, see Fichte (2021).
6. The full name of the journal is *Berlin oder der preußische Hausfreund*.
7. That Fichte advocates specifically Pestalozzi's theory and methods in these

dialogues further underlines the democratic and cosmopolitan tenor of his thinking. Pestalozzi envisions a child-centered pedagogy guided by a child's natural developmental inquisitiveness and desire to learn. Starting with the paradigmatic mother-child duo as the basic building block of education, Pestalozzi makes education available to all children of the entire citizenry, with every mother as the child's first teacher. Using a child's common human development as the basis of educational theory means that every child, from all classes and nations, is valued not as an empty vessel to be filled or a clay to be molded, but as a full human being with a natural developmental path to be enhanced. To promote Pestalozzi's pedagogy as a German national pedagogy thus promotes a cosmopolitan attitude that applies to members of all nations equally while also treasuring a groundbreaking, and specifically German, contribution to modernity.

8. See Fichte 1971, 530–45.
9. See James 2015, chapter 6.
10. For an example of a common antidemocratic interpretation, see Zöller 2015, who argues for the "manifestly antidemocratic republicanism of Fichte" (95).
11. Important exceptions are Fichte 2015 and Fichte 2025.
12. Karl Marx, "Theses on Feuerbach."
13. The editors of the *Gesamtausgabe* (GA) point out that Fichte uses an example of the musician to illustrate the role of the scholar in the 1811 lectures, in contrast to his earlier 1805 invocation of a sculptor. The editors speculate that Fichte's choice of this metaphor could have been due to the presence of Beethoven at his lectures in August 1811. J. G. Fichte, *Gesamtausgabe*, ed. Erich Fuchs, Reinhard Lauth, Ives Radrizzani, and Peter K. Schneider (Fromann-Holzboog, 1999), II/12.312.
14. This view is expressed most clearly in his 1804 *Wissenschaftslehre*. See Fichte (2005), especially lectures 1–2.

## Works Cited

Beck, Gunnar. 2008. *Fichte and Kant on Freedom, Rights, and Law*. Lexington Books.

Fichte, J. G. 1971. *Fichtes Werke: Band VII. Zur Politik, Moral, und Philosophie der Geschichte*. Edited by Immanuel Hermann Fichte. Walter de Gruyter.

Fichte, J. G. 1999. *Gesamtausgabe*. Edited by Erich Fuchs, Reinhard Lauth, Ives Radrizzani, and Peter K. Schneider. Fromann-Holzboog.

Fichte, J. G. 2000. *Foundations of Natural Right*. Edited by Frederick Neuhouser, translated by Michael Baur. Cambridge University Press.

Fichte, J. G. 2005. *The Science of Knowing: J. G. Fichte's 1804 Lectures on the Wissenschaftslehre*. State University of New York Press.

Fichte, J. G. 2009. *Addresses to the German Nation*. Edited by Gregory Moore. Cambridge University Press.

Fichte, J. G. 2012. *The Closed Commercial State*. Edited by Anthony Curtis Adler. State University of New York Press.

Fichte, J. G. 2013. *Addresses to the German Nation*. Edited by Isaac Nakhimovsky, Bela Kapossy, and Keith Tribe. Hackett.

Fichte, J. G. 2015. *Lectures on the Theory of Ethics (1812)*. Translated by Benjamin D. Crowe. State University of New York Press.

Fichte, J. G. 2016. "On Machiavelli, as an Author, and Passages from His Writings." Translated by Ian Alexander Moore and Christopher Turner. *Philosophy Today* 60 (3): 761–88.

Fichte, J. G. 2021. *Contribution to the Correction of the Public's Judgments on the French Revolution*. Edited by Jeffrey Church and Anna Marisa Schön. State University of New York Press.

Fichte, J. G. 2025. *The Doctrine of the State*. Edited by Jeffrey Church and Anna Marisa Schön. Oxford University Press.

Fuchs, Eric. 2010. "Fichte: Stammvater des deutschen Nationalismus?" *Fichte-Studien* 35: 267–84.

James, David. 2011. *Fichte's Social and Political Philosophy: Property and Virtue*. Cambridge University Press.

James, David. 2015. *Fichte's Republic: Idealism, History, and Nationalism*. Cambridge University Press.

Kinlaw, C. Jeffery. 2006. "Law, Morality, and Bildung in the 1812 Rechtslehre." In *"Praktische Philosophie in Fichtes Spätwerk," Fichte-Studien* 29: 67–78.

Leon, Xavier. 1927. *Fichte et son temps*. 2 volumes. Colin Press, 1922–1927.

Siep, Ludwig. 2017. "Revolution, Nation und Individuum in Fichtes philosophischer Entwicklung." *Fichte-Studien* 44: 141–51.

Turnbull, G. H. 1926. *The Educational Theory of J.G. Fichte: A Critical Account, Together with Translations*. University Press of Liverpool.

Verweyen, Hansjürgen. 1975. *Recht und Sittlichkeit in J.G. Fichtes Gesellschaftslehre*. Verlag Karl Alber.

Zöller, Günter. 2009. "Menschenbildung: Staatspolitische Erziehung beim späten Fichte." In *Bildung als Mittel und Selbstzweck: Korrektive Errinerung wider die Verengung des Bildungsbegriffs*, 42–62. Verlag Karl Alber.

Zöller, Günter . 2015. *Res Publica: Plato's Republic in Classical German Philosophy*. Chinese University Press.

Zöller, Günter. 2020. "Freedom, Right, and Law: Fichte's Late Political Philosophy." In *The Bloomsbury Handbook of Fichte*, edited by Marina F. Bykova, 261–76. Bloomsbury.

# 1

# The Application of Eloquence to the Present War (1806)

*Translated by Anne C. Reitz*

[76][1] [VII.505] Modern thinkers often find eloquence even in what is not said. Here, we understand eloquence primarily as actual speech; we will discuss the first thing mentioned further below.

It is well known that everywhere and always, throughout history, where there has been eloquence and an ear to hear it, it rouses the armies to victory even in war, and often one word has defeated armies. Even if we could have forgotten it, the enemy has shown this to us, even up to the most recent events.[2]

Indeed, we take for granted here as reasonable that in the present war, nowhere, from the highest leader down to the lowliest subordinates, is there a need for encouragement or inciting, since surely all hearts burn abundantly, inflamed by a cause unprecedented in all time. Nonetheless, independent of that task, the far purer, and more beautiful function of eloquence always remains: to intensify the spark already ignited into a lasting, free and deliberate flame, and to preserve the sacred fire thus, that it might, at any moment, be fanned appropriately.

Eloquence in this spirit, that presumes prior understanding, only counts on the foremost members of the army, and on the best, who are capable of pure and clear reflection. [VII.506] Not originally inflaming, it can only expose to contemplation once again what the best man really is and how he thinks internally. It wants only to make intelligible for him, in words, what disappears for the active man in the course of uninterrupted activity, holding fast for lasting intuition the beautiful image, the moment of greatest inspiration conceived in him. Eloquence wants only to pursue that contemplation that anybody would just as well pursue himself if he had the time for it and precisely by doing so, to fix those considerations for one's own clear reflection in life, for one's own unshakable consistency, as well as fixing them for easier communication with others.

The first thing incumbent on someone who might offer to administer this function of speech would be the presentation of evidence that he himself understands the significance of this war and is seized more by this interest than by the interest in his own life [72] or by any other interest. The author of this proposal sees the present war in this way: It should decide the question of whether what humankind has achieved since its beginning — through thousandfold sacrifices to order, legality, morals, art and science, and with a cheerful eye to heaven — shall persist and grow according to the laws of human development; or whether everything the poets have sung, the wise have thought, and the heroes have consummated shall be swallowed up by the bottomless maw of an arbitrary will that absolutely does not know what it *wants*, other than to be unlimited and ironclad. The judgment on this has finally, after others' thwarted attempts, fallen to that very state in Europe that has come furthest[3] in possession of all of those goods of humankind that are at stake, and to which the preservation of them therefore must matter the most — just as if it had quite actually developed to this purpose in recent times, and thus retained its significance. The question is whether the [VI.507] speaker offering himself knows in what way the great task can be resolved victoriously.

The author believes: unfailingly, if everyone, from the highest to the lowliest completely wills what they want, with the same ironclad energy with which the enemy wills, and wills only that and nothing else besides, and does not think of peace while at war. In short, if everyone takes as a motto, not, as the enemy once did, "Victory or Death," (as the latter will come even without our intent and he who is to act must never want it), but instead just simply "Victory." The question is whether the speaker offering himself is himself so powerfully seized by this interest that we may expect of him that his speech will spring from the heart, lively and enlivening. The author knows that he does not want to live except in possession of what is at stake, and that only the hope of being able to contribute something to the attainment of the purpose tears him away from occupations that arouse his activity far more and spurs him to this offer.

[73] Concerning the outer form, this author would fall back on the old and familiar form of a preacher (superficially that much more feasible, since he once studied theology and preached widely), in case people might be put off by strangeness and novelty of form, in this age when everything is modernizing and the enemy threatens us with new evils marching on in revolutionary fashion, however much the freer form of a secular state orator strikes him as more appropriate to our times: a state orator around whom the best have gathered, on certain days, such as Sundays, for serious and solemn contemplation of their next, great calling, following that topic indicated above, which seems to promise conversation that never runs out.

So much about unmediated eloquence that, flowing face to face, animates most powerfully.

In terms of the other kind, that requires letters as a vehicle, proclamations are to be issued to the army, either in order to recognize and to applaud their rightness, sensibly and with determination and discrimination, or to recommend moral discipline to them in the provinces they pass through, and good ethics and order, so that we not only threaten, but also that their good will be won simultaneously. Proclamations are to be issued to the inhabitants of the provinces that our military campaign meets that make them familiar, and friendly with our intention not to rob or subject them, but to give peace, freedom, and repose back to them.

Although it may well lie beyond the boundaries of the mandate I am to undertake, even yet I wish to be allowed to add, for the sake of completeness, that in mentioning the function of the talents in this war for humanity, it seems to me that a manifesto will also be delivered at the opening of the war that clearly and unambiguously expresses the aim of the war, protects us from all other intentions in an unsurpassable manner by and for ourselves, [74] and thus ensures us in the general opinion of Europe, a not unobjectionable ally, the best there can be for us.

[VII.508] We will have to confess that the time has finally come to fend off the proposals of a petty, calculating cabinet policy from this holy battle; and if we are really decided, then we are to attest to and disclose this decision unambiguously!

## Notes

1. Pagination references are to J. G. Fichte, *Gesamtausgabe*, ed. Hans Gliwitzky and Reinhard Lauth (Fromann-Holzboog, 1994), II/10.71–74, with page number in brackets, and to J. G. Fichte, *Fichtes Werke: Band VII. Zur Politik, Moral, und Philosophie der Geschichte*, ed. Immanuel Hermann Fichte (Berlin: Walter de Gruyter, 1971), 505–8, with VII and then page number in brackets.
2. Reference to Napoleon's proclamations and military orders.
3. Fichte refers here to the confederation of Saxony-Weimar, the Electorate of Saxony, and Prussia.

# 2

# Patriotism and Its Opposite

## *Patriotic Dialogues (1806–1807)*

*Translated by Anne C. Reitz*

## [393] Preamble

The[1] essays I cite in the following preface of July 1806, appeared in a Berlin journal[2] that was even worse than such journals are normally allowed to be, with the exception of several very good essays[3] that wound up there due to some fakery to be discussed straightaway. In addition to the conspicuous striving to hustle the highest persons by using indecent flatteries contrary to true respect, this journal aroused indignation primarily by trying to pretend that these highest persons took a particular interest, as if these persons would let its coarse baloney and spiteful badmouthings of other scholars be laid before them, or that its articles, equally crudely worded as muddled in thought, would be to their taste. The examples cited in the conversation are borrowed from this journal. The reader will easily gather from context [394] what the preface meant. Other concerns and considerations soon emerged and thus the essay remained unpublished until now. I will let these temporary references stand as contributions to contemporary history and simultaneously as examples of what is not to be imitated but rather avoided. In regards to the content, I consider it not yet out of date or antiquated. The necessity of supplementing the earlier composition at the present time, with the attached conversation appearing second, speaks for itself.

— Königsberg, June 1807

# Preface

The composition of the following conversation was first prompted by several essays that were brought to the attention of the author unsolicited, and through the equally unwelcome invitation to make certain contributions. By now, he considers its content to be important enough to share the essay that thus came to life.

[395] Finding the rules according to which a literary composition comes to be is best left to the reader. But I have some feeling that, as regards the following conversation, not every reader will manage this assignment very ably and peculiar misunderstandings could thus arise. For that reason, I find it appropriate to note explicitly that what I recognize as the only possible patriotism of our time and of our nation is explained through its opposite here, and that for this reason its opposite had to be distinguished by strong and powerful features. In reality, this image aims at those whom it resembles, and those whom it does not resemble are not meant. For me, personally, it would be most favorable if nobody could be found who resembles it. As the rules of such a composition likewise require, all the features of this opposite are further amassed onto one person, without meaning to insist that these features might be united somewhere and found together in reality. Finally, as this must likewise happen if an appearance is to be made intelligible, the innermost principles and the foundational maxims of this contrast have clearly been permeated by the concept, made visible, and elevated to the level of reflection. We are far from believing that this clarity and this deliberate purposefulness take place in those who act like this, in which case they really would be devils. In fact, we instead simply consider them poor sinners, who know not what they do, irresistibly pulled onward by their dark inclinations and by a love they themselves do not understand. Every image of backwardness, if done consistently, necessarily looks like the exaggeration others always accuse us of in these instances. But they forget that we did not mean just to deliver their portrait, but rather much more to extract the inner spirit from their sinful body. Incidentally, we would like to believe that if they just once succeeded in glimpsing themselves in their true form, and the hidden principles and necessary consequences of their mentality, they would be horrified at themselves. May the publication of this essay contribute somewhat to provoking this curative horror at the sin.

[396] Now within these limitations which justice and fairness[4] demand, I would think others could very well allow us to say without shying away what they themselves do not in fact shy away from actually doing, since obviously the act that is surely visible without our mentioning it causes far greater nuisance than the subsequent naming of the act. And although absolutely nothing prevents those who maintain control over public book publication because of their official position from personally belonging to one of the two main parties often in conflict, they can, however, only assert the interests of their own party if they themselves step forward as authors. But as public persons they have no party and they have to administer to intellect (which, in any case, applies

to them far more rarely than does ignorance) just as much as they cater to ignorance every day, tending to its needs at every whim. They are also not authorized to refuse any single tone from becoming loud just because it strikes their ear as foreign and paradoxical. That's how things should be in my view. Whether such things can be found in actual practice remains to be seen.

— Berlin, July, 1806[5]

[397]

# The Patriots

### First Conversation

A. *Embarrassed, and anxious, rocks in his chair, looks at the clock.*
B. It seems that my continued presence is annoying you. You want me to go. What's going on?
A. If I may speak freely, I would request you visit another time. The clock has struck five. This hour is scheduled in my daily agenda for my practice of patriotism. Of all my duties, I like least of all to miss this one!
B. Now, surely there's no real hurry for that. — Practicing patriotism? However do you do that if you are patriotic?
A. I inform myself about what new public institutions and ordinances have been made, probe their wisdom and then finally praise that wisdom loudly and publicly.
B. Then do you always find these institutions wise and praiseworthy?
A. That goes without saying. A good patriot should only praise, and always praise, and praise everything exclusively just as it is. If, counter to expectation, something might be found that isn't completely praiseworthy, then it is to be passed over in silence. That's the way for the beautiful bond of love and trust from the governed to the government and back again to be knotted and tied, I say. Our praise for the government really must be eternally flattering, and government can know nothing other than that trust in the government is only the expression of the general mood.
B. Let's leave out the governed, who — if it's true that they are governed wisely — will surely proclaim and glorify the beneficence of their government most naturally with the display[6] of their happiness! With respect to your wise government, I would hope that, precisely because it is wise, it will [398] quietly and seriously proceed on its course from goodness (if God has granted it any) to better and ever better, without taking notice of your songs of praise. Were

it foolish and vain enough, as you assume, to put up with your panegyrics, we would fear that you would corrupt it with them and that it, believing it has attained the goal, would lay itself to rest and give up striving for the more perfect. And then you would have produced a highly pernicious effect with your good, patriotic belief.

A. But patriotism must surely exist, and it must surely be something and must need to be practiced. I wouldn't know how else one could practice it other than in the way I've described.

B. How about if, at this point, a person were to think that there is no patriotism as separate actions and conditions existing for themselves at all, just as there's no religiosity in separate actions and conditions that exist for themselves? But what if a person thought instead that patriotism should just be the abiding element and the foundational form of all our civic life, just as religiosity is the abiding element of our higher spiritual life in general?

A. I can't quite understand you on that point.

B. My opinion is that every individual should do his part, with all his power, in his own place and situation, and that then, to the extent that everything's going well for every individual, everything will also go well for the whole, without any effort on anybody's part and without the help of any special patriotism. With that, internal affairs will be well ordered. From there, anyone who is neither driven by his profession nor justified by his intellect in dispensing advice about external affairs, would simply defer to the highest authority[7] for creating and maintaining for the state that self-sufficiency and independence, dignity, and commanding influence that it can and should have in international relations and for ordering its external affairs accordingly. Beyond this, every individual can further be convinced that through his and others' dutifulness, even these affairs will be suitably advanced.

A. Yes, I certainly thought you would find the chance to apply that old saw that everybody should just fulfill his responsibility in his place and [399] to remind us of honest Luther's adage: if each would learn his lesson, all will be well in house and state.[8] But that's nothing. We already know that and don't want to hear it again. Anybody could do that, but we want to do something special and exceptional, something additional, an *opus supererogativum*[9] where special merit and honor can be gained. That's why an even more special and more expressive patriotism has to be gained for us, since we're always disposed to see the distinctions[10] that the theorist makes in concepts depicted in life as well, since otherwise they wouldn't have any reality.

B. Well then, we'll just have to see what we can do for your patriotic fervor for a pure patriotism, but in a candid way and with clear cognition! — Without a doubt, shouldn't patriotism be an opposite and further determination of cosmopolitanism?

A. Maybe.

B. We would therefore comprehend patriotism if we first knew what cosmopolitanism is and saw how it's further determined by patriotism?

A. May also be.

B. Cosmopolitanism is the ruling will that the purpose of the existence of humankind be achieved within humankind, that this purpose be achieved first and foremost in that nation we ourselves are members of, and that success disseminates from here outwards over the entire human race.

A. Well now, I'll accept that.

B. If you look even more closely at the established concept, it'll make sense to you right away that there can't really be any cosmopolitanism as such[11] at all, but that in reality, cosmopolitanism would inevitably have to become patriotism.

[400] A. I'm not a friend of taking a closer look; I have my reasons against it. But by now this claim of yours so closely corresponds to my own wishes that I'll put up with you bringing the concept in closer.

B. Wherever it's the ruling will that the purpose of humanity be achieved, this will doesn't remain inactive, but rather breaks out, works and takes effect in a direction. But it can only intervene in its nearest environs, where it is and lives as a vital power. So now as certainly as it lives in any given state, these environs are then within the possibilities for effectiveness of the state in which it lives, and this state separates itself from the rest of the world through its own, organic unity. Thus, the effectiveness of each of its good citizens issues forth, and namely in its own medium, according to its own laws, and within itself. But at the point where it separates itself from its surroundings, it also puts the dam holding itself together as a unit in front of this effectiveness. And so then, each and every cosmopolitan will necessarily become a patriot, due to his limitation within the nation, and anyone who is the most forceful and most active patriot in his nation is, precisely for that reason, the most active citizen of the world, in that the ultimate purpose of all national education is surely always that this education should spread across the human race.

A. If I really understood a single word of all this — which is in fact not the case, since all the world knows you lack the talent for lucid lectures — then I still have really no insight into how I could gain the patriotism through it that *I* would very much like to have, the patriotism that's meant to become my own.

B. To have insight into which patriotism you could make your own, you would first have to understand the meaning of the point in time you live in and then the point in space you move in. Only with that would you be able to comprehend in which specific way the ultimate purpose of humanity is to be achieved onward and outward from the point in time you live in and from the nation whose member you are . . .

[401] A. Have I really not yet told you clearly enough that I comprehend or understand nothing at all of what you just now said, as I am not especially understanding now? Anyway, I'll put up with how you keep on telling it to me.

B. Then I'll first and foremost interpret for you the time that you just can't help living in. Everything that's happened up to now for the development of humankind has been accomplished under the guidance of the murky instinct for reason[12] that seized and inspired a chosen few and further shaped humanity with its effectiveness. This instinct is extinguished within the human race and across the entire cultural state, and genius has died out and thus nothing more can be expected from it for the human race. Your most fleeting glance informs you of this. Genius reveals itself only in new creations. But what has our time created that's new? Our political undertakings are imitations of former times. Our artistic aspirations are echoes. A source from which life originally and freshly emerged is no longer available to us. In place of this murky genius, unknown to itself, science has stepped in, and ever since reason stopped operating as a murky instinct, and in the form of unmediated life itself, it has clearly been permeated in its unity by the concept. Even this appearance of science is itself the reason for the silencing and the disappearance of the instinct for reason, for this instinct was in its essence only the fixed, extant possibility of future science. But where it flourishes into reality, the extant possibility is annihilated, and from then on, the spark that breaks out of humankind anywhere is no longer within humankind for that very reason. The source of genius, through which alone humankind has been formed until now, has run dry. Science stepped into its place. From then on, only by this clear science and according to its clearly visible laws and only by deliberate skill,[13] can humankind be led further forward, onward from that [402] point where the murky and thoughtless art of genius abandoned humankind.

A. Your liveliness is sweeping you forward. You're having visions. You claim that reason has, in its unity, been clearly permeated by the concept, and that this happened in our time and before our very eyes and not the least notice was given, neither to me nor to any of my acquaintances! Beyond that, if we were to grant credence to your claims, a total transformation of humankind and all its relationships must have happened. This would virtually contradict the axiom I and all my acquaintances give our firmest belief to: that the world always stays the same and nothing new ever happens under the sun.

But anyway, don't let yourself be interrupted, just keep going instead. It seems that your talks are very comfortable for sleeping through, and I hope that I'll fall asleep to it.

B. The fact that neither you nor any one of your acquaintances took notice of the truly great event of our time — which only now ended the time of creation, set humankind on its own feet, and declared its coming of age by happenstance to every paternalistic authority — comes about because you can't be told about this event only as an external[14] one, but instead have to take part in it as an active contributor yourself if it's going to reach us. With respect to you and your acquaintances' axiom that the world as a whole always stays the same — well, that scares me so little that I consider it, even completely independent of the perception you mean to counter with it, but just taken by itself, to be the greatest absurdity that human lunacy ever hatched and that your and your acquaintances' laziness take for good.

In the meantime, I beg your permission to continue the discussion we have already begun, and it occurs to me to interpret for you the place in space in which you find yourself.

Is it not true, you are a German?

[403] A. No, not a German, I don't want to be a German. I am Prussian, and even more, a patriotic Prussian.[15]

B. Just understand me correctly here. The separation of a Prussian from the other Germans is artificial, founded on arbitrary structures brought about by chance. The separation of the German from the other nations of Europe is based on nature. A collective language and a common national character mutually unite the Germans and separate them from others. Each particular German, and, since you're talking about Prussia, every Prussian, only becomes a Prussian by passing through the German, so that only the true, genuine German is a genuine Prussian. It certainly goes without saying that, as I already said, the Prussian-German can only move and be effective within his own borders, which of course, the organic unity of the state of Prussia gives him.

A. A collective language for Germans! There's a concept. And their national character! Do Germans even have a national character?

B. At least our forefathers tried to dedicate themselves to making noticeable seriousness, perseverance, the search for honest profit and a striving for the essence more than the appearance of things their characteristic nature. I can't claim to know whether the present German generation could make those labels their own with any luck, or whether they would even want them, if one were to offer them, even without any equivalents. But how would it be if precisely this would be seen from the very first as education: an education of the humanity within the German, an education such that he restore, and indeed with deliberation, his national character, and specifically that character already described, should it somehow be lost. That character, of an upright seriousness about whatever, in the eternal flow of time, is now the order of the day, might well be his natural one.

The German living and working in the unified Prussian state will now intend, and work to effect, that [404] the German national character emerge first and most perfectly in this unified state, that it may spread out from here across the related German populations, and then from them outwards, gradually, to all of humanity, occurring as of its own accord, and even without his intention. I wish for this as a German-Prussian patriot now, with a warmth that neither you nor anybody can surpass. What, on the other hand, the Prussian, as pure Prussian, is or signifies, as opposed to the rest of humanity, and how, he, as a Prussian, could have any interest besides the just mentioned interest of the Prussian-German, that the parts of the monarchy remain united as one body politic, that it flourish in good, internal prosperity, and that it claim its due rank in the European order of states, and how anybody could contribute to this purpose in any way other than by fulfilling his obligation in his own place, I confess, I don't grasp. Therefore, I'll just discard that completely, since I only admit what's clearly comprehensible. I'm convinced, that murky and confused concept of a distinct Prussian patriotism is the spawn of a lie and clumsy flattery.

Let's recap! The patriot intends that the purpose of humanity be achieved first in that nation where he is a member. In our time, that purpose can only be furthered by science. Accordingly, science and its greatest possible spread, right in our own time, is the very next purpose of humanity, and humanity cannot and may not set itself any purpose other than this one.

The German patriot in particular wants this purpose to be achieved among the Germans first, and then only from them should that success spread outwards across the rest of humanity. The German can will this because science began under him and is recorded in his language. It's plausible that the greatest ability to grasp science will lie within the nation that also had the power to engender it. Only the German can will this because only he can realize — by means of the possession of science and the understanding of our time in general that has thus become possible to him — that this is the very next purpose of humanity.

That purpose is the only possible patriotic purpose; accordingly, only the German can be a patriot. Only he can include all of [405] humanity in the purpose of his nation. In contrast to that, from now on, ever since the extinguishing of the instinct for reason and the entrance only of egotism into clarity, the patriotism of every other nation will prove to be selfish, mean-spirited, and hostile to the rest of humankind.

A. Science, I hear, science, over and over. It's hard to grasp how humanity can be aided very much by the acquired possession of some abstract formulas and principles.

B. Do I have to repeat that in science, the laws according to which humankind must be systematically further educated (that is, reason) are understood and clearly permeated? Must I repeat that art premised on the possession of this science will really order and improve all human relationships from now on, progressing surely and systematically according to the rules of that science? That's why we're not talking about the possession of some dry formulas just to have those formulas, but about the science and fine art of the real endurance of the human race. For example, in order to stick with the next object of your patriotism: how do you and your acquaintances believe states are really governed?

A. By experience, by routine and above all through divine mercy. When difficulties occur, a person looks up in the chronicles how wise men before our time behaved in similar situations. People have their maneuvers, etc., but then later it turns out that things were just governed without anybody being able to say exactly how it was done.

B. Looking up in the chronicles can't help anything and has never helped anything, since the past never repeats in the same way, and as certain as the measure previously taken was suitable for the situation then, it is as unsuitable for the present situation, for this is necessarily a different one. Just as little has routine ever helped anything, and for just that same reason. Often, the invisible genius of regents combined with experience and routine, which alone had become visible, and everything that was done right in former times was done through this alone. This genius seems [406] to have disappeared from humanity, like all genius, and from now on, governing has become an art that has a solid and unchangeable science. Both need to be learned thoroughly, and without this learning nothing wise will come about anymore. Instead, everywhere there will only be regression, worsening, and decay.

A. Learned, like a trade?

B. No, not like a trade or mechanical learning, but learning from clear, scientific reason and understanding. In the same way that every particular branch of the art of governing — for example, leadership in warfare— is an art that has a strict science. In short, there are no more human affairs at all from which the spirit has not been extinguished and died out and which do not await new life solely, exclusively from science. From now on, therefore, all devotion to the affairs of humanity can be directed exclusively towards the expansion of science, since all other human affairs are included and treated in it.

The particular German states can now compete with one another in this, the only possible patriotism, each grappling with all its power in its own sphere, the Prussian in his. Victory will attend the state that struggles more vigorously.

A. That might well be good for the few scientific people there are in Germany; but for the rest of us, that's not patriotism. Because out of every hundred of us from the educated classes, at least ninety-nine are the greatest imbeciles and idiots. We've never heard that science has any influence on the ordering of human affairs and affairs of state, or even, as you say, that this ordering is based solely on science, and we'll never believe it. And if you just might want to say that out loud, you can certainly count on inexhaustible laughter echoing back at you.

B. Just the same, even though you are all imbeciles and have decided to remain so, you can still demonstrate your patriotism by a deep respect for science and scientific seriousness. Of course, he who is already at home in science isn't asking for your respect, but among the undecided, many would be inclined to take science seriously if it counted for something out in the open, too. [407]

A. With all due respect for your scientific devotion to your office, I must nonetheless note that it's leading you to deliriums. How could we even have respect for science without giving up our respect for ourselves, we who are imbeciles, and without harboring in our hearts a low opinion of ourselves, which might still happen in any case? And how could we further show this respect for science externally in our behavior, without unleashing the whole world's disrespect on us and openly inviting it to disdain us? That's what you're hoping to persuade us of?

B. I should really think that if you just quite decisively gave up your claims to understanding and science, and loudly attested to your disdain for excelling in this area, nobody would impose on you this intolerable measurement for evaluating your worth. After that, you would go out into the world with a tolerable amount of honor based on your remaining good qualities that we're hoping for, especially your genuine respect for the understanding you currently lack.

A. Once again, delirious! Right, if only we could all give up our claim to understanding! But the misfortune is precisely there: that nobody can be such a blockhead that he really wouldn't prefer to see himself as rational, and so the being who wouldn't at least like to be seen as rational is not so easy to find. One would sooner grant another person any other advantages — of birth, of class, or of wealth — than one would sincerely admit another person's advantage in understanding and talent. And of course, jealousy of another's understanding is always that much greater, the greater one's own lack of understanding is, in that whoever is conscious of his own worth in any subject more easily allows others to shine in their own, but whoever has no understanding of his own at all will also not put up with anybody else's.

B. Since by now you in fact have no understanding, as you admit, how will it be possible for you to create a believable appearance of it?

A. First and foremost, the foundation of our edifice is writing. We write because, for the time being, it's the surest way to document that one actually possesses understanding. [408]

B. But then again, writing itself requires understanding. How are you getting out of this circle?

A. I see that you're stuck in the cardinal mistake about writing. Understanding is so scantly necessary for it, that the less understanding somebody has, the more abundantly the writing flows. And so, for the person who has none, it will flow the most copiously of all.

B. I beg you, explain to me how that's possible.

A. Consider: so much of all kinds of writing has been written in our language that this language practically writes itself, and the words just line themselves up in rows and columns without even trying. We've read various things, and still read various things every day, that are all mixed up. So then afterwards, when we sit down to write, what we've read occurs to us again, although fortunately not just as it was printed, since we've never read and grasped it just as it's written, but rather changed in such a way that it looks like something new. Now we don't have anything more to do except interpret this stream of memory and ideas coming to mind with a busy and bustling pen, and the task of writing is completed just at the point where the flow stops. — Do you care to consider for yourself whether, during this operation, any sort of function of that which people like you call understanding steps in? — But should someone with understanding want to write a book, then he would first have to contemplate his object, arrange and sort through the materials, and design a plan for the whole thing, all of which is certainly an utter loss of time and power for real, professional writing.

B. I certainly grasp well enough how a document, as a physical product, can come into existence in that way, but I still don't grasp, without your better instruction, how a work that arose in such a way can look like it's rational, which is, after all, the actual intent. I don't comprehend how a work, unaffected by understanding during its production, can allow understanding, intention, and reflection to peek through afterwards, only once it's finished. It can't be otherwise but that which comes about through blind chance [409] remains blind, without internal unity or plan. The concepts that you didn't determine and didn't make clear likewise remained undetermined and unclear such that no one, and you yourself the very least, know what you wanted to say, since you didn't know it right from the beginning as you wrote. It can't fail but that your whole thing[16] will ultimately tear itself apart, eradicate and cancel itself.

A. First of all, only very few readers know that unity, clarity, precision and internal coherence need to be in a book. It is exceedingly seldom that a reader happens onto the idea of really wanting to understand a piece of writing, and that he's then struck with understanding. Instead, as a rule, all writings are consumed just like we, too, consume them: to use a casual skimming to seed our imaginations for our own, similar products. So then, in the case that the unreasonable demand of understanding might nonetheless be imposed on us, we have a heroic, universal means[17] that simultaneously guarantees the sure attainment of all our other goals and crowns us with the most glorious success.

B. I'm getting pretty anxious to hear about it.

A. We resolutely deny, completely and forever, that understanding is possible, that it ever actually existed in time or ever will actually come to be. We declare the claim that there is a fixed and agreed-upon truth to be not only an inanity but also simultaneously vicious insolence. We declare as an indisputable axiom that the unalterable fate of the whole of the human race is to be thrown around in the same aimlessness, confusion, and contradiction that we also find ourselves in. We teach that there is absolutely no exception, nor will there ever be, that each and every one of us is, without exception, a poor sinner, and in this no one person has an advantage over another. Now, you may show us proof of as many of our imprecisions, inconsistencies, and contradictions, as you want, and we'll respond triumphantly: Were you just so uncomprehending that you [410] expected anything else? Did you really not know that it's a work of human hands; and can any human work turn out other than imprecise, inconsistent and contradictory?

You see what fraternal equality and what fond tolerance arises from this system. We lower ourselves to everyone's level in order to raise everyone up to our level, and to seek solace with everyone. You see what a joyful gospel this doctrine is for everybody whose attitude is aggrieved and dejected by the sense that something might be out there that's leaving them behind. It assures us their acclaim forever.

B. But does this claim, admittedly bold and fundamentally repairing any damage to you, get by so completely without opposition?

A. Very little of that is lacking. By far the most enormous voting majority stands in favor of the truth of our gospel. A very small number hovers, undecided, between the yea and the nay, in one minute trending surely enough towards the nay, when for instance an enthusiast for understanding has just worked them over, but then in the next moment trending once more towards the yea, after that person has stayed silent. But those who would decisively contradict us and accept a fixed truth — who even believed they had found it — are easy to count up. And we're really trying with all our might to make their lives miserable for their dogged opposition.

B. But if there ever were such people, and still are, who purported to possess a fixed, agreed-upon truth, and actually put forward such truth, then how did you get anywhere with only mere denials? In that case, you will surely have had to analyze and refute the doctrine that those people put forward as truth?

A. Nothing less. We just said, in a nutshell: It's simply not true, and they don't know more than we do. They can't be serious about their claim, but instead it's a pure joke. Only if they beat their breast and said, "we, too, are just poor sinners like all you others," would they be serious. Since, once and for all, there can't be any understanding at all and no truth at all, [411] then it is understood wholly and immediately, without any further investigation, that they, too, wouldn't have any.

B. Earlier you also mentioned making life miserable. Just how do you do that?

A. We have plenty of means for that. First of all, we publicly denounce people like that precisely for the fact that they claim[18] a fixed and agreed-upon truth.

B. Does your public[19] really take it so badly?

A. Admittedly, if we only said it in the phrases we just used, that might have little effect. But the art consists in turning it just so that it looks belittling to the fools. Because each and every fool is annoyed and his hate provoked whenever somebody is pointed out to him who seems to claim to be smarter than him. For example, have it printed that a man called his system the maximum of intelligence,[20] and then every fool who reads it — and our writing is only meant for fools — thinks, " then he also deems himself more intelligent than me" — and he gets incensed.

B. Well, I would certainly believe every newly found truth to be a maximum of intelligence in the subject of this truth, as something altogether unchangeable and to which nothing can be added. Thus was, in his time, the inventor of the Pythagorean theorem the maximum of mathematical intelligence. Whoever gets jealous about it might only consider that, by appropriating that same truth on the spot, he can put himself into possession of that maximum, and displace those first sole possessors!

A. But he wouldn't be a fool if he thought of that.

B. Don't you sometimes encounter a sort of gross ignorance with statements like these?

A. Almost always. That's how one of us makes that man with the maximum of intelligence — who provoked even further ridicule when he wanted to teach the Berliners [412] to live blissfully to boot — into a philosopher of nature, when of course it's known that he disputes natural philosophy. But what harm does it do? He writes for readers who mix up Fichte and Schelling.

Further, we sneer at scientific striving and its seriousness.

B. You make fun? How can you? Could you have wit where you haven't any understanding?
A. We can do without it completely. The goodwill of our reader substitutes for it. He likes nothing more than to laugh, and likes to laugh at nothing more than at understanding. So, we give him sort of a signal that we would have liked to laugh at this or that spot, and then he'll laugh all right.

That's why we like to tell anecdotes cutting down grand reputations. Nothing, for example, gives us more pleasure than rustling up a little joke by Kant, something the good bachelor said to a friend at a merry moment, and being able to report it in print for posterity, years after his death.[21]
B. Why does that give you so much pleasure?
A. In that we're looking down on the man, half with pity, in this single remark, it looks like we're simultaneously looking down on the *Critique of [Pure] Reason* from the same height, too. The reader will personally shift into the same optical illusion, and he likes that. At that moment, we and our readers come to be on a first name basis with the great Kant, and we delight in nothing more than dragging a great man down to our level. — For the same reason we also say about *Gall* — whom we likewise [413] envy for the sensation he's caused — for him it all comes down to a lot of two-Friedrichs d'Or coins.[22]
B. But do the scientific people always let you slip all this by?
A. Almost always. Their contempt for us is so excessive that they seldom cast a glance at our scribblings. And if they really do just once, and respond to something, how are you able to deal with us? We are certain we're jotting our scribblings down, for foolishness has set a thousand pens in motion before understanding finds a single one.
B. But now if the one is found after all?
A. Then we'll scold them ourselves that they didn't ignore our essence with the usual silent contempt.
B. Yourselves? But then wouldn't you die of embarrassment about it, and get hissed at by your readers?
A. Neither of those. It then becomes completely apparent that we ourselves know very well, just as our readers know, too, that our essence is nothing serious at all, but just a farce instead. But we consistently strike a serious man as something not to be messed with at all.[23] [414]

Besides these authorial devices, we also have others to whisper in people's ears in social settings, devices that add first the actual commentary and then the practical application to our writerly efforts.
B. I'll allow you to keep quiet about that. From everything you've said, it emerges clearly enough that you get to work quite properly systematically, etc. According to everything that you've told me, the actual fatherland your patriotism is fighting for, and whose flowering and prosperity it seeks to promote, is the kingdom of ignorance and stupidity,[24] whereas the foreigner and enemy that you seek to oust is understanding and science!
A. That's right.

B. Your patriotism is accordingly the exact inversion of the one that I described earlier. Thus, just as I said that the separate German states should compete with one another for the prize of scientific character, just so do the patriots like you all compete with all the other German states for the prize of ignorance, frivolousness, and un-German sense?

A. That's right. [415]

B. And to what extent do you believe you've succeeded up to now?

A. With respect to ignorance itself, it might be hard to retain and substantiate our advantage over the other German states. But in view of the clear and conscious pride in ignorance and the firm determination to remain ignorant and to become ever more ignorant: at least in the capital of the Prussian monarchy, there are living exemplars whose equal you would seek in vain in the entire rest of the cultivated world.

B. I see through your system completely and believe that you cannot possibly fail to find success with such excellent means. Indeed, if you succeed, all the states, as well as the whole current cultural state, will go to ruin because of it. If Germans don't take on governing the world through science, then the Tartars, the Negroes, the North American tribes will take it over after every kind of torment[25] and put an end to current ways.[26] But until then, you'll thrive through every change, assured in honor and prosperity, because foolishness is popular everywhere and if the German doesn't shake it off, then surely no other European nation will shake it off. Then Europe will become one single, continental foolishness and ignorance.

A. We simply don't believe that our doings will have that sad result for everyone, and none of those like you are going to persuade us of it. We very much want the happy success for ourselves that you likewise tout; and thus, we simply continue and, at the same time, keep an immaculate conscience through our ignorance.

    In the meantime, the fundamental principles and rules of our method have unexpectedly, and beyond all my hopes, become clear to me during this conversation with you, and a perfected art of this method has almost formed within me. I wish the other disciples of our art could also share in this advantage. To this end, would you perhaps allow me to publicize this, our well-tended conversation, in print?

B. It's at your service, with no limits.

A. Oh, superb. You give me courage to dare another request of you.

B. Request away!

[416] A. Fundamentally, it could seem, and I'm certain it will seem, as though you had attacked us and shown very little respect at all for our whole work and essence. I foresee that the situation could turn out in such a way that it would bring great comfort to us all for you yourself just to denounce the conversation that just now happened between us two.

B. I foresee it, myself. But how do you intend to do that?

A. I will attack you partly about what you said yourself, and partly about what I said. That latter, although it's the innermost soul of my life, actions, and drives, I really, usually take care not to express. But you've coaxed it out of me with your feigned impartiality. To begin with, you yourself have just now denied the possibility of a concrete, specific Prussian patriotism. We believed until now that we could charm our way in with this concept.

B. Did you succeed?

A. We ourselves don't really know, but we believe so.[27] You tried to annihilate the concept of an exclusively Prussian patriotism and, God willing, that's the first thing that'll turn out bad for you.

B. It's true, that I denied the reality of this concept, because I don't completely comprehend what it might mean. Or just explain it to me in a comprehensible way. You'll find me highly teachable and highly willing to take back my mistake.

A. Yes, well, whoever ventures onto the field of clear concepts with you is lost indeed. You'll never get me there. Instead, I'll attack you precisely because you claim to grasp everything clearly. I'll say you're completely missing any feeling, any sense, any tact, those senseless words with which we manage to help ourselves through any [417] scientific trouble. I'll stir the pot and mix up trouble with the loveable sentiment of mutual trust and the trusting love that you tried so hard to eradicate, and with similar figures of speech until your ears are ringing, and every fool in the city and country considers you a monster and a moral freak.

B. I believe that will happen.

A. Further, I'll show that your ways of thinking are most unpatriotic. I'll draw my evidence from the principle that a patriot must always praise. But what you've wheedled out of me looks like criticism and very harsh criticism, at that.

B. At most, a criticism of you and the folks like you, of your ways of thinking — that you've never clarified to yourselves — and of your scribblings. But then, are your scribblings the fatherland?

A. Of course not. But I'll know how to set it up so that the majesty of the state seems to be attacked whenever our botched scripta are under attack.

B. If I were to uncover the source of all evil at home, in the state and in the world, and just wanted to improve it with strict criticism, then wouldn't my endeavors be highly patriotic?

A. Wanting to improve? Hand on your heart, do you believe that anything would be improved by this conversation?

B. Since you implore me, of course I must admit that I consider folks like you completely incorrigible, and likewise, I admit your supreme power over the reading public to be indisputable. In the meantime, I thought, what can one more vain attempt hurt, after so many, countless, vain attempts, and so in the name of God I attempted it. It would only be right, and I wish it from the bottom of my heart, that this attempt could improve something.

A. Of course, I'll ascribe completely different intentions to you. I'll say that you just wanted to air out your spleen, since everybody knows that the entire rational world is laughing at you, at how you just wanted to get yourself established with your recommendation of science and that you believed yourself to be science personified,[28] [418] and that for you, nothing at all is right except you yourself. I'll say for the second time that you considered yourself the maximum of intelligence, and lots more stuff like that. You can be sure that all my readers will take me at my word.

B. I don't doubt it. What more do you want from me for that purpose?

A. You should promise me that from now on you'll ignore, with implied contempt, all these and additional smears that we'll inflict on you.

B. Why should I do that? I understood that you're so sure of your public that nothing I could say against you would get them riled up.

A. Quite true. But not to the extent that it wouldn't seem to this public that you might be right for as long as you're speaking. Only once I comment on your speech in my way are you then wrong and I'm right again. For this public, whoever gets the last word is right. Now without a doubt, it would always be an easy thing for me to rebut your last speech once again. But still, that would cost me some effort, and the same for you, too, that we can both relieve ourselves of. So therefore, it's my wish that you just let me have the last word in a nice way. I would surely get it, anyway.

B. I believe you're right. So, with that I now happily give you my word, my faithful gallant, that I will ignore all your further smears in silence.

## Second Conversation

C. Going back to the first conversation — that's how you thought about patriotism a year ago, in the time of the deepest and most secure peace — as it seemed to the masses. Hopefully, you think differently today, as you've also acted differently in some ways since then.

B. Differently, hardly — but maybe now I find it necessary to expand the same constant, unchanging thinking to other objects.

C. I could anticipate that answer. "Principles don't change in time or in any event of time: only the application of them is determined by the material that time provides." — Who doesn't know that saying? But is it really supposed to be only an expansion of the sphere of your thinking, and not maybe more of a modification of the principle itself, one that has proved inadequate to you? That's something I wouldn't put past you and that I think I notice.

B. Let's see. My thoughts about patriotism certainly assumed the state in a lasting peace and examined it under this assumption in two ways. Partly, with regards to its form, it must be firmly responsible for itself and must persevere. For this purpose, and according to my lasting opinion, nobody can do more than carefully meeting his obligations in his place and in just the way that is required of him — every action beyond that would only cause disruptions and disorder in a well-ordered, precisely calculated state that's appropriately engaged in all its parts. And that the state thus continuously brings forth its own rebirth to a higher and more spiritual life within and secured by this, its persevering form. The latter, I said, is possible since the visible extinction of the instinct for reason only by clear science and an art of reason[29] founded on clear science. Therefore, whoever wants to do even more for the state than merely what the obligations of his class and profession entail can do so only either through the active advancement of scientific clarity or, in case his ability in this fails him, [420] by attesting to science with sincere respect. All that in peace. But it's completely otherwise when war threatens the continued existence of the fixed, permanent form within which alone all continuing development of civic life is possible, and the citizens are prevented from fulfilling the duties of their professions and vocations in the customary, ordered way. Then the higher life that is attacked in its provisionary environment must surely pause a moment, above all else in order to assure itself of its spiritual rule over the disputed position. At that time, the entire state comes under a revolutionary strain, and the citizen must do more than is requested of him and more than can be requested of him only within the sphere of the concept of right. Now, active patriotism, free self-sacrifice, and a sense of heroism step up in place of the lawful obedience that was previously singularly allowed. Property, the good and regular administration of which previously best served the state, gets sacrificed now. Life, that was previously to be maintained for as long as it could be for all civil purposes, will now confront danger. For the state is not in its natural situation, but is in an emergency instead, and with that the well-being of all is threatened. An exact accounting of what each individual should do is not possible now: the state needs everybody's power, and the earlier this is completely put into action, the earlier the conditions of order and the legal distribution of the burdens sets in again. But its power is put into action completely only by each individual offering his all. Thus, the citizen should do more in war than in peace. By the same token, particularly in a dangerous war, he should let some stuff go that, in his full rights, he can and should do in times of peace, perhaps for the greatest well-being of the whole. For example, discussing whatever might still be done for better basic organization [421] is really not on the daily agenda if the ground for all real or possible organization is shaky. To bring this up, bitterly and squabbling, for all the world to hear, especially in such times, and thereby even further cloud the moods of the already dazed, confused masses looking for objects of vengeance for their distress, would at least be judged as not acting very prudently.[30] If there are family disputes between us, then let's settle them when the existence of the family as such will no longer be endangered. To use just precisely the time of a general emergency to extort what one believes would not be granted in good times would be a very unworthy profanity for an educated person.

C. I have to admit that with the distinction between tranquil and dangerous times, you've pulled yourself out of this mess well enough and have rescued your logical consistency. But what about your unconditional tossing out of a particular, and pure, Prussian patriotism? Today you are certainly a Prussian only, and certainly wish only this state and its allies good fortune and victory?

B. But this, too, is solely out of necessity, because all the other German populations seem compelled to forget their Germanness and to give up on defending German independence.[31]

C. For now, my questions to you have only related to secondary matters. I have one more, far more significant objection to your system of patriotism.

The instinct for reason, you say, has been extinguished over the whole present human cultural state, which I'll grant you, since I foresee that you would say to him who would disavow it: he just doesn't understand what you meant by instinct for reason and has absolutely no cognition of the relations under discussion, and it is initially incumbent on him to achieve first the education through which alone that understanding becomes possible, before it's appropriate for him to join in talking about this matter.

[422] B. I certainly would say that.

C. Since now every benefit for humankind could come solely from reason — and I grant you that from the heart — thus you expect from now on the cure and the recovery of our race only from a clear science of reason?[32]

B. That's it.

C. I have really been wondering that you haven't discovered the obvious circle in your speculations that holds you captive, like someone blind as a bat.

B. You have discovered an obvious circle in my speculations? That's excellent. I know one, too, as well as its solution. Develop your thoughts. I want to see whether they coincide with my own.

C. Isn't this true: You hold that Kant, first and alone among all mortals, discovered the principle of the science of reason, clear self-reflection and self-understanding, and that later on the *Wissenschaftslehre* recognized this principle, expressed it definitively, and systematically and consistently implemented it in the sphere of the very first principles of reason.

B. That's what I believe.

C. Do you think that Kant has been understood?

B. Kant tossed sparks of truth and of better cognition out in all directions of science and to innumerable minds, sparks that compounded with lingering basic misconceptions and so made the misconception somewhat more bearable, but then also more powerful and persistent. But penetrating his principle and making it a medium of pure truth and clarity has been granted solely to the author of the *Wissenschaftslehre* among all living people.

C. By the way, do you know that people resent beyond words such pronouncements like that last one? That you offend your colleagues in the field of philosophy with similar pronouncements such as that, and fiercely incense them, along with the whole world? And that people interpret it as a self-conceit in you that borders on insanity?

B. I even saw in advance that it would come to that before I had ever even done such things and I've been prepared to bear this as my unalterable destiny for fourteen years now. In the meantime, this cannot remain unsaid: for since I want to bring them to comprehension, I can't leave them [423] thinking that they already understood it, as they in fact do believe. Further, since I am the one who wants to teach them correct comprehension, then I just have to say that I myself understand it. It can be just as little proven, since the proof of not-understanding could only be shown to him who really understood it. At the same time, if it could be shown to anyone else, then there would be someone who understood it, a thing just now being denied.

C. So then, pronouncements like that don't just slip out of you in an unguarded and passionate mood, but really you pronounce such things in good consciousness and with a considered purpose?

B.[33] Unfortunately, I must confess the latter is the case. —
Now, as much as I freely acknowledge the bad light that puts me in, and bear it, I also certainly cannot absolve others of all unfairness against me, in that I, in my place, wouldn't take it badly or feel offended in the least if they in turn said that I don't understand what I in fact do not understand.

C. Well, don't base too much on that last bit. You easily bear it when people say you don't understand whatever you didn't like learning and understanding. But you are accusing people of not understanding what they have studied for half a lifetime and what they would really give anything in the world to understand. Those are very different cases.

But let's turn back to our intended subject! Only one person, then, understood Kant. And so, then again, how many understood this one person and his doctrine?

B. The *Wissenschaftslehre,* too, scattered out masses of sparks, just like Kant, but nobody I'm familiar with grasped it in its principle. But this not being familiar to me is decisive here, since it's certain that if anyone had this cognition, he would surely not keep it secret.

C. Well then, I just ask of you to stop and think, finally, just for once! It's been more than thirteen years now that you've offered this *Wissenschaft*. What have you not [424] written, debated, and fought in your time? Which form and what tone have you left untried? And with that, you've had extraordinary luck. With a book[34] that you yourself recognized as bad, even as you were having it printed, and that afterwards was publicly declared bad, even by you, while its author was presumed for a while to be Kant, you suddenly won a name for yourself. The first notes that rang out over your new discovery stirred up expectations, and almost every sect looking for a leader was inclined to gather under your flag. And, as far as I can gather from the various judgements, they don't even bring up awkwardness of expression and speech, like with good old Kant, who couldn't write.

B. What? Kant couldn't write?

C. That's how it is, as you can hear from the mouths of our mature and immature folks who can write.

After that you believed it would pan out better as an oral lecture. Which form, and turn of phrase in this oral lecture have you left untried since then? In how many places have you not stood at your podium, and whom have you not lured into your lecture hall? And in this, too, unparalleled luck accompanied you everywhere. — And now you say, after these thirteen years of work and effort in all directions, that 'nobody, absolutely none of all the living, understood what [425] I actually want to make comprehensible to them, and which is the only thing that matters.' Then shouldn't you, as a man who wants to be seen as sensible, finally see that this universal, this ongoing not-understanding that blocks every applied means of communication couldn't in any way be accidental, but there must instead be a principle at the bottom of it that always necessarily results in it? How can you hope, if you want to use understanding for just a moment here, that what has proven itself completely impossible will be possible if you still keep on acting in the same way as you have up to now for another thirteen years — and, were it possible, thirteen times thirteen years in any one of those thirteen years?

B. Oh, friend and faithful advisor, I certainly don't hope! Who told you I'm hoping?

C. Then why not rest and let humankind go however it will, and just take care that you yourself get by tolerably well? You must have lots more ways to spend your time and that of others. Translate something, give lectures about history, write satirical dialogues for which you surely seem to be lacking neither the mood nor the material.

B. *Verum nequeo dormire!*[35]

C. *Ter uncti transnanto Tiberim*[36] — I could continue the quote. But now seriously and back to the point.

    Do you therefore admit, that it's not in any way based on an especially ill will, but instead much more that it's simply impossible for the present generation to grasp the principle of the clear science of reason?

B. Unfortunately, I'm compelled to accept that last comment.

C. And where do you situate the reason for this impossibility?

B. In the intellectual and moral depravity of the generation.

C. But where do you situate the reason for the all the other evils of humankind, which — following the extinguishing of the instinct for reason — await their healing from science alone?

B. In that same intellectual and moral depravity of the generation.

C. And thus, the circle in your speculations becomes clear as day. The very [426] depravity in need of a cure is, precisely because it is depravity, incapable of it. If, as you claim, this cure is the only one and there is no other to be found, then humanity must succumb to its evils without salvation, which is now completely what it's looking like. And you are a doctor who may be able to invent a remedy out of the blue, but only when someone else stops him from using it does he actually admit its impossibility.

B. The situation operates just exactly like you're saying: And you're completely right regarding the circle you've diagnosed that reproaches my speculations, to the extent that they're summarized in the conversation you read. But how about if I knew the means to fill the gap that's left?

C. Your fundamental claim that science is the only remedy for healing sick humanity can only exist together with your present avowal that this science can't reach the people where they are, and with the fixed assumption that they

nonetheless can and should be helped, if you know of another, second remedy. This second remedy wouldn't heal humankind of its illness for now, but would first of all heal it of its inability to acquire science for itself, and only after that would a complete healing be carried out by science being brought to the people from then on.
B. That's my opinion.
C. Then you would have to know how to present, in pure isolation and independent of the rest of the generation's depravity, the particular reason for its lack of receptiveness to science, and to indicate the sure means for removing that reason.
B. In fact, that's how I intend to proceed.

The purpose of science is to bring the fundamental source of truth and reality per se, in their absolute point of unity, into the free possession of human beings. From that point of unity, every particular truth and reality descends as a further determination of the first, according to determined and equally recognizable laws of a further such determination. The cognition and the free possession of that said point of unity is not inherent in the human being, [427] but must be acquired. The highest thing the human being has earlier on, prior to this acquisition, is a mere substitute, a shadow and specter of reality, which, in this situation where he has nothing higher, he necessarily takes for reality itself. Consequently, the very first matter that you must undertake with him in order to bring him to cognition of the truth is this: to pierce this shadow as a mere shadow for him, and thus destroy it.

Now the last and highest shadow that all of humanity except for Kant took for reality — and the greatest upswing in cognition consisted not in ripping apart and dividing even this shadow again, but instead grasping it as a solid unity, as, for example, Spinoza did — this last and highest shadow, I say, is *being*. Kant exposed this as an empty shadow and began to destroy it on all sides in his assorted writings, without, however, really tackling it at the root.
C. In hearing this, plenty of places in Kant occur to me that can only make sense under the condition that he recognized being as completely empty and void. Yet I don't know of another author who has understood Kant like that.
B. In that respect, the *Wissenschaftslehre* has been understood better,[37] and this is therefore surely an advancement of universal cognition. After a number of years, we have finally discovered that this completely destroys, exterminates and dissolves being into absolute nothingness. But now you think: that must be wrong after all and can never again be intended seriously by that science, since being really does exist. And so then, some people help themselves by wanting to safeguard this being from transience[38] with the addition of absoluteness — but with that they only take away from it its purity and simplicity as a shadow, position it one level lower, and [428] make it into the shadow of the shadows. Others attempt a deeper analysis of this concept, in case perhaps a more fireproof part might be discovered in it.[39] What never occurs to anybody: that after the destruction of this actual void — a void that clearly wears the stamp of death in its perseverance and calm and that can be reawakened

to life and to activity only through a manifest contradiction — nothing of the void remains in any way. Rather, only then does it come to the only truly real thing, *to immediate life itself,* that *lives,* not simply *is,* persists and exists, and much more plainly destroys any such being that also doesn't exist outside of itself, but within itself, just like all being.

C. Then tell it to them like that, as certainly and as clearly as you just now told me it. — Not in being do truth and reality reside, but only in immediate life itself. The former is only the shadow of the latter — whose origin from life you'll probably also explain?

B. But of course.

C. Immediate life itself, in living, is to be understood as the highest and most absolute. Does that not suffice? I should think everyone can understand that. It's also immediately convincing, if one just considers for a moment what you [said] above about the persistence of being, and that only with a new work of art, one that actually contradicts the first principle, can we once again bring in life and activity, that people really require anyway.

B. Unfortunately, that doesn't suffice. Because now, as immediately as they get it, they certainly think this life to death again. They think it away as a lifelessly existing and persisting thing that real activity attaches to only now and then, as an *accidens*, and they surely have another word, but not another meaning.

C. Then how else should they understand it?

B. Like this: that they think it without thinking it; that it doesn't come into being and die away outside of them, but that they remain one with it. In short, I can surely give you the word — they should get it not by thinking, but through living intuition.

[429] C. Tell me, can you express yourself differently than I just now expressed myself? Life *is,* and it *is* the only thing true, real etc. in itself?

B. Not at all. Because even language is located in the region of shadows and what's been elaborated collapses with being as its first and immediate shadow. Therefore what I express is never my intuition itself; and what is to be understood in my expression is that which I mean rather than what I say, just like we really do always operate in life. It's completely essential that language come to an end at the principle of real science and that communication in words about this principle not be possible.

C. So then, neither can your protege express himself otherwise. Then how can you know, and prove to him, that despite the fact that he talks just like you, he nevertheless didn't understand you?

B. In the following way: the immediate intuition of actual life is itself *spiritual* life as the first modification of it per se, and directly at its root. But the previously mentioned further determinations of truth and reality, with all their schematic addenda, are completely contained in these roots, and flow completely easily and clearly into each person who has only become that intuition or that spiritual, fundamental life itself. Or in other words: we can't grasp the principle of science without becoming it ourselves, for if we were not to become it, then we would only have thought the principle, that is, killed it and displaced it in a mere shadow, outside itself. But if we have become it, then we have become simultaneously an artist and a self-creator of science in all its further determinations. Despite the fact that for this reason we can't communicate in words about the principle, we can certainly nevertheless communicate very easily about its results, and here the agreement in words surely can't deceive. Whoever can't immediately take up the thread where the teacher lets it fall and continue the deduction in an orderly and correct manner has understood neither the principle nor the first results, but has merely memorized words.

C. Then that's what you base your claim on, that among all the living there is no one who has understood you, in the actual meaning of the word?

[430] B. That's what I base it on.

C. And completely opposite the approach of other teachers, you are more meticulously concerned with showing that we don't understand you than that we do understand you. You don't get indignant that we don't understand you, and aren't afraid that your ability for representation or your doctrine itself will get blamed, or that people will say, how can something be valid that no human being understands?

B. That's how it is; and I'm not in the least afraid of these judgments, either.

C. And the result of all this, if you've gotten as far as results, is . . . ?

B. . . . That the reason it's impossible for this generation to get science is that they neither share in nor are receptive to an intuition of immediate life. The highest spiritual operation[40] they can swing themselves up to, where they're still most excellent, is thinking, that is, the projecting out of themselves a shadow of their inner life that they then look at and content themselves with, rather than the thing itself. Usually, it doesn't even get as far as this thinking, but really just stays at daydreaming, meaning at the arbitrary creating of shadows from the elements of shadows in the first place.

C. The entire pre-historical world also lacked, according to you, this intuition of immediate life up until it finally blossomed into reality and clarity in Kant. And I therefore don't see how you want to reproach only our generation for this deficiency and even especially, how you want to link this deficiency even more closely to the extinction of the instinct for reason that you've put in pre-history, and to our whole intellectual and moral deterioration that has never been so deep in any previous time. But you have to do this anyway, if we're not to find gaps in your view of time, and ensure that thoroughness and succinctness are not missing in it.

B. And I plan to do that. Don't let it escape you that I deny not only our generation's participation in the intuition of life, where they have the same fate as the whole of prior history, but also their immediate receptivity for it. That latter I wouldn't necessarily deny to pre-history at all, [431] in that I think Kant and the *Wissenschaftslehre* would have been grasped by the ancient Greeks, maybe also by the Romans, and in the Middle Ages in every country where religious superstition wasn't too oppressive, certainly even in Leibniz's time, and before Locke, the Encyclopedists and our Eclectics and Popular-Philosophers begun to educate the era.

But our generation isn't immediately receptive to the intuition of life because, from the moment of their first development on, absolutely all intuition gets completely yanked away from them and they are driven away from it into shadows and fog with considerable art, which skill our education consists of. The child's organ barely develops to its first babbling when it presents an opening to our art, already lying in wait, and thus the child gets words instead of things and phrases instead of sensations. Soon the spoken words, a schema that is still too near to intuition, are transformed for him into dead letters, until these, too, lose their solid forms through familiarity and the children are swimming in an ocean of unformed letter-elements as their real world. And thus, education has already achieved one of its primary ends. The highest art of this education is this: surely not allowing the pupil to linger a moment on any shadow of lower potency — since that's lost time for the goal of education and laziness and stupidity in the pupil — but driving him quickly on to the shadow of the shadow, and again to the shadow of the last shadow, and on and on. The genius of the pupil resides precisely in this skill for hurrying along. In this way, only a fog-and-shadows world remained for the generation, without any kind of core of intuition, truth, and reality supporting it. But their higher scientific endeavors consist in once again refining, filtering, and sublimating the designated shadows of highest potency, thereby raising them to an ever-higher power, and then in coupling these reactants with each other so that they beget a fog-world completely purified, where possible, of all truth and reality. [432] Of course, this business can be continued ad infinitum, although the intended goal of obtaining a fog-world completely purified of truth will nevertheless never be completely accomplished. There are valiant, albeit poorly informed men[41] in Germany who think the *Wissenschaftslehre* is a high mistress in this art of sublimating the fog and who, out of a murky feeling that it needn't be so, are therefore heartily ill-disposed towards it. I honor and love the source of this aversion.

Now, is it any wonder, or could the result be any different, than that those who have never, since they've come to consciousness, found themselves in the condition of intuition in any field of knowledge, can't enter into the highest intuition of all and into the source of all other intuitions? But that instead, they persist in the shadow and fog they grew up in and have lived in? How could such persons notice and correctly comprehend the finest and deeply hidden operations of spiritual life through which, for example, being comes about in the first place, and the awareness of which is ultimately required for the annihilation of being as such? They who quite possibly haven't even conceived of a single chair leg correctly in their whole lives, and how it's truly there? They really know absolutely nothing at all, and they haven't been allowed to linger anywhere until the point of knowledge, but have instead always been driven on to temporarily memorizing yet another thing. How could they ever know of knowledge itself? A generation like that and science live in completely opposing elements. Science doesn't seem to them to be something like development, further education, or anything similar; it seems to them to be like something born anew, and that's a pure impossibility. In contrast, if you take human beings who simply know something correctly and precisely because they grasped it in living intuition and made it their free property, then it's already in a shared element with them. They only have to augment a faculty that they already actually possess and that always remains the same, and elevate it to the last level that it can achieve, and this [433] elevation of an already given, fundamental faculty isn't even very hard.

C. According to that, you find the reason for our generation's lack of receptivity to the doctrine of truth, that is, to science, in its education, which results in the generation always being whipped further, with deliberate art, from truth and the immediacy of intuition to mere substitute shadows, and ever forwards into this shadow-world. Thus, you find the reason for their lack of receptivity to the doctrine of truth, that is, to science, in the lack of receptivity for all truth that's forced onto them.

I don't want to bother you with a derivation on the rest of the deterioration of the generation because of these circumstances. Since the one and eternal truth is the only thing that binds human beings to a unity of convictions[42] and immerses those humans as one in their eternal wellspring, then it's immediately clear that, where truth has been wiped out of the human race, and every individual only lives in his self-created fog-world, pure selfishness must inevitably become the only driving force in human life, and civic mindedness, morality and religion must inevitably disappear.

But I would love to hear from you just how the extinction of the instinct for reason might succeed from that same root cause.

B. In the following way: Just as the essence of science consists in further developing and shaping the truth given in immediate intuition according to a law, with deliberate art, and within clear consciousness, so, too, does being driven by the instinct for reason consist of a truth, given in immediate intuition, likewise developing and further shaping itself, without any evident intervention by the individual and in dim consciousness. And now because reality resides in life, that truth seizes the life of the individual and lives its own life in him. Now it's clear that where there's no intuition at all and for that very reason also no truth, one cannot develop itself, just as little within dim consciousness (on the path of the instinct for reason) as within a clear consciousness (on the path of science). Thus, it's clear that a generation without intuition, just as it exists and lives completely without reason, would also have to live without the instinct for reason.

In fact, even the shadows and fog within them carry the sign of their descent from life and of their relatedness to reality, in that they themselves also [434] stir themselves, move and shape themselves, occasionally with great agility and colorful, bustling activity; of course, always and inevitably in dim consciousness and precluding deliberate art, in that shadows only last in the dark, anyway, and clarity stepping in would destroy them and replace them with the essence. Commonplace imagining exists in this liveliness of the shadows, to which the independent thought and all ideal creation of such a generation necessarily remains limited. And so, in its form, effusive daydreaming,[43] as the self-development of an unknown within dark consciousness, is exactly the same as the stimulus of the instinct for reason. But in their essence, they are completely different, partly because truth is at the base of the latter, and dreams and shadows the former, and partly because the latter grasps real life and shapes it according to itself, while the former only gives birth to theories that nobody dares take seriously in life or invest themselves in.

C. This would certainly bring another question to mind. But another, more opportune time for putting it out there might still come up. For now, let's first outline everything that's been said together, as a unit.

According to you, the education of the generation is the root of all their evil generally, including especially that of their lack of receptivity to a clear science of reason, and the state of education specifically that absolutely doesn't allow the pupil to linger and take root in intuition, but instead drives him away from it to shadows, and to shadows ever more removed, ever further from reality. Accordingly, the remedy would consist in getting rid of this type of intellectual education absolutely and completely. In fact, you might even mean that if intellectual education ever claims to exist and to mean something, it should strike out on the exact opposite path, and lead its pupil to intuition and really fix them there and let them take root in it. That's how truth will reach the generation once more for a possible instinctive development, [435] as will the skill to reign freely with the organ for truth, with intuition, for scientific development.

B. That's what I'm saying.

C. I'm afraid you've gotten into a new circle. If the whole lot of the entire, currently living generation is ruined for living intuition, then how do you hope to find teachers in this generation who can instruct the coming generation in this art of intuition?

B. That's precisely the infinitely high, great and triumphant thing about this idea, that this art need not be taught, just as it also couldn't be taught, but that only direction is required and that anybody can quite easily comprehend the rules of it and can give this direction to whomever might be missing that art entirely in their own person. The nature of the human race has not yet run dry, has not been rooted out. Luckily, our children are still born like all children of humankind have been born from the beginning, with the ability and drive for intuition. They themselves don't desire the shadow-world: it's only our unholy art that drives them into it, against their resistance. This art should be abolished and another should step in instead, to guide them appropriately in intuition and thus fix their hold on reality and develop their freedom to manage intuition appropriately. Not a single other thing is needed than, above all, your conviction that things behave as has just been postulated and secondly, that you then learn the rules of the art of guiding intuition correctly and in accordance with the natural order. And learning these rules is not hard.

C. Are you hoping to convert the generation even just to the first thing, that things are so? Do you hope ever to bring them back from the unconditional esteem for that single thing in which they see spiritual talent, namely that skill of leaping to the more abstract shadows from the simpler ones?
B. Whether we can hope for it or not, let's just calmly await the results. It surely has to be said sometime, and tested by being said, [436] since this is the final means for saving the contemporary, cultured state from ruin. At least, I'm not alone in saying this, fortunately, and not the first. It's been said before, thundering in our ears. And here again, it's the German nation, to which the first author[44] of the proposal belongs, to which the proposal was first made. Even among all the other European nations, the German nation is the first to be trusted in being capable of the necessary self-reflection and self-denial, and also, on the other hand, the necessary teachability. So here we are again: if the German nation doesn't rescue the cultural level of humankind, then any other European nation will hardly do it. But if the level of culture doesn't get rescued by this, the only agreed-upon intermediary left to it, rescued for the higher and absolute remedy, for science, then the second human cultural level will go down in ruins just like the first one went down in ruins. Then the question is whether new cultures will arise from savages and barbarians after millennia, and whether these, too, will fall to ruin or will maintain themselves more worthily than their two known predecessors.
C. Enough with the indoctrination! Let's stick with what's at hand: You aren't the only one, and not the first, either, who says this? How am I supposed to understand that?
B. And I'll go even further: I'll say that this art of guiding pupils' intuition has already been pretty fully outlined to the public, and is being diligently carried out elsewhere.
C. You certainly don't mean Pestalozzi's[45] theory, that has children [437] rote-learning words and expressions they don't understand? They say he is in fact trying to introduce an unbearable mechanism, one that, precisely as in your previous words that I thought were a criticism, gives the barely babbling child a word instead of a thing, etc. Do you mean this man, who himself acknowledges his total ignorance and clumsiness in all things, his gloomy empiricism,[46] and his absolute inability in any philosophy? And he isn't just sort of being modest with these acknowledgments, whose literal truth is clear as day in his writings. This man, who seems not too fond of philosophy in general, but belongs among those who think of it as the art of diffusing fog to the finest possible mist. A philosopher, the author of the *Wissenschaftslehre*, recommends this man as the final savior and redeemer of humanity!
B. Pestalozzi, too, you have to get to know by his own words, and not by any accounts from his reviewers. As you can read for yourself in his own admission, necessity forces him to that rote teaching of words not yet understood, which is inadvisable and definitely doesn't belong to the essence of the method [438] but much more contradicts its spirit and its origin, and which,

by the way, doesn't have the disadvantage in this context at all that it shows in every other.

Pestalozzi's thought is infinitely more and infinitely greater than Pestalozzi himself, just like every truly ingenious thought's relationship to its apparent author is. He didn't think the thought, or make it up, but eternal reason thought it within him, and the thought made the man and will further make him. In the history of the revelation of this thought, as it appears in Pestalozzi's writings with a truth that speaks for itself and with a pure, childlike simplicity, we could demonstrate what we said above with sensuous clarity: that a truth, once it has seized a human being, continues to form itself in dark consciousness, without knowledge or free effort on the part of that human being, finally breaking out nonetheless to light and clarity despite the most powerful obstacles. The soul of Pestalozzi's life was love for the poor and neglected; his love became so blessed that he found more than he searched for, the singular remedy for all of humanity. That at the same time he found the sole means for educating a generation capable of understanding Kant and the *Wissenschaftslehre* [439] will seem miraculous, even to himself, if he hears that I've said it, or even might sort of make a light bulb go on in his head about the actual point of the *Wissenschaftslehre*.

It's in this sense, then, that you first have to grasp Pestalozzian thought, in order to understand it correctly and to appreciate it: not as the intellectual education only of the poor and oppressed, but as the absolutely vital elementary education of the entire future generation and of all the generations from here on out. Although the latter, higher view is not at all foreign to him and he often expresses it in the description of the implementation, too, the first, limited view still keeps getting in the way, even of the author himself, as the essential one. This is partly because he himself started with it when he organized his practice, partly because he seems implicitly to assume that this oppression and impoverishment of the greater majority will always remain and dares not see that, wherever his education becomes the national education, that oppression would quite soon and inevitably fall away. Finally, despite all of his aversion to alphabetics,[47] he nonetheless places far too great a value on it for the populace, precisely as a weapon against oppression. All of these other features that belong so little to the fundamental idea that they really contradict it, and which have roused the greatest offence and even put current education in a position of nobly opposing the new pedagogy, arose simply from this predominant consideration for the exclusive needs of the majority of the people.[48]

Secondly, it's imperative that we track the fundamental idea itself down to its roots to give the practice the foundation that it presently lacks.

C. The practice whose principles you recommend lacks a foundation?

B. And it does such good service, and benevolent nature gives a boost, too, just like it also certainly does for what's even worse. But if the system is to appear in its full value and as what it is, as the elementary education of the whole human race, [440] then it must be given this foundation for its practice.

C. Make your meaning clear.
B. Of course Pestalozzi and his followers and colleagues know nothing other than that being is the ultimate and the absolute and the truth, and that nothing transcends being. They thus initiate the development of intuition with the objective things scattered about the space. They would have known that all reflection and all education towards freedom of intuition emanates from the subject.
C. Pestalozzi says the same thing you're just now saying very decidedly and emphasizes it insistently. Precisely in this regard, his first elementary tool for development, his *Book for Mothers*, is occupied with the child himself and gives him awareness[49] of his body.
B. He says it, and quite certainly sees, with his sense of truth, that it must be so. But he doesn't understand what he's seeing and, as he explains himself and as it becomes practice, he says and does the opposite! So, is the child's body the child himself? Pestalozzi surely doesn't believe that. The child thus becomes objectified to himself, and in fact is objectified to himself far too early, because according to the regular course of development that P. sticks to so seriously and quite rightly elsewhere, the child must first learn to use his body and should get to know it before he is to separate it objectively from himself. If P. had [441] been able to find any other application for his correct assumption that education has to emanate from the subject, then he would certainly have discovered that this beginning with awareness of the body contradicts his own fundamental principle.

There is still a second fundamental principle of the Pestalozzian theory, as correct in itself as it is incorrectly understood and applied by the author himself. The correct understanding of it would have gotten him past the point of criticism and sorted things out right away. According to Pestalozzi, among the three means for helping a human being get from dim concepts to clear ones (we want to let him have his language, but in place of that we would say instead, helping a human being to freer and more reflective intuition), sound is at the forefront as the medium of words and language, the latter of which he actually means.

Observed more closely, this is simply not true in the sphere that Pestalozzian development is based on. The figure of an object in space has become clear, that is, it has come into the reflective freedom of intuition, in that you can reconstruct it in all its parts completely precisely, and thus renew it at will. With that, clarity is then complete and whole and no possible component can be added. By retaining a name and word for it, you simply get the ability to communicate[50] about it with others, but, while it thus relegates us to a completely different sphere, [442] the intuition itself is not augmented by it. Language behaves like that in general in relation to the entire objective world, from the shape of the simplest line up to the most complex operation of reason. It is only the medium of communication with others and the element of harmony in a spiritual world consisting of diverse individuals. But the sole medium for self-communication in this objective world is the free construction in intuition. In contrast, the sort of language use that P. recommends, as a readymade framework for ordering intuitions, is more correctly the medium for making an abrupt transition and for early mouthings[51] to which Pestalozzian theory, where it moves forward consistently, is quite justifiably so very hostile. This use of language imposes itself on Pestalozzian theory because of the previously mentioned interim worry about the populace. And yet the Pestalozzian principle is true, and an infinitely deep truth lies within it — it's just true in another sphere. Indeed, not language but speaking itself — that is, *that* the human being speaks and is to be expressed — is the very first medium for the development of self-reflection. The child sits there in a muffled chaos of all his feelings that all incessantly blur into each other. How does he ever pick out anything singly and separately from this stream, and himself emerge from the flood and be born to his own concept of I-hood?[52] What gives him the need for this singling out and the impetus for it, and for this generating of the self by itself? Obviously, the necessity of *expressing*, in his absolute helplessness, the most pressing, most immediate threat to his own preservation to the people who are at his side and ready to help but who relate to him by absolutely no other medium except that of [443] language. In all higher spheres, language is only a principle for the further education of the entire human race by the more advantaged individuals; here alone is it the absolute, creative principle of a spiritual world in the first place.

And just like with intuition, perhaps of an object in space, what is unique about a feeling is isolated from all the rest of its infinity in this clarification of feeling, and permeated with freedom, and reconstructed. Accordingly, reflection is present for this, and the self in its entire essence. The difference from actual intuition is only that this reconstruction of feeling is bound to simultaneity with the real feeling, whereas the reconstruction of actual intuition prevails unbound, through all time. And then that accordingly, we can't arbitrarily produce in ourselves for example, the taste, of sugar, in the way we can recall the intuition of every form in any instant. For this reason, too, it is feeling alone that truly binds to reality, or, better yet, to truth and law. In contrast, the intuition of spatial limitation posited by Pestalozzi as the very first cultivated intuition is only a second shadow, a shadow of the shadow.

According to this, the primary business of education would therefore be the management of reflection on these feelings according to a solid rule and in a graduated way that develops reflection; and this would consequently be the foundation lacking in Pestalozzian theory. The ABC of intuition, which is always free, would have to be preceded by an ABC of reflecting on non-freedom, the recollection of which is thus the absolute beginning of all freedom. That ABC would constitute the actual *Book for Mothers*. The child would first of all have to be made capable of indicating definitively whether he is hungry, or better yet, sleepy, whether he tastes or smells, etc. whether he smells roses or carnations, hears notes from violins or flutes, etc. because precisely these features are what's actual and finally objective and real in the primary physical world,[53] whereas space, and especially the schemata of even higher abstraction, are merely schematic forms of that objectivity.

[444] C. Then indeed, you do admit, in opposition to the categorical claim from your earlier dialogue, that even since Kant — you will surely have tacitly excepted him and dated things starting from him — someone driven by the instinct for reason has invented something truly new that has never existed before?

B. It could seem to be know-it-all arrogance if I insisted that Pestalozzi must be seen as Kant's contemporary and neither his successor nor instructed by him in any way, in that Pestalozzi was certainly seized by the spirit and swept away long before the Kantian spirit manifested itself with any clarity, and that likewise, according to all available evidence, Kant had absolutely no influence on Pestalozzi's development. I don't want to seem like a know-it-all, so therefore consider everything that you require to be admitted.[54]

C. So then your meaning is that if basically all the people in one state association[55] were to receive this primary education, as you call this proposal brought by Pestalozzi, that is, if this education became the national education — that's what you mean?

B. Yes, of course. People talked a lot about national education before there was an art of education. Now we could have it — give it to the citizens and you'll get a nation at the same time, and this education will have proven itself as a national education in the highest sense of the word.

C. If this were to happen just so, would the people first of all be healed of their confusion,[56] and from all the vices that stem from it? And beyond that, would some few among them become capable of making the science of reason and the art of reason their own, as the sure guarantors of the regular and uninterrupted progress of humanity towards its vocation?

B. That's just what I mean.

C. And you hope to persuade those who are the heads of the nations [445] that you will have grasped even the thought of an education for their nation, and that they should make the decision to spend what's really necessary for such an education?

B. As I have already explained previously: I can't even make up my own mind on what's to be hoped for or not to be hoped for, and of all the dark places there might be in my body of knowledge, it's at least the only one that I intentionally tolerate, and where I don't want clarity brought.

But I know the following and can raise as evidence an ordinary math example: Assume a state that had fifteen years of peace, and during this peace spent everything that it could pull from its land in those years and that it could spare from other indispensable expenses on the maintenance of its army, an army that, as can happen, totally loses in the first battle[57] after the outbreak of war. Instead of that, suppose half of the army had resigned and the cost of the maintenance of that half had been turned over to a national education as Pestalozzi and I conceive of it. I intend to show that with the outbreak of war, this state could have excused the other half of its army too, and would nonetheless have had a nation to bring to arms, one that simply could not have been beaten by any human power.

C. You may be right in that case, and since you've so brashly decided to hope for exactly that, I don't want to disturb you any more in your sweet, cosmopolitan dreams.[58]

# Notes

1. Pagination references are to J. G. Fichte, *Gesamtausgabe*, ed. Hans Gliwitzky and Reinhard Lauth (Fromann-Holzboog, 1993), II/9.393–445 with page number in brackets.
2. *Berlin oder der Preußische Hausfreund. Eine patriotische Zeitschrift für gebildete Leser jedes Standes* ("Berlin, or the Prussian Gallant; a Patriotic Journal for Educated Readers of Every Class"), published beginning in April 1806.
3. Fichte may have in mind submissions by Johann August Zeune and Friedrich Delbrück, friends of Fichte and occasional contributors to the journal.
4. Billigkeit
5. This preface was presumably written after the draft of the first dialogue. The German editors of the *Gesamtausgabe* reasonably speculate that the last paragraph was added to address the censors.
6. Schauspiel
7. Behörde
8. The last line of Luther's "Small Catechism," yet Fichte himself adds "and state" at the end.
9. A supererogatory deed
10. Absonderungen
11. Kosmopolitismus überhaupt
12. VernunftInstinktes
13. besonnene Kunst
14. fremdes
15. (FICHTE'S NOTE) This is how I would be answered in Berlin, anyway, where I drafted this conversation. My German reader in any other place could be answered in the same mode: I am a Saxon, Bavarian, Austrian, etc. And continuing so forth, as applicable.
16. euer Ganzes
17. heroisches UniversalMittel
18. I. H. Fichte's edition of Fichte's complete works contains additions to and variations on Fichte's text. We include the most important of these in the footnotes as "SW addition."
SW addition: And we also have plenty of means for their external combat. First and foremost, we denounce that type of people precisely |by letting] our audience [know] that they claim a firm and agreed-upon truth.
19. das Publikum, that is, the reading public or community that attends lectures.
20. A reference to Friedrich Schelling and his Naturphilosophie.

21. "The Prussian Gallant," p. 23 (19 April 1806): "Anecdotes. In a Conversation with the Famous Philosopher from Königsberg, Kant, the discussion turned to the fair sex: 'A woman,' said Kant, 'has to be like the clocktower, in order to do everything punctually and by the minute, and then on the contrary not like a clocktower, not announcing every secret out loud. She has to be homey like a snail, but then on the contrary not like a snail that carries everything she has on her person.'" Page 55 (10 May 1806): "'Good, that you're coming!' Countess K. called out to the savant, Kant, as he was entering, 'Since you are such a great judge of human character, can you, perhaps, determine as soon as you first enter an unfamiliar house whether the husband or the wife wears the pants?' 'Oh, yes,' 'How do you claim to know?' 'You see, my dear Countess, once I notice that an exemplary quiet prevails in the house and absolutely no disagreement comes up, I conclude that the wife governs absolutely. Since women don't rest until then.'"

22. Franz Joseph Gall was a German anatomist and one of the inventors of phrenology. A two-Friedrichs d'Or coin circulated under Frederick the Great and was worth about 10 Thaler. See "The Prussian Gallant," p. 23 (19 April 1806): "That we can judge human beings according to the formation of their skulls, is a joke; but that a lot of two-Friedrichs d'Or coins aren't bad: that's completely serious!"

23. The original manuscripts contain both changes made by Fichte and subsequently by his son Immanuel Hermann Fichte, which can't reliably be distinguished based on their handwriting. The editors of the GA, Hans Gliwitzky and Reinhard Lauth, only included those alterations that, according to their best judgment, can be attributed to J.G. Fichte. In a number of places text is crossed out in the manuscripts.

Crossed out in Fichte's text: [B] Besides these written means of information, you'll probably have still more in your dealings in life? Wouldn't you also like to share some of those with me?

[A] Gladly. One of the most common turns of our conversations is that we assert about anyone in whom we notice a scientific leaning that he's messed up in the head and he's also messing up other people in the head, especially young people. The more high-class, grand and influential somebody is, the louder he says it.

B. But now if the entire conduct of the man shows a quiet, healthy, solid understanding, then how do you get belief?

A. Nothing is easier! For the masses, only the person who thinks like they do has a healthy understanding, in that no doubt only they have a healthy understanding, really. But whoever thinks the opposite of their thinking is crazy, since if you claimed to assume otherwise it would follow that they are crazy, which of course just cannot be.

Add to it that we all spread lies about the men we don't like.

B. So you lie, too? Do you do that just on your own, and come away unscathed?

A. So very much on my own that the same person who would have had to issue an alleged directive, if it had been given, himself circulates further that some directive has been issued about something that the man we're talking about would in fact never have thought of.

B. But now what if the defamed hears of the defamation and rebuts it? [414]

A. Partly, our lie is funny, although its truth is serious, and the public loves what's funny much more than what's serious. Besides that, they wish that the first bit might be true, because they're happy to see pretensions towards understanding humiliated. And thus, the whole world believes our lie, but nobody his truth. In a corrupt public, you can safely defame others. Such a public only believes what's bad, because it only loves the bad.

B. According to all this, you go out looking, properly systematically and with clear deliberateness, in theory and in life, for the extermination of all respect for science and indeed of all seriousness and for the spread of thoughtlessness and disrespect?

A. Can we do otherwise? We want to claim respect for ourselves. But we can only do that if understanding, which we don't have, doesn't matter, as opposed to foolishness and thoughtlessness, which we have in full, that matter more than anything. We want to please the masses. The unfailingly permanent condition that we can always take for granted in them is hatred for understanding, and science. Therefore, we please them unfailingly when we give them occasion to let off steam on those ideas.

B. You're surely also looking to bring the documents composed according to such foundational principles and for such purposes to the attention of high, and the highest, persons, and would like, if you could, to share with them your contempt of seriousness, thoroughness, and firm science, as well as your thoughtless perspectives on human relations?

A. We would like nothing better than to see the latter succeed.

B. You also try to bring your slanderous fictions about the men you don't like to the same high persons?

A. We have always made the most candid effort to do that.

B. Then have you earned belief, and what effect has it produced?

A. On this point, I don't want to explain myself at this time. The main effect we're still waiting for.

24. Unwissenheit und Unverstandes
25. SW addition: drudgeries from nations beyond Europe, that
26. dem dermaligen Wesen
27. Crossed out in Fichte's text: B. I don't know anything about it either. But I, as a genuine patriot and understanding admirer of my king, hope and believe that the king has as much taste and education, and as much of the blood of his truly genius ancestor, Frederick II, that he properly scorns you as a clumsy scribbler.

A. We hope the opposite; and it'll be on your head that we're right and you're wrong.

28. Fichte points out that it is a common misunderstanding of his day that his *Wissenschaftslehre* is about particular "individuals" who "for example, produce the entire material world and the like" (1811, "Facts of Consciousness

Lectures," *Gesamtausgabe* II/12, p. 71). See, for example, Karl Heinrich Leopold Reinhardt: "Poems," Berlin 1806, p. 284: "The wise always renounced their own systems actively; Not so, indeed, the Fichtians, for whom everything comes down to — their ego."
29. VernunftKunst
30. besonnen
31. Crossed out in Fichte's text: but instead seem even to fight through for Germania's subjugation. But I hope indeed, that this is now itself only an appearance and that this evil appearance will disappear and so I'll continue now, simply in the hope of the victory of the just cause, as a Prussian in Prussia, to embrace the entire German nation, and in it this entire human race, with love, in hope and faith, despite that I thoroughly do not love their actual conduct but rather hate and scorn it with my whole heart.
32. Vernunft Wissenschaft
33. The manuscript erroneously has an A at this point.
34. *Attempt at a Critique of all Revelation*, Königsberg, 1792. — Upon its publication, many assumed the *Attempt* was authored by Kant.
35. "I truly cannot sleep!"
36. "Let those [who need sleep] oil themselves and swim across the Tiber thrice." —Horace, *Satires*, II 1, 7–8.
37. Marginal note: "better" written above "was more fortunate"
38. Allusion to Schelling and his followers, including Hegel.
39. Allusion to the realist opponents of the *Wissenschaftslehre*, Bardili, Reinhold, and Jacobi.
40. GeistesOperation
41. Allusion to Friedrich Heinrich Jacobi and his school.
42. Einigkeit der Gesinnung
43. schwärmende Phantasiren
44. Urheber
45. Johann Heinrich Pestalozzi, 1746–1827, educator and author. Fichte read Pestalozzi's works from a young age, as seen in his 1788 work "Random Thoughts in a Sleepless Night." He studied Pestalozzi closely again as he was preparing the Patriotism dialogues. Pestalozzi's theory would become important for the theoretical background of Fichte's educational theory in the *Addresses to the German Nation*. Much of the following exchange alludes to Pestalozzi's work *How Gertrude Teaches Her Children*.
46. SW alternative: egotism
47. das Buchstabenwesen
48. des großen Volks
49. Kenntnis
50. verständigen
51. Maulbraucherei, a Pestalozzi neologism meaning using your mouth without an understanding of speech
52. Ichheit
53. an der ersten Erscheinungswelt

54. Crossed out in Fichte's text: I can't hide in passing that I think, not without exalting, and when I look at the "present relationships" of the immediately present appearances, not without a melancholic feeling, that the last who so thoroughly encompassed the needs of the entire human race on both extreme ends, were both Germans.
55. Staatsverein
56. Schwindel
57. A reference to the Battle of Jena and Auerstedt.
58. Crossed out in Fichte's text: In contrast you see how you solve the following objection, in order even just to save your theory as a mere theory. Now if a national education such as you desire is established and thus everyone who has been through it thereby becomes receptive to the science of reason and the art of reason, at least according to the premise, do you intend to raise every citizen without exception to that art and science?
B. In no way, rather always just such a large percentage of them that the state continuously needs; and namely we'll choose them according to higher and more convincing ability, or, where even this isn't decisive, let chance decide, which then counts as the same as God's will.
C. And the others?

# 3

# The Republic of the Germans (1807)

*Translated by Benjamin Hofmann*

[377][1] A depiction of the present age from[2] a historian: "The youth considered themselves unconstrained, not considering that they could grow old themselves. They were right. The older [one gets], the more cowardly, the more spoiled [one becomes]. But this was due to the fact that they were solely dependent on instinct, without the art of courage, of learning, of acting, and so forth. When they made it past 30 they should have been beaten to death: because as much as they came to terms with themselves, the continuation was nothing but a worsening of themselves, others, and future generations. Hence it is the case that the world gets worse as it ages. Everywhere it is apparent: the world's famous men had earned honor in their youth. Later they got worse. But it was only natural fancifulness.[3] They neglected to channel it, to elevate it to a clear and level-headed art. Age and experience only provided egoistic prudence[4] of selfishness, of insight into universal evil and of the resignation not to want to be better than others. Hence what was better about youth was merely lack of understanding, impudence, imprudence."

Princes: not evil, but immensely unwise and ignorant.[5] To let oneself be robbed with impunity yet comfort oneself that one would always have enough to eat, counted as heroism with them. They did not know that something other than their meals mattered (not that that they would have resisted it — they just had never heard of it, such was *their upbringing*.) Among their courtiers this was heresy, high treason, and they made sure it would not reach their ears. [They used] disgusting compliments. No frankincense was too strong for their nerves. The princes felt no shame at being praised when only once they neglected to play a particularly bad prank, or when they — after a life full of cowardice and ignominy — for once manned up.[6] They lack the most common concepts and emotions. For their ministers, all foreign policy was diplomacy, [but really it was] espionage and half-lies, dissimulating and meandering through the world. The internal [politics was] *to make money*, without knowing what they [should] do with it. Of education or religion they knew nothing. [378]

[They had] principles, such as increasing the population through facilitating divorces and through prostitution. Their military: at most the junior officer was good for something. The higher ups, behind the front lines, gave up the fortresses and capitulated out of cowardice. [Consider] what documents come from this age. The landowners who do not give anything to his countryman, [but rather] gave the best to the enemy. Only fear moved these dignified leaders of the stock. — Studying [higher education]: they went through it, whatever may have stuck. Their preachers are for the most part without religion themselves, and the city priest is a moocher, jokester, jester, [while] the country priest is a crude tenant, wild like his horses and bulls, talkative like the starlings, the catechism memorized on the whole, [but] completely confused and insecure. The jurists: you could lecture them but they would not understand. [Their] cases [are mainly] about non-facts. Not that they would have been able to enlighten the obtuse parties: even [for] those [parties] who were enlightened they obscured clarity and simplicity through their juridical performances. Even where it was better, it did not go beyond the knowledge of civil law, and the blind superstition in it. [It was] a miracle when they rose to spirit and reasons. Those who could have understood it [civil law] organically in the whole of the state could easily have been counted. Hence they became what held back all improvements. In general they were averse to everything new, because that would have required learning, but they had learned everything but *learning* itself.

*Trade*: to doubt that everyone should be at liberty to draw the maximal profit from the misery of his compatriot sounded like inexplicable nonsense to them.

The higher the estate, the worse [the person] — [this arises] from precisely the principle that because he matured earlier and became on the whole smarter, he had more independence to satisfy the egoism that was growing inside him, [which was] authorized by the state through religion (which had itself become eudaemonism), through general morals, through shamelessness and the lack of a feeling of honor. They knew no other use of life but enjoyment and never heard anything else or listened to it. That the opposite opinion was enthusiasm[7] they knew with the vast majority. Only in the lower estates could, precisely through pressure from above, some rightfulness and some religion prevail. One liked to refer to them for consolation. [379]

The officer was embarrassed to speak his language properly and with articulation. After all, one could have thought him a pedant. He affected a lisp, rattle, and mistakes: for these seemed elegant to him.[8]

[380] The protector[9] must hear the small council, before which he can also appeal in accordance with his responsibility, but he is completely free in his decision.

[However, he] remains subject to the final judgement [before God]. Facing him is a *clean slate*[10] that no subsequent age can take away. [He undergoes] *suspension* until the outcome (in which it must be assumed that he saw many things that the councilors did not). Should a successor have been crowned before this suspension is over, then a golden nail is driven into the line and a spot left empty. The large council decides on this, if it is not, after consulting [this matter], judge in its own case. Then there are the *notables*, i.e. those from whom the large council is chosen.[11] The councils complement one another. The people elect the notables through voters in a variety of ranks.[12]

Which subjects do the councilors decide on with the protector? 1) foreign affairs, war, peace, alliances, acquisitions, e.g. colonization. 2) there are other subjects, e.g. changes to the constitution or to the laws. For these the whole condition of the state has to be viewed more determinately. The plan for internal progress has to be made very precisely right from the beginning, [and be based on] universal equality.

Ministers, emissaries, governors of provinces. I believe they should be alternated, like in the Roman senate. One can refuse an office *when reasons are offered* (otherwise one is condemned as lazy by the censor), other than the protectorate and the spots on the councils. But one cannot put oneself forward for them. [Yet] wouldn't it be better if the governor of a province serves for a lifetime, to know their nature better? — Stop: this is never quite the question, [but rather] one gets used to it. [381]

The governor[13] generally supervises the improvement of culture, education, warfare, the judiciary, finances. It goes without saying that one [should] send those who fit a particular branch, e.g. one who is familiar with shipping to the shoreside provinces.[14]

He sends official reports to the senate and protector.[15]

The following applies to that matter: from time to time, those two have to set themselves certain common ends to be executed in due consideration of the circumstances. In light of these [ends] they should question the governors.

*Estates*. Farmers, craftsmen, businessmen (foreign trade is conducted by the state), *scholars* and civil servants. But now the last? Preachers, judges, [all] advocates. Yes. This should be the first rank.[16] Doctors, medical facilities and conditions. Teachers and professors. But these happen also to be the writers, the continual educators[17] and maintainers even of the mature nation. Their prerogatives are very large. But they are required to remain at the general [level]. How do the latter relate to the senators? They are invited to be members, and can come, as soon as they want. They can also send their impressions in writing.

Still [what about] other assemblies and committees? I should not think that this was part of the council, e.g. supervision of farming and manufacturing. [It] does require an assembly, education. Judicature is merely positive. But they too can propose laws. Military constitution. Also religion. All [of these] are in the *senate* whose special institution has to be described more closely.

There are general assemblies, and those for special provinces: all flow together in the smaller senate. That simultaneously contains the presidents, and the general supervision.

Where are there collisions? Between all improvements and the personal civil [382] right.[18] A permanent principle and guardian ... standing military and the other branches. During wartime the latter are secondary. The nation is sustained through warfare. Who would be interested in peacetime in disturbing the latter? There only remains the permanent estate of the army. (How to quickly mobilize the army is *res actionis indaginis*.[19]) So it must be always. Everything in its place. Whoever has to march knows it and receives orders. The remaining ones follow in double time. Every German citizen is *soldier* and *farmer*. The war needs surgeons, but where to get those quickly? More generally, [it is essential to] strike the right balance between war and peace. 1.) Are rations present for years that cover for the loss of farming? 2) Must the war be continued on foreign soil?

The essence of war. In peacetime the protector, between sowing and the harvest, annually travels to the provinces. The senate wishes him happy travels, conducts war deliberations, and otherwise reviews [its business]. — The other controller is the governor.

Now to the determinate organization of both senates, and the other assemblies.

How strong would the smaller senate have to be for Germany and what does it have to do? 1.) Election of the protector, as designed. 2.) Foreign affairs, as above. 3) Higher [level] internal politics, [involving the] progress of the whole.

First [we must] clarify the mediating role of the ministers, emissaries, generals, governors.

Ministers are first and foremost scribes of the protector, not councilors. His councilors are the senate. If he wants to, he is permitted to conduct specific negotiations with specific [councilors]. The emissaries too are nothing more than his messengers. Where do these come from and what status do they have? Non liquet[20] before settling other questions. Precisely who determines [membership in] the assemblies? Answer: they recruit themselves. Thus they also submit their presumed need to the Studies Commission. Their superiors, however — presidents and such — are appointed by the protector. These are now viewed from two sides. The councilors have no executive force, but only and conditionally negative [force]. Ministers, emissaries come from the assemblies, [and] they have the status of privy councilors; they can become [members of] it after their possible exit. *Generals*: The army is dealt with by the protector, hence appointing generals seems to also fall to him. But [that] the army appoints its own officers[?]. This I should not believe, [since] it requires *higher education*. So [let us assume] that the officers recruit from among themselves, and from them finally the protector [emerges]. A part, one half of the army, could never amount to a supreme commander[21] [383] unless they let themselves be admitted into the corps of learned officers. Governors are the internal emissaries between the council and the protector, who watch one another. They give advice to the presiding senators without being able to force them. The matter goes to the protector. Both *communicate*. How to maintain the peace between the two of them? Here the emissary of the protector is the weaker one, because he risks indictment and–such that the protector does not antagonize the council–dismissal. For they can fight about *opinions*, not deeds, and the protector ultimately has the executive [power], so it will remain.

Every governor on the side of the king is a general. This is where they learn the warriors' art of government. How do I bring the councilors back into the war? They are from the assemblies. Are they not soldiers too, since everyone is a soldier? Of course: they come along to the war exercises and are sent into the field during wartime by the senate itself, which allocates a number of spots [for them]. Good. But first: can the judge, doctor,[22] and preacher go on a [military] campaign? No: but [they can be part of] provincial maneuvers during the holidays. Hence the military constitution is without exception.

Education: it can be completed between the ages 8–14 by the farmer who learns farming at the same time. "I did not want so much [education]: I only want it until [age] 12." Response: it is for the body. Whoever aspires to more can be let go earlier. Here [there might be] knitting to practice one's fingers, sewing and such, [as well as] reading, writing, math, religion, law, natural science, physical education. Music would be abandoned to the higher [subjects]: or [could] it be added to the general plan? It appears: no! This is bad. What to do? It would be possible through hiring a music teacher. / but in year 12 it is too late. With a certain order it is possible in the ninth [year].

— But: the brainy kid skips classes, and thereby finishes earlier. Whoever has finished with 12 years in his courses would be ready for another. What more does the *urban citizen*[23] need? Technological knowledge and skill. Where does Latin belong for the scholars? Answer: I think they learn general grammar, French, Italian until age 14. In the [case of] these [languages], it comes as far as it can. [384] The directors of the learned schools evaluate [the students, and] indicate how many are qualified. The colleges determine the presumed need. Either greater aptitude or lottery decide. The rejected become urban citizens, artisans and such.

Hence [they will attend] the learned school until 20 years [of age]. Here the main judgement [is that of] *Iudicium necit*.[24]

The remaining ones enter subordinate services.

The internal [structure] of education, honor, and morality.

Self-sufficiency: Girls are only removed from their estate through marriage. They too learn farming. [In] this [case, they serve] only with the boys and as their assistants.

The men knit, and so no one has a stiff hand. Everyone learns to swim, to dance.

[They must learn] to endure hunger and thirst, coldness and heat.

Punishment in the educational institutes. Laziness has to be made up for [by sacrificing] the leisure hours. For social transgressions: shunning [during a] ceremonial welcoming back. [For] breaking *secrecy*: to be put before the censor: they will keep silent about this, [as] it will be noted. Similarly a *dishonoring punishment*: What would be appropriate for this? For example a cilice.[25] Whoever inquires [into this, or] ridicules [the person wearing the cilice] has to wear it too. For the first [infraction] one can pray it [the cilice] away.[26] Later, unchastity, flippancy, smaller breaches of trust [all deserve this penalty]. — It is forbidden to go to the toilet in public, instead they have a pot and closed chambers. [This is intended] to increase [their sense of] shame. [They] stand under censorship.[27]

[It is] better to discuss the means to redress [these infractions].

[Here are] lessons for the parents as to how they are to keep their children [in line] until the 8th year. [Educate children] according to the same principles [they followed]. Those who were raised [properly] in this way will turn out [right] by themselves.

*Country farmers*: the state alone is the proprietor of the soil, and it gives each country farmer his field for a lifetime. However, possession is not inherited. Children inherit the [field's] inventory, [but not the soil]. The state is required to help supply everyone his livelihood. *Servants*: a compensated child does not inherit [anything]: they have given their due to the community. Someone must have his inventory. [385]

Marriages are indissoluble. What is to be done with adultery, which cannot be avoided completely, as most of the soldiers are married when they are in the field? No inquisition against it is [permitted] ex officio.[28] Those [adulterers whose spouses] have forgiven [them] are also forgiven by the state. The husband is counted[29] as father of the child. [The case] is twofold again. [Was it] in the *presence* of the husband or in his absence, when she surrendered to the other one?

In the first case, the wife whose husband was never absent will have her hair cut off and she will be banished from the community and her name incinerated [from the public record]. She can then serve as a maid or something of the sort. In the other case [where the husband was absent], she will be removed quietly. The adulterer, if he is a bachelor, or his wife is absent, will [also] be removed quietly from the community. If his wife is present, [he will be] *publicly* banished and his name incinerated. He is *dead*. What use are such people to the state? Answer: as executioners. The stubborn women [can do] commode cleaning, street sweeping, and so on.

Measures against *forced marriage* [include] annual public admonitions. She who was talked into [a marriage] can tell the clergyman: he [should] be the mediator. He is also the mediator between spouses. In general, no marriage can be blessed without a private conversation with the clergyman, or his wife (who should be an honorable woman). [She should] be a teacher: more of this at the right time.

[Let us consider] other sins against the flesh. Prostitution will not be tolerated publicly. [For example,] masters [of the house who take advantage] of [their] maid servants. The censor [is to] report [it], remove to the country side [with] the clergy. Pregnancy outside of marriage requires marriage. But [instances of] rape? — No: She exits the *community*. — The lad too: [he is sent] into foreign services. She is reported to the censor, and no one else knows about it. She marries someone similar, but she may not betray him. It is said: the *censor* knows about [that] one.

Oath. [These are to be made] without superstition. None are [to be] absolutely negative. Punishment of lying under oath [includes] relegation to the islands amongst the savages.[30] Same with traitors to the country.[31]

[There should be] beauty of public buildings, canals, streets, churches, schools, alleys, gardens. This is especially to be seen in the cultivation of the land.

The *Olympic* Games. I should think during physical inspection [for military service] one could be evaluated to participate in the games. Only he who has never been censured can become the censor. Speaker, reader, musician. Where do the artists stand, [386] and how are they awarded? They are always something else. Are there not for example those who are scholars by profession? Yes, *academics*. — How learned institutions recruit is understood. [They recruit] from the teachers.

Teachers, who commit major transgressions, will be transferred with a notation by the censor of the place.

University: overall from no pre-cut cloth. [Only] after a trial year do they choose their subject. The theologian must be poetic, have pure morals, voice, a good education. The jurist can be of a prosaic nature, and the medical professional of natural humanity. A philosophical faculty as such does not exist. Whoever stands out through astuteness and eloquence becomes it, [or] through ease and aptitude with what is difficult.

Are particular military studies required [to develop] astuteness with high sharpening of the senses and physical prowess? These become artillery officers, and generally officers of the standing armies with whom they do their exercises. In war [they are] the leaders. Nothing speaks against combining the military academy with the university. They have gone through the first school studies.

A large *school commission* is required. I think this is in the large assembly, since it is generally for the protection of the constitution. The small [council is] for moving [the constitution] forward.

Organization of the country. Cities in the center, villages produce for them, including enjoyments if the land yields them. In their proximity the *primary* schools, [and] general schools, middle schools, [as well as the] elected, chosen schools.

What is the provincial directorate? Where *trade* is [to be], and the *large factories*. This should be [covered in] the *middle schools*. Hence it does appear as though a higher tier is missing.

How do I want to organize *trade*? 1) foreign [trade], of course, is conducted by the state. What foreign products stream into the country will be sold on the state's bill. It delivers it for free and hence a pound of coffee costs the same in the whole country until the state raises [the price]. 2.) Internal trade: it appears to disappear mostly. Every object is produced in the cities of the region in which it grows — hence exchange would only be for fabricated goods[32]. Hence how to remove something from there should be dictated. [The] answer is [through] organized [trade]. In every commercial city there is a house that trades in the wares, [and] in the provincial cities they are its commissioners. The wares [therefore] cost the same everywhere, one rounds up [or down]. [387]

In harbors there is no private activity, but only the official exchange[33] [sanctioned by] the state. If any private activity [occurs], the state inherits [it]. They stand under its control.[34]

Main foundational principles: To educate humanity, all races equally. [To ensure] the land [needed] for their dignified occupancy. [To provide the] guarantee to all peoples to go about their work likewise.

Borders. Poles have become Germans for the most part, and the others may emigrate to Russia, and so forth. It is a main principle that only the *German* can be a *citizen*.

Germany barely has gold and silver, nor does it need either of those. On the other hand, it traded the plentiful iron that exists in its country to nations that did not know [how] to appreciate it.[35]

Whoever dies because of insubordination or desertion has atoned: his remains we took back in. He will be buried: His earth has been returned to the Earth.

The female teachers are usually spouses of the teachers: they are educated in seminaries. — But [they are] also chosen through the channels of decency, love, and strength of speech. In short, the community of the graceful. Let the women in higher estates learn foreign *languages* and such things if the parents want it. This would be [taught] apart from the learned schools for boys. — Against [the wishes of] the parents she is.[36]

[388] Does this appear to be an inconsistency? Why would I not leave this business to the state as well? Answer: Because it cannot be supervised and new branches develop. So one should leave some freedom [here]. But the businessman should provide an accounting, and send an annual report.

How do things stand with medical and law schools? With regard to the former there can be no subordinate [authority] just yet. With regard to the second, there is a local assembly in the city: it is called the local city assembly, in which the matters are dealt with that the justice of the peace cannot dismiss. In this assembly, there is also a justice of the peace, who reports to the district [authority]. The same [should go for] the physician who can employ people whom he stands for.

The provincial city has a governor and reports directly to the council: the reports of the councils constitute the decree.[37] The same [councils] have provided this and also report. How can one learn through mere reporting whether someone can govern? Oh yes! [One can learn] if he is at the same time a soldier.

The provincial city. — Only the highest appeal applies to it, the large council and its committee. — Report on their own initiatives in legislation to the small council.

Situation of the rest of Europe. England and the northern empires. Italy, Spain, Russians, the French. The latter harmless.

Asia: Italy, towards the East (the Magyars), Serbs, Rascians, but more Greeks, have German protection.

Of foreign wares there are repositories. [These are] not produced in the colonies because the soil has to be cultivated first, and the motherland should not be depopulated.

*Tax system*: Only on the soil and no other tax: that is, that has to be established. Reserves are always there. [During] the peaceful years [they are] safely used: in these [years, levy] *war taxes*. During war, [these taxes should be] lowered. Everything in proportion. Land tax. I came through well. — Spots for [military] exercises: natural or artificial.

Meadows that are then cut.

Borders: Switzerland, Holland. Netherlands. North and Baltic Seas: Canal near the Eider.

Above the Memel. Then Weichsel, Warte. Schlesia, Bohemia, Moravia, Austria. [389]

So internally, what of the large provinces and Adriatic Sea? How are the borders there?[38]

And[39] which [city should be the] capital? This [one] off of one of the large *rivers*. Through the Eider, the Baltic and the North Seas are united. This points to the Elbe: Magdeburg is a little too far West in this case. It will probably remain Magdeburg. This [will] provide a great unity with the North through Havel, Spree, canals. It will have to stay like this.

Can Elbe and Main be united? There is the Fichtel Mountains, the Thuringian Forest. It would have to go through the Weser. Weser and Elbe would have to be reunited in *Lower Saxony*. [This] only leaves the Main and the Weser, which will work. Then the waters are all connected. Of the Rhine and Danube, we have already talked.

Provinces: From North Prussia, Brandenburg, Lower Saxony, Upper Saxony, plus Silesia. Bohemia, plus Moravia. Austria. Coastland. Franconia. Upper Rhine, Lower Rhine, Helvetia.

This seems to be correct. Forestry. Hunting. Mining is not to be overlooked. Fishery. Especially at the coasts. Shipbuilding and maritime schools. East Frisia. [390]

Thus it appears. What is not written down, is thought. Do I want to try my luck?

Winery requires more hands. Hence only half [can] be taken as soldiers. For this a particular school is to be established. How to organize the maintenance of this branch? There is a public cellar. [The vintner] puts his reserves in there and sets aside something for maintenance. [He] can borrow on it. [There are] good and bad regions [for winery], so how [best] to distribute? [This] is a tough challenge. Answer: Generally, only where the location is exquisitely good should wine be cultivated. Other hilltops for fruit, and plants for consumption. The *valley for tilling*.

Now I get to work and in this order. 1) General preliminary report. [Should] the first chapter be about religion or *education*[?] I contend the former is to be told first because education in turn builds on it. From education, [other] *institutions* then follow.

The first chapter ought to be the general foundational principles. Furthermore I believe I can continue working.

But no I cannot. I have to read *Pestalozzi*.[40] This will only be presented as well as it can be.

Basic goal: All-around educated human beings with complete equality of descent, such that the inequality of individuals is only determined by talent or fate. Their state [is] the most educated. [To] secure their *independence*[41] [it is essential to] guarantee other peoples [the ability] to form and develop according to their national character without constraint.

Feminine education. The legislators' perspective on them. The relation of the Germanic tribes to them. Worship of the virgin Mary.[42] "The male virtues of clear prudence, courage, adamant strictness and solidity should, within their boundaries, be added to the foundation of female virtues, that of revenge, belief, and love. Hence the female nature was the actual foundation and its formation the foundation for all other education."[43] The boy is [said to be] wild, destructive, egoistic. Already in her games, the girl will provide order and be helpful. [391]

Foundation of female chastity. The man's drive not to be loved but to be esteemed. [They are] told that in the case of forbidden consent they despise only that something small leads to something bigger. How to develop this drive to esteem in a timely fashion? Answer: If a boy is insolent assign him the blame, [or,] certainly, a cilice. The decent ones are permitted to supervise the boys' laundry and such.

The accomplished female teachers receive the golden cross (sky blue on gold), and are called mothers, almost seen as holy. Their transgressions against chastity are suppressed, they are passed off as dead and sent to the colonies. To become worthy of their love is the goal of the clergy. Whether they are beautiful is no question.

It is part of this [process] that they were nurses. The wife of a doctor usually is one too. They are good doctors. In this case they may accompany their husbands in the army. I want to have boys taught knitting by the mother of the house. She is also responsible for cleanliness, and other maids [stand] under her leadership.[44]

Fortune. What they thought about it. How they actually depended on God and then also taught.

*Humility*. To doubt one's ability when another is chosen or is assigned a way of life or office counts as *cowardice*. To boldly trust oneself [counts] as courage. One is allowed to lash out [at another], but one is subject to censorship. [392]

To try to determine one's estate, through pleas and such, belongs to ignominy.

Order against *cowardice*. The lawmakers themselves find it difficult [to accomplish this]. But, they ask, whoever did not become brave through our education and the spirit of the whole nation, how cowardly must he be, and how would he have fared under any other nation?

Which [deeds] of the protector fall under censorship? 1) When he illegally gained office. 2) When he showed disfavor or aversion against persons, or even let himself be bribed. 3) [when he] has suppressed messages, which serve the knowledge of the citizens. He must sign the accusation. So that nothing is noticed he invites the censors from time to time, [pretending] he needs their advice in the election of ministers, governors. The tact that is observed in this.

If the protector wants to allow a dispute to arise with the censors, he will be dismissed if they prove [their case]. If they do not prove [their case] they are exiled. It's always a scary matter, which calls for much consideration.

If a censor himself gossips, this will be dealt with by the rest of the assembly like the unchastity of the teacher: quietly but [they become publicly] dead and [actually] exiled.

The female teachers [are] a true standing clergy. The masculine principle is the progressing, forming, newly creating one in the spiritual world. The feminine one [is] that which gives stability.

The feminine religious principle: that which unites human beings and instills love and pity. The masculine one: that which strengthens heroic virtue, as should be carried in the breast of the one who decides to die. But *aliquid fit*.[45] [393][46]

Rod and cilice without mercy in response to the maids' sneaking [uneaten] food[47] (who, by the way, are not spared nor [seen as] exempted from temptation). After the cilice [they are] locked in for two hours. Then the rod, then another two hours locked in. Then good advice and a kiss, delivered by the mother. Love of the maids, the graceful. The more you need them, the better the example spreads. The boy is by nature selfish. Love makes the maid incredibly astute and inventive. The man first has to objectivize things.

Nice traits of the Germans. Frequently the fields of widows or of those whose husbands are absent at war, are tilled, cut, and so forth before the break of dawn. Such that one does not know who helped the poor spouses. A borrowed calf, a wagon, a horse, and such things, tied up in a similar manner.

*A punished and violent* [man who is] is comforted and married by the sister of the victim. Punishment of the graceful.[48]

The woman who remains faithful to her disgraced cowardly husband. His heart breaks.

"Announcements" of a *murderer*. He chose death like the dying. He wanted to be dead for the mortal. May he live in the memory of the All-merciful.

Of a coward: His memory and name are extinguished in the native land. Incinerated the sheet [of paper]. When he dies, [he is] incinerated without ceremony and his urn is buried without a name. Proclamation: A citizen without a name has fully passed away.

Of someone who lied under oath and who has been banished to the savages: His word was without the truth and he has ceased to speak our language. / Banished. [394]

Concerning the one who has been punished because of subordination: He is free to desert, and he receives five hours for this. He has done enough for the law of war with his blood and earned his honor. His remains are among us. This after his life has been extinguished. We remain lovingly silent about the rest.

The double-doors of the hall are open like the brown of the citizen's files, or is it a curtain open? (So it is!)

A deserter: He betrayed the paternal country that trusted him. His memory is extinguished, earth has been returned to the Earth.

[ . . . ] Furthermore he was punished for this. I would have to pay with something else for my transgression.

The intention of merely letting go. They erected . . . The legislators who intended to build on this religion of love the general civil love insisted that he who claims eternal life for himself should publicly recognize the same ability in his fellow citizen, whose belief is close to his own, and that nothing be taught that hinders the possibility of this general belief. They demanded this acknowledgment as a condition for acceptance into the citizenry, put it in the civil baptismal formula[49] and required teachers of all confessions to specifically teach this proposition. Whoever does not believe in a future world for himself we cannot expect to have different beliefs about others. He has no religion at all that one could require of him and we are quite certain that we can cope with this one through civil law alone. But whoever excludes his fellow citizens of other confessions clearly regards them as lesser and his preferred belief for better. And it is certainly impossible that he could esteem and love them just as much as those he recognizes as shared heirs of bliss in a future life. This supposition [395] is resisted by teachers of a certain confession. Fortunately a large share of the laymen have stood up against their clergy. And so the majority accepted this proposition and some opposed were banished from the realm.

So come to terms with their behavior, according to the [ . . . ] Protestant [ . . . ][50]

Preliminary thoughts.

Their aptitude in philology[51] qualifies them to teach the savages. How do they compete with them in the training of the senses?

They use materials for war sparingly. It would be easy for them to conquer the whole world, but they will refrain from such an idea. They know that they only exist in contrast with others. Conflict with the third protector who constrained the Moors in Africa too much. It happened that the Moors united with the Negros and made them more warlike.

Because many men go to war and die there, how [might we] establish a relationship? Through polygyny in the colonies. One chooses the most inferior ones, those born out of wedlock and the like.

There is no punishment for infanticide, because it is impossible.

[396] It did not become known if suddenly, as if by a miracle, these princes and this nobility changed, and, having recognized that they are completely unsuited to lead the nation, voluntarily lowered themselves to achieve equality with the [lower classes], thus enabling an entirely new organization, whose closer description is the purpose of the following work.

## Final End of the German Constitution

The lawgivers, whom the Germans tasked with judgment [about the final end], established the constitutional council. Through this council the lawgivers laid down the following very determinate account as the standard for all subsequent eras, an account of the final end [of the constitution] and how the special provisions that they have made are related to it. We will frequently help ourselves to this authentic account.

In part, we wanted to provide humanity an all-around education as far as time permitted it. Because [we are] concerned with the whole, we must treat the tribes with absolute equality, but the inequality [makes this difficult]. This equality of the tribes — that they are Germans — was not modified [in our constitution] and must be included in our observations, in the life of another [nation,] but turn back in upon themselves. In addition, by right it is capable of resigning all of this.

This education is not limited, but contains the possibility of higher education.

In regard to their external [character], firmness and independence [are] of equal weight, because providence did not endow them with that drive to render it also harmless to others. As a negative force it became solid.[52] Because of it we were reluctant to deny its immeasurable power that one also could not deny on the grounds of all-around education.[53] [397]

Hence we believed that only one [tribe] could claim its distinctive being for itself, but will never be permitted to force it [on others], [and] that not without reason do [they] want to be in the midst of others, who insofar as they have received a meager education, want the latter, and believed it was their vocation.

## Religions of the Germans

### Religious Denominations of the Germans

The legislator identified the three well-known denominations.[54] They deemed it necessary to recognize [and] clearly articulate a fourth one, and to elevate [it] to the true civil religion, that is, [elevate it] to the legitimate religion for the functioning of the state.

This new one was called the general Christian religion with the German name, leaving the Greek one for the Catholics. It differed [from other denominations] in that it recognized the doctrine of religion of Christendom [as true], because and insofar as it would find it [to be true] with its own reason. By contrast, those who stayed with the old [denominations] admitted that they did not [find it true based on reason], but that they [believed] it on the credit [of authority]. They commemorated the person of Jesus with all honors, but did not engage with the ridiculous historical dispute, but forgave everyone and recognized him [alone].

In a dialectical discussion it emerged when the opponents [of the new religion] did not succeed with the worn retort that they believe [Christianity] to be true both because they understand it and at the same time because Jesus taught it, that those who do not want to show [it to be true] do not understand [Christianity] to be true, [not] that they are drawn to it by themselves, but instead . . .[55] [398]

Because we ourselves, as what is essential [about us], firmly believe ourselves to be Christs[56] [in the sense of the scripture] we strive and advance our worship to become him in reality. On the other hand our fellow citizens from the other side confess that Christ . . . [57] is of a different kind for them and that they not only cannot become equal to him but also cannot make anything of themselves [yet can] still be permitted into the Christian community.

Apart from the above . . . ,[58] [let us consider] the public application of this system. We would probe their account more deeply through the following:

*Bow deeply* before God: but he should *do it himself.* The first condition of all education is unrestricted independence. This type of independence means that the human being recognizes no obstacles other than the ones he gives himself through a will guided by clear insight.

Ecclesiastical goods belong to the *citizens*, not to the *denominations*.

[399]

## Episode about our Age, from a Republican Writer

One captures the life of past human beings in one go if one understands it as a growing deterioration, caused by the increasing age [of the people] and [people increasingly] climbing higher [in the] estates, factors that get worse with every generation over the previous one. The older and more refined the man is, the worse one could usually assume him to be. One could also safely expect that after the passing of a year the whole mass [of the people] would be much worse than it is today.

The first fact is due to the following reason. In one's youth the progressing development of life gives the human being a desire to be active and to have an external impact, and certain tendencies of his rational nature and determinations of this striving are released. This activity is not guided by knowledge of the surrounding world, [yet] expectations are measured by it. As such, this activity either remains completely without success or at least far behind the success that was expected. The courageous and fiery youth might try several times, but eventually he will be forced to turn inward and admit that human beings are worse and less susceptible to influence than he had assumed. And because it was only nature, not the clear insight of reason, that drove him to his activity, and that drove his youthful fire, he easily resolves to give up the useless attempts, [and] to do as others [do], not wanting to be better than them. Careful observers from that age have left testimony that they observed some youths enter the world with the most fiery resolutions to start something new and better, [but] once they entered the world of business they became as lazy and sleepy as all who entered the usual streets[59] and never again thought of further cultivating[60] themselves. Their activity was due to the restlessness of youth and their talent due to [youthful] fantasy, and [neither] was captured in virtuous principles to be maintained as eternal property through sober art. As such, with the fading of youth men lost the semblance[61] of life and spirit, as women lost beauty, and they sank into laziness and stupor. [400] Age and experience merely gave them the wisdom of egoism, the conviction of universal evil[62] in themselves and in others, such that, when they came to [develop] understanding, one saw that what one had been inclined to consider good dispositions of their youth was merely their lack of understanding and they came [to understand] themselves clearly and purely that they were void of all that is good. Once they were beyond thirty years, we should wish for their death for their own honor and for the best of the world, because from then on they only lived to worsen themselves and their environment.

All appearances from these days exhibit this basic tendency. The youthful geniuses of such eras, as if they had been sure that they would never reach mature age but would ruin themselves in advance [of maturity] or sink into childish imbecility — hopes that as a rule did not deceive them — admired the youth alone and deemed it exclusively capable of any business. On the other hand [they] despised as unfit the more mature age, and every new master in art or science believed himself to be better than the existing masters just because he counted fewer years than them. And they usually were right, because the advantages of mature age, somber clarity, and free art of right willing, and capability for [pursuing] any purpose in fact were rare occurrences in those days. The same geniuses made it plainly known that they were resting solely on their nature and their genius, and if someone had avowed that he also requires industriousness they would have ridiculed him as depraved by nature. Whoever had entered the higher circles of business, or made a name for himself in the world of writers, had usually done so on account of his first jobs or texts. Later the former would only be retained because one once had [hired] them and [they would be] advanced according to their years of service, but no sensible superior, looking for new youths for the job when the business required it, would have hired them. The [older people in the job] became increasingly shallow and mindless, or better, it was much more evident in them what had previously been concealed by a certain freshness of youth. For some more time they benefited from [401] ancient reputation until they were given over to deserved oblivion. So [it was as well] in the armies. The valor, expertise, and attentiveness in little things, which was still present in these armies, usually did not reach higher than the subordinate officers. The higher and older commanders were staggering about in lazy carelessness and had no knowledge of the condition and the movements of the enemy. [They] let themselves be encircled without realizing it and even after they discovered it they neglected to man the mountain passes where they were attacked. And after the defeats that were bound to result from this had followed, [they] negotiated shameful capitulations and without resistance handed over the fortresses, frequently to the deep chagrin and strongest opposition of their younger subjects.

The relative increase in evil in the higher estates was for this reason. The higher a child was due to his birth, the sooner and in a more cramped manner did the life of human beings appear before him, and their corruption, which he understands to be morality. What initially surrounded him was bad and it could not have occurred to him that there might be something honorable in the lower estates, which he disdained, nor would others have given him this thought. Hence he had by birth the great relief to gain a clear experience of human beings relatively early. How could a drive to be something other than everyone else have fallen into his soul? Because of his privileges, wealth, and his subordination of lower, popular classes[63] under him he had an unlimited sphere in front of him in which to develop and satisfy his egoism and raise it through ongoing satisfaction to a higher and higher faculty. [This happened] without any countervailing force, neither from the state, in which what was not forbidden was permitted, and which offered little to the higher classes and rarely or never knew — or even wanted to know — what they themselves were doing against the prohibition; nor from religion, which had also transformed into a doctrine of pleasure; nor from public morals, which agreed completely with this perspective that life only consists in enjoyment and considered the opposite perspective foolishness. Against this [402] the lower classes could never achieve any clarity about life as it was then, because of their limited knowledge of the relations of life, and because the higher classes pretended to [have made] various miraculous achievements for the whole, as well as to [be in] the possession of some virtues. Furthermore the higher estates, who were keen to maintain religion among the people if only they were spared it, imposed on them a religious belief about the prospect of a different life. Hence the lower classes could never sink so low, but the higher ones could sink deeper, the closer they were to the zenith, the more they inclined toward the abyss. Given all this, one could say only about a few individuals amongst them that they were evil or violent, because the majority lacked the power for this; for the most part they were merely stupid, and without knowledge, cowardly, lazy, and base.

One saw princes in these times who counted it as heroic courage and greatness of the soul when they calmly watched the subjection of their closest blood-relative neighbors, the narrowing of their own borders, and the partition of their most loyal provinces. They despised those who could not [calmly watch this] as weaklings. Whatever bitter indignities they experienced they took comfort in the fact that they would have enough to eat and to drink for a lifetime. It will remain absolutely impossible for our contemporaries to believe that in light of such occurrences any prince could ever have been so stupid and coarse only to focus on himself, and there only on [his] need for food[64] — until we remind them of the education the princes received. Occupying themselves with strenuous mental exercises, we believe, could endanger this life so valuable to the world, and the seriousness required of them would perhaps leave external marks and damage their former appeal to the ladies. Hence one limited the higher education of the prince to conversational French, horse riding, the art of presenting a rifle, and, if it was very thorough, a little bit of music and drawing. [Consider, by contrast, the suggestion] that through possession of the ancient languages [403] they would inhabit the honorable spirit of the peoples of antiquity, that they would order their concepts, and bring the understanding, as an artificial tool, under their free control. [Or the suggestion] that they could even gain an idea of the state through a foundational study of philosophy, or of their relationship with their people, and of their duties. Whoever had dared to make these suggestions, he would have soon made his home in an insane asylum. Thus educated as and made into regents, they passed their lives with the joys of intercourse if they had any imagination, or, if they lacked it, they lived in sullen brooding until the day came when they were presented as fathers of the fatherland to the most loyal-hearted and gaily applauding German peoples, the day after which they continued their lives as before, [but] now wearing the prince's cap.[65] The courtiers made sure that no word reached them, telling them that they have duties, that it is not due to their arbitrary will whether they want to govern in accordance with or against reason, that they belonged to their nation as much as it belonged to them, and [that] at the very least one could demand of them that they do not become the nation's ineradicable eyesore and stigma. As such, one could not say about them that they thought their peoples their property, and [that they considered them to be] a game for their arbitrary will, because in truth they thought nothing about this at all, but were born and lived and died without ever raising the question as to why they are there.

This unbelievable stupidity was also evident in other appearances. They could have made mistake after mistake for a whole government, mistakes that were now laid bare for all the world to see, but the moment they showed a temporary impulse to man up, or not to commit an ignominious deed, the most rapt panegyrist would appear, seemingly lacking words and images to laud these exemplary deeds as born of the regent's wisdom and courage. They would not feel the deep shame that this brought on them, and no example is known, in which they objected to this.

Their ministers were deserving of such princes. These [ministers] too usually had not gone through a fundamentally scientific education, neither had they made the free power of thinking their own, but instead had [404] focused with some studiousness on what was then called Chivalry Studies[66] and they knew about other things through ragged fragments they had picked up when passing through lecture halls — if they had come close to them [at all] — in assemblies, in coffee houses and theaters, and what had stuck with them while travelling. When the need arose, instead of free thinking they reshaped these fragments in their spirit into a new idea on the basis of the two rules which concern the whole wisdom of the state of that era, which we will state shortly. The management of external relations was solely focused on what they called diplomacy, which — except for the science of espionage, the eliciting of secrets, listening to gossip, none of which served a purpose other than being able to file a report on them — consisted in the art of drawing out the need for a crucial decision as long as possible, based on equivocation and vague explanations, in the hope that in the meantime chance would perhaps intervene and make the choice, releasing them from the harsh compulsion of having to think and will for themselves.

The art of internal administration was even simpler and consisted simply in the science of acquiring as much cash as was possible. They did not presume to reflect much on this money and its worth, and one was regarded badly if one tried to convey to them that they cannot eat gold and silver, that under certain circumstances they could be much richer with half these metals than under other circumstances, that it seems to be higher art to create such favorable circumstances, and that in borrowing money today one should consider whether one can repay it tomorrow. They were also wholly indifferent in choosing the means to this highest purpose of government. They would poison public morality at its root if that is what it took to grab a penny from a poor maid through gambling. In general it was lost on them completely that educating the public to religion and morality is the foundation of all government. While they did want [405] religion for the common man, as noted above, they did not at all know what this is, hence the knowledge of the means of furthering this end fully eluded them. They believed themselves to be acting innocently enough when they paid priests and consistories according to ancient custom and origin. If one dared to expect them to do something for the education of the people — which was unbelievably wretched — they made the excuse of having no money. And so education, religion, and morals had to be replaced with the one, and quite simple, tool of the rod. Incidentally, in this respect, there were principles of government wisdom in circulation as means to increase population, such as the one that recommended making divorces easier and leniency about prostitution.

The population, increased through such means, as well as all the money, of which one could never get enough, together flowed into the enormous maw of the standing armies, which could never be large enough, and which left nothing for any other expenditure. The wisdom of this use of the money can be seen when a state over a decade of deepest peace provided its armies salaries, uniforms, and weaponry, and let them exercise diligently and without interruption, then at the first outbreak of war in the first battle the army completely collapsed and when the resistance was not completely abandoned, a new one had to be formed. As we have discussed, this happened literally not once, but several times, not to one, but to several of the prominent Germanic tribes, certainly proving that it does not occur merely by coincidence but follows a law lying in the nature of things.

The highest estate, the nobility, was usually to constitute [the officers for the army], as shown above, such that this estate had to become necessary. With few exceptions all the officers in the armies came from this estate. As such they avoided most urgently the appearance of a fine upbringing or a scientific education.[67] They believed one could by no means count as a brave officer without impertinent and coarse strutting about and arrogant defiance against other estates, alongside specially practiced mistakes in pronunciations and language errors. [406] One learns from documents of these times that several of them deserted during battle, that those, who were not included in the capitulations, submitted to the enemy from afar, so as to avoid becoming prisoners of war as well like their comrades. One [also] sees the portrait of others who enlisted children of their country in the service of the enemy hung from the gallows. Despite this, one does not detect in the privileged estate a diminishing of arrogance, nor [does one see] the lords getting the idea to remove the estate's exclusive privilege [to serve as officers] and try hiring other citizens. The same nobility had, again with very minor exceptions, the only pure landownership that existed at the time. One knows from documents from those times that the landowners only gave meagerly and with reluctance what they were required [to give] to their compatriots who were marching through. But these same landowners would, half a year before an enemy came to them, decree that to host the enemy cattle should be slaughtered, white bread be kept at the ready, and spirits be stocked. It soon became clear that this subset of the people, who only governed through fear, could itself only be motivated by fear.

In addition to the regiment of these princes, these ministers, and this nobility, the following external circumstance also contributed to Germany's ruin. The German national assembly[68] had long lost its power and two key powers had arisen in the nation, which — after a bitter war was concluded — jealously watched each other. The remaining smaller states seemed to quite naturally belong to one or the other, depending on their location, denomination, and interests. Had those two key powers understood their and the nation's interest, they would have recognized and established a separation and unification caused by nature itself through resolutions, and they would have placed the parts belonging to them into a military and diplomatic union with themselves that would preserve the civil independence of the [these] smaller states. Thereby Germany would have at least united itself into two large wholes, and the sources of jealousy and [407] future war between them merely would have to be carefully removed. One sword would have kept the other in its sheath and both would have instilled the requisite awe abroad. But, far from such an understanding of their true interest and from insight into the laws of higher government wisdom, they committed a number of mistakes in government in a short time without having a single healthy thought lying in between, such that they were in the position to thank God for their mere existence and to only live for the day and to feel themselves relieved of a great burden if one day passed without their demise. Instead, it fell on the smaller German states like a trick to play [the role of] the powerful [state] and do themselves what the larger ones should have done: to increase their earnings and their armies, to complete their lands, to enlarge their territories, all at the expense of their German neighbors. If a neighbor's village or office seemed convenient nothing was spared to acquire it, and when it had been acquired, to acquire another office or village that had been made convenient by the [initial] acquisition. There was no evidence of any reflection about the purpose of such an enlargement within the fold of the very same nation, nor of a thought as to what they might need the largest possible expansion for, should they actually achieve it. Instead, they appeared to be guided merely by raw and blind greed, or a stupid misunderstanding, which could frequently be applied to their situation. The means for acquiring such an office conveniently located for them were all the same to them as long as the purpose was served. They groveled in front of foreign countries and opened to them the womb of the fatherland. They would have groveled in front of the Regent of Algiers, kissed the dust of his feet, married their daughters to his natural or adopted sons if thereby they could only reach high office or the title of king. Driven by their wild greed they did not think that the foreigner [408] would despise them, nor [did they think about] how they would fare if the foreigner had invaded the land himself without regard for achieving the desired office.

## [409] The Republic of the Germans at the Beginning of the Twenty-Second Century Under Their Fifth Magistrate

Introduction

There came a time when the German nation had declined so far that some of its princes betrayed their country to foreign states, others who did not do quite as much of this themselves watched in shameful cowardice and laziness and declared it good that the peoples, under a trusting delusion that it is their duty to endure their princes' desire [simply] because it is their desire, were completely exhausted, shamed, and used as a blind tool by the cruel moods of the foreign states, even as they pit Germans against Germans. In this condition the nobility showed itself to be the first estate of the nation solely by being the first that fled when there was danger and when, abandoning the shared cause, sought to earn the mercy of the common enemy through shameful groveling and betrayal. The writers had also broken away from the nation, either through cowardly silence or brainless admiration of raw power and through vapid flattery of the common enemy. Because only these constituents of the people were noticed, but secretly and quietly tolerated by the remaining masses, all of Europe judged that the Germans, as a quite despicable nation, fully deserved their fate. [This] judgement [was shared by] the arrogant and raw power that was crushing them, which found itself quite justified to give misery its due.[69] This judgment was even [shared] by both of the remaining upstanding classes, which we just named, who were heroically prepared to [410] share the punishment for the universal guilt that they did not contribute to.

We do not know whether these princes and this nobility suddenly and miraculously recognized that they were barely, hence not at all, capable of leading the nation, and so driven by a sense of equality with all others, voluntarily lowered themselves down and offered a helping hand to the new order. Or whether the nation organized itself, as though hit by an electric shock and favored by circumstances, and rid itself of the princes and nobility in a good manner and with the support of the few honest ones from the named classes. Only this much is certain: some time after this decay, the German nation whose history in the interim is lost (with the exception of a few shallow remarks by foreigners, which bear obvious signs of being wrong) reemerges without hereditary princes or nobility and under a constitution whose description is the purpose of the following work.

## Ultimate Goal of the Constitution of the Germans

The legislators of the Germans have stipulated, in the archives of the upper assembly for the instruction of all future times, a very determinate account both generally of the ultimate goal they had in mind in their legislation and in particular of how each decision they made follows from that ultimate goal. To explain their laws we will frequently reference their own authentic interpretations verbatim.

With regard to the first aspect [the ultimate goal], they say that the purpose of our legislation was to fully develop humanity in the nation we have come to advise, as far as the era allows. For this to occur equally in the whole nation, not in an [411] arbitrarily chosen part of it, the absolute equality of the tribes would have to be introduced. Clearly and in front of the world's eyes, the unavoidable inequality among individuals had to be caused by difference in talents or through a fate comparable to the will of God. Hence this equality of tribes was demanded, positing that it would not already be achieved through right alone, by the purpose of education, which is undoubtedly the basis of all rights.

We have adhered to this concept of the education of the human being in general and no further determination of it was needed, considering the fact that it is *Germans* to whom we would be giving a constitution. The latter concept did not come up, other than in the happy observation that the Germans, the first before all Europeans, would let themselves be given such a constitution, because only they — as a nation free from the urge of other peoples to display exquisite [taste] towards the outside [world] and to only feel great and honored in comparison to others in their surroundings — have the most power to retreat back into themselves and quietly rest with themselves. Hence even individuals, even [those] with recognized and permitted rights for the highest offices, were easily capable of relinquishing [their rights to high office] for their person if it were necessary, and remaining in the lowest one, so as long as the right of their tribe remained undiminished.

The second key consideration in our legislation was that the means to the intended education we introduced should not be limited to a [specific] point where ongoing education would have to stand still, but that they would contain the drive of progress and elevation into the infinite.

With regard to the nation's foreign relations, we have two main considerations. First, that the preservation of the state, its constitution, and its independence from all foreign violence and influence be secured and that these are beyond question internally and above the attempt of invasion from anyone externally. Thereafter we believed that a nation, which like the German one, strives to maintain and defend its unique being, but not to [412] impose it on others, was not unintentionally placed in the center of peoples, who once they have reached even a meager part of education immediately display this aspiration. In the eternal plan of the human race as a whole, they were [rather] destined to be a bulwark against such constant invasiveness and to guarantee not only for themselves but for all European peoples that they can walk their own way to the shared goal. In this regard and in firm confidence that we will not be called to account for this [claim] in front of the tribunal of the whole human race, of which the German nation is only a single part, we have placed an immeasurable power in their hands.

## Religious Denomination of the Germans

The legislators found the three familiar main denominations of Christianity[70] in the landowning estate. They deemed it necessary to authoritatively declare, recognize, and elevate a fourth denomination they knew about to the universal civil religion, to accompany and legitimize government negotiations. [They did this] because they knew that all freely educated men who had ever deliberated about this matter [religion] would be favorable to it [the fourth denomination], a circumstance that would exclude them from all public devotions and which would therefore put the state in a situation in which neither its most honorable citizens nor its own dignitaries believed in the ideas[71] on which they [are required to] act. Leaving the Catholics their foreign name, the disciples of this [fourth] denomination called themselves universal Christians. The scholars amongst them did justice to Jesus Christ, [by claiming] that he was the first among all [human beings], and as far as can be seen, to know and teach the highest endpoint of all truth without having received any instruction himself. However, they insisted that they [413] did not deem this teaching true, nor that anyone should deem it true, because Jesus had taught it, but only because and insofar as one feels internally compelled to recognize it. They even refrained from imposing the profound respect for Jesus that had arisen from historical investigation on anyone who either did not want to undertake such historical inquiries alongside them or [thought that] the same inquiries led to different results. Instead, they recognized anyone as a member of their faith who believed with them the content of Christian theology, or whichever name that member might give to it. They refused to be drawn into the question raised by their opponents as to whether this cognition would exist in the world if Jesus had not existed, because it could never be resolved, and even if it could [be resolved] would never lead to a reasonable application. When it came to a heated dialectical discussion between them and their opponents, the attempted excuse that they believe it because they understand it to be true, but in addition because Jesus had taught it (or posited the other way around), was exposed in its complete absurdity for all to see. Then, those who had not already decided to convert to their [side] had to posit as their distinctive teaching the confession that they did not accept it [Christian faith] as true, nor that love or a wish draws them to it, but that they believed it merely based on the word of a man mostly unfamiliar to them. Hence the first ones called themselves Christians as such. As one of the first representatives of this denomination says, "[We are

Christians] not because we follow the relations of the times, which are over, but because we firmly believe ourselves to be Christs[72] in our being and disposition, and urge ourselves and our [fellow believers] to become the same in reality. Meanwhile, our fellow citizens from the other side believe that Christ is of a completely different being than they are and that becoming equal to him, even finding truth in what he found to be true, is impossible in itself and an aspiration toward a foolish impudence. Hence their relationship to him, which they nonetheless defend and also want to impose on others, could most appropriately be called Christianism."[73] [414] The Christianists, in the heat of the argument, appropriated this name — just as the Lutherans once had [appropriated] theirs — leaving the name of Christians for the former.

Aside from the reasons already mentioned above about the public recognition of this denomination, the legislators have explained more deeply: "The first condition of all human education is unlimited independence, which consists in not recognizing any constraints other than those that are posited by clear insight and one's own will. Whoever must will following an alien insight, is not free. The system of blind belief in authority where it is not due to despotic minds is due to slavish minds.[74] No constitution for a free people may make a rule that seems to impose limits on a person's insight as a condition for civic status, nor [may such a constitution] silently allow [such a limitation] to stand."

The legislators then closely followed this principle of liberating the conscience. They established a cult of this universal Christian Church, but also left the cults of the three remaining denominations completely intact as they were, and left it open for all citizens [to decide] which they wanted to belong to. Incidentally, they conducted the remaining civil religious trials, treated more deeply below, without exception according to the new manner, but with the freedom for everyone to recapitulate, or even anticipate, the execution [of the trials] in his own manner. Only one circumstance almost caused dangerous unrest. The legislators, intending to ground universal civic love on a religion of love, insisted that everyone who hoped for another blessed life for himself, acknowledge each of his co-citizens, whatever confession he may belong to, as capable of the same blessedness and that no teaching contrary to this principle may be tolerated by the state. They made the public recognition of their principle a condition of admission into the citizenry. They placed it into the public procedure for baptismal rituals.[75] They demanded of teachers of all denominations that they explicitly teach it. "If someone denies," so they declared on a certain occasion about this matter, [415] "or even doubts, another life for himself, we cannot expect of him to think more of others than for himself. He is without any religion and without either the good or the contrary dispositions that it instills, and [so] we will legislate in a way that we can get along with him even without religion. But whoever claims to know that a blessed life awaits him and his co-religionists, while he excludes others who are his fellow citizens, clearly deems himself and his own better than the latter and, contrary to his assurances, it is impossible, and should not be believed, that he esteems, loves, and is inclined to serve alongside those from whom he expects to be completely separated in another life as much as those with whom he expects to live through all eternity." We hope that as the readers become more familiar with the spirit of the mandates of these men and with their successes, they will increasingly understand that they cannot skip over this point. A certain portion of teachers of a particular denomination resisted the mentioned imposition. Fortunately, the better part of the laymen of their congregations, driven by a nobler sentiment, declared themselves in opposition to their teachers, and so the disputed principle was accepted by the majority of the laity of this church and those who remained opposed were banished from the realm.

Not all those teachers of the two Protestant denominations who had been present for the beginning of the separation had died, and for reasons which the reader of our account might detect himself, the members of these congregations had joined the universal Christendom. The third denomination has long remained separate, but now that the parents and for a good part the grandparents of the entire living generation [416] have undergone the new education only a few dispersed Catholic congregations remain in some Old Catholic provinces, whose members are surrounded with the same love and whose cult is maintained with the same care as those of other communities.

The main precept for the teachers of Christians, as we will call the main [religious] community of the Germans from now on without qualifications, was that it actually is religion, into which they initiated their pupils and with which they entertained their adult members, instead of morality, or politics, or the theory of happiness, or if they felt like it, the art of agriculture. For them, and those who agreed with them — for whose needs this new church had been established — religion was the cognition of our being solely in God, and our eternal existence in him, and the certainty that he most immediately reveals himself in us, in his translucent clarity, his steadfast firmness, his strict order, and his all-encompassing benevolence, constantly flooding around and through us and onto others. Because they considered the Bible to be the national book, and also believed that especially in the so-called New Testament there are books, which, if only they were not measured with a one-sided standard, no other book in the primeval world nor in all posterity[76] could be compared to. On this topic, others believed that precisely because of [the Bible's] indeterminacy it could easily be molded into the correct opinion, so they instructed these teachers to tie their lessons, whose content and confirmation by the way they had to create themselves, to the Bible, for the memory of the people and the nation and for the sensuous enlivening of it. Meanwhile, they rejected, following their basic confession, any conclusive authority on the Bible.

How religion was first brought to the youths will be covered in a later chapter. For now we want to speak of the application of what has already been covered in the era determined above, transporting ourselves with our reader into the open plaza of some village church, which overall resemble the churches of city districts. [417]

The church of the smallest village that [can] be granted a church [is], (for reasons and employing means that will be discussed at a different time), a pretty building usually a dome elongated in several areas. The locations of those churches are not determined according to the geographical points, but according to the capacity of the place where they stand, which probably also determined the variation of the domes, and which is usually at a moderate height and always chosen to give the entire region a beautiful central point. They are surrounded by a round, open plaza closed off by walls. With regard to its main decorations it should be remarked that the Christian Church, immediately after its recognition, decided to cremate the bodies of the deceased, in a manner and with festivities that, should we come across an appropriate moment, we will not forget to describe. The Christianists continued to bury theirs underground, but after burial was proscribed by the law in certain cases, which [we will discuss] in time, even the Christianists started to cremate. And there are those who claim to know human nature well, and who remark at this point in their history that the transition to this manner of burial was also the transition to universal Christianity. So it then happened, that, behind the shelves with horizontal receptacles, which are rounded in accordance with the shape of the wall and which carry the urns of the deceased inhabitants of the village, one sees urns that are without a doubt empty, because the bodies have long been decomposing in the ground below. The families of the deceased have attempted to do them this service, and this is a little deceit of love, the sort of act the German republic does not like to reprimand.

Every citizen's urn, wherever he dies and however high his status, will be sent back to the cemetery of the village in which he was born, and will be placed there. One can see there on the highest shelf: "died for the fatherland in the fields," and then the names on the urns; or on the second [highest shelf]: [418] "advised the fatherland through clarity and understanding;" or on the third [shelf]: "lived peacefully as a good housefather, a good housemother, produced and raised well-behaved children for the fatherland, proved to be beloved and good to his fellow citizens;" finally one also sees shelves without headings or names on the urns.

The part of the [cemetery] yard that is not covered with these shelves is — now that no more bodies shall be buried — a charming garden full of trees, plants, and foliage, sent from all directions of the sky.

The peculiarly romantic spirit of this nation, on its wide rambles through the world, still cannot help itself but long for the place, where its eye first awoke to the light of day, and where its ashes will peacefully join other ash. And [it longs] to send to this place seeds or cuttings of that which stirred its wonder in the distant realm of plants. Hence one can see plants from all regions able to develop — aided by the preacher who is always also a good botanist — in the place that awaits the ashes of he who sent them [the seeds]. The inhabitants of neighboring villages undertook pilgrimages to these sites to view these gifts and compare them to their own. Thus develops in these country residents a tender love for plants and a keen eye for their observation, because what their rational nature loves and esteems the most connects with it.

In the inside of a church, there is one setting, contrasted with the other [setting] where the choir is, that is always covered by a curtain, which neither falls nor rises when opening or closing [it], such that by closing it, the lower and upper ceilings and both sides interlock and concealment and unveiling occur as if by magic, and nothing happens during it that could displease a trained eye. The space thereby separated is called the hall. From its center the pulpit arises in the requisite distance, roughly going to two-thirds of the height of the internally visible dome. In front of it [stands] a simple altar, whose side walls and decorations help to hide the stairs to the pulpit. [419] Opposite from this, the seats of the congregation spread out on the floor and in amphitheaters, well-ordered and higher than everything else, and the choir almost touches the arch of the dome. Nevertheless, the legislators of the Germans began starting the year in the spring, [which it deemed] rational and purposeful — just as another European nation used to,[77] but was later found undeserving of it — so they left the Sunday in place, which is incidentally a very purposeful time[78] [as] a gathering day for Christians, and did not interfere in this temporal order.

The celebration of Sunday consists in the following. During the shortest days, when it is midday, and during the longest, maximally two hours after dawn, the bell is rung to [call to] congregate. No healthy [person] easily stays away, as [this] is connected with certain punishments.

The congregation gathers in the front court just described. The clergy is already in the church, standing in front of the altar. As they notice that the first [congregants] have gathered, all doors are opened, the community enters, and all take their assigned places while soft instrumental music lifts their spirit to devotion. When all have entered the music ends, and suddenly the hall opens. In the hall lie rifles in their own determined place, as every German man beginning in the 20th year and, with few exceptions, until his death, is a soldier with an assigned rifle. The village's justice of the peace appears before them, holding the flag. Because what happens next, with which the public celebration begins, are civil actions, it was found fitting that the basic symbol of citizenship, the weaponry, would be visible to them and form the basis of the scene. [420]

The first act is the internment of the dead. When, in which manner, and with which celebrations the bodies are cremated and their ashes collected we will report at a different time. In the act that we are now describing the urns are already on the altar in front of the clergyman when the church opens. Because this internment is a universal civil act, in the beginning empty urns were erected and buried for those whose bodies had been buried according to their particular church custom. This institution, from which no one could be excused, may have contributed to move the many more quickly to accept cremation and with it universal Christendom. Names are announced by the clergyman in the order in which the urn has to be placed — whether he [the deceased] died fighting for the fatherland, or if he supported it otherwise through advice and action, or, where this is the same, according to the earliest date of death. From the civil record the biography of the deceased is read. We can comprehend this better by news, that, when accepting a male or female child into the community, the name that it receives is recorded into a page of this book and from then on, as things happen to them, or as official reports are received from afar, these are recorded onto the same page: his advancement in public education, his estate or office, what he has contributed to the good of the whole through them [the estate or office], if he went to war, which battles and victories he witnessed, etc. Recordings continue until his death, and in this same manner. After this reading [of his biography], another empty sheet of paper — as a symbol for what might be recorded about the deceased before the court of morality — is thrown into a pan next to the altar, in which a flame of pleasant-smelling woods burns under the words: "Should the flight of heavenly desire have occasionally been hampered by the earthly shell, he now has shed the shell. [Now let the shell] be erased [421] from our remembrance and that of all mortals," words which are slowly and festively spoken by the entire community. Delaying, as we mentioned, our treatment at length of the aforementioned court of honor, we only note here, to facilitate understanding of the above, that this court in its meetings actually consigns to the flames all remarks and proceedings about citizens, whose death is officially reported to them, and it would be considered unbecoming, other than in the case of one person mentioned further below, to delay this. This symbolic destruction [extends] without exception even to those persons, whose names almost certainly never appeared in the records of the court, indeed, even to those who are not subject to it [the court] in order to instill in the citizens the holy awe of this court, and the thought — focusing attention on ourselves — that anyone could expose him, and finally the conviction that the stains that are thereby revealed cannot be redeemed through penance like other offenses, but can only be freely forgiven by a harmonious community, and only after one's death. [This] also [serves to] portray death in the friendly shape of a universal redeemer[79] and reconciler, an intention that is also visible in some of its other institutions.

And thus, if there are several urns, every individual is carried forward. When these acts have been completed, a soft music intones; the priest lifts the first urn, and the two eldest of two other [families] stand by his side, until the procession is positioned to leave. When the hymn, which we call by its first words "May Ye be Happy" and which contains a congratulations to the departed, as well as all others [who deceased] on the state's territory since its inception. And for the living it contains the wish to mature through doing and bearing [children] until they become worthy of resuming the interrupted shared existence with them. [Then] the procession begins slowly to walk through the main door, opposite from the altar and opening by itself through a hidden spring, and the procession places the urns on their designated shelves. The tears of love and gratitude, gifts, wreaths [422] covered with thankful tears are delivered by individuals to the urns after the congregation has dispersed, [all this] we do not want to mention here.

Such is how public burial in general is conducted. How to proceed in extraordinary cases, we will cover when dealing with them. ([For example,] one does not like to bury someone who was punished for cowardice alone.)

They festively reenter, stand in front of the altar in reversed order with the clergyman in the background until the hymn has concluded. The eldest separate out and go to their seats and for some moments there is a festive silence.

Now the doors open again and the oldest and most honorable women of the congregation enter and with quiet decorum step to the altar one by one, carrying in their arms the newborn children to be entered into the congregation. Because the induction process is different for the two genders, but the legislators nowhere wanted to permit even the hint of a privilege of one gender over the other, the difficulty that arises here is resolved. The time of birth decides. If the first [child] born in the past week is a girl, the induction of girls is conducted first, if it is a boy then that of the boys.

The preacher speaks loudly and distinctly: "it is on this day, in this hour of this family that our fellow citizen was born: a son, a daughter, who shall carry the name [of this family]." During this speech the [female] citizen who is holding this child takes a few steps forward, separate from the others and raises the child up so that it is visible to all. The page that is shown [of the civil record] is dedicated to his or her life. To avoid delays, which would put the priest in an uncomfortable situation, it is assumed that what was first said has already been written down by the priest beforehand.

One of the eldest steps to the wall of the altar, and glances, turned away from the people [423] [and], standing in the same direction and upright, signs his name on the page sideways and says with a loud voice, e.g. Jakob Ehrenberg, son of Maria Meyerin, daughter of him and her, has her page in the civil record. Same with the others: every time one of the eldest steps in front to sign the prepared page.

Meanwhile, the bearers of the children who are to be inducted first have gathered into a small group to the left of the altar, and to its right [are] the others, as long as this is possible without a lack of propriety. The preacher puts his hand on the first child, leaving it there for the entire ceremony that follows and says: "we call you Maria Meyerin" (the surname is also spoken), which the whole congregation festively repeats as a sign that we, and through us the entire fatherland of the German nation recognizes you *as a being capable of reason* (the latter is repeated by the congregation), *as sharing all rights of our citizenship* (repeated), *as co-inheritors of the eternal life for which we hope* (repeated.) This [is done] with every child. When he has reached the last, he raises his hand and swings it in an arc back to the first and from there back again, leaving it to rest in the middle of the arc and says: "Live, grow, prosper, may the page reserved for you become the story of a virtuous life, may a band of love proceed from you extending to the entire circle [of people] in which you act, may valiant sons and daughters take your place, should you be taken from us." The entire last speech is repeated by the congregation. Upon mention of the sons, towards whom the preacher now turns in this case, while the bearers of the daughters remain in the closed circle, the first ceremony with the laying of the hand and the use by the congregation is unchanged; the second one, however, with the raised hand, is called thusly . . . [80]

[424] National attire: 1) The principles regarding clothes are well-known. Expressive, liberating trousers and jacket at work. Mere details of personal

presentation as such do not have anything *national* [about them]. Only the color could be [national in character]. Then the decorations, the hat.

Working clothes. Deciding [their] color. Those who do not take care of the human body are despicable. Red blue black, the negro should wear the latter. Brown-grey is the true [color] for the European. Business attire: long trousers up to the stomach. Again short sleeves. Jacket, shirt, to be buttoned, in the same color. For the worker: *darker* [colors], so as not to show the dirt. Raw not *smooth*. (Can also be *without sleeves*.) *Women*: *A bodice* is appropriate. The skirt of the latter is in the way during certain activities, supporting the legs and so on during certain times. They remain attached to it. They can have *trousers* for work. Stop — [only at] certain times. Good. It will be introduced that they stay at home and wear skirts.[81]

Performance attire: A coat, with or without sleeves? With the form of a Swiss priest's robe, [or] like a Saxonian Priest's robe down to the feet. (Because this dress is not for walking.) [Made] from slightly *lighter grey*, and the stuff can *be smooth*.

For the women the same.

Now [on to] hair and headdress [style]: (Beard?) 1) Hair. Growing it by itself would be enough to have a natural headdress. a) It is cumbersome not to be able to take it off. b) Its daily upkeep and cleaning costs time. Hence cutting it is better for both genders. 2) The headdress is not really *attire* but an umbrella and parasol fastened to the body (Head and face should not be covered, and custom will make it so that he does not need one in a pinch.) Our round hat is solely made for this one. (Caps, turbans, and the like are barbaric. Think of the Persian and [425] Greek skulls. War may then have its *helmets*.) Our natural hats are purposeful insofar as they do not immediately encompass and express the form of the head.[82] The necessary cover is the hair. There is no reason why the two genders should be different in this regard. The custom[83] until now is without reason. 3) Beard. One could cut the hair on one's head just as one cuts the beard! Without a doubt the custom arose from the desire to appear youthful. (But this is not the inclination of the youth itself.) More precisely, cleanliness and ease brought it about. The clash over *woolen* garments with the old. This is not the case with the linen shirts of the moderns. One can cut it shorter in the summer than in winter. Hence, the rule: one [should] cut it roughly as much as the head hair. Cut it off [completely] where it is uncomfortable.[84] This creates a polite difference between the genders given the similarity in their apparel.

Where to attach nationality? 1) Is this *portrayal* of apparel, the thoroughly *similar colors* (even across estates), the *beard* and so on not [appropriately] regarded as sufficient? If others imitate [it], it will clearly be called German garb. One has grown accustomed only to take the *arbitrary* to be *special*, not the *natural*. It must be dishonorable to wear something else.

2) But what about the *work* apparel? This one has cut and color as well. This all seems to have occurred. 3) One only wears *official* apparel when conducting official business. It consists in a ready-made *collar* just thrown over the national garb which should be taken off after conducting one's official [business]. We

have here the *teacher* (preacher, professor, principal. These are completely alike.) Only during public exercises do the professor and principal wear their badge, not during usual teaching. The preacher [wears it] always during public assemblies. Judges. What else? Nothing. The king? Where does he have to appear in public? 1) During the coronation. During formal visitations. His councilors [are] there [with him]. Black for the teachers (color of the collection) [426] *White* for the judge, [representing] innocence, incorruptibility. Red [for] the regent, [which is] imposing. The higher estates [are] never without a robe. 4) The military. The work apparel with the requisite weaponry. The divisions may have their *insignia* [on the uniforms]. But the apparel retains the national color. 5) As a matter of fact, no one should present himself to the others unless [he is] in [his] gown. So that walking is not obstructed, it should be packed like our soldiers pack their coats. 6) Only he who has been declared manly wears this gown. Until then the work apparel.

This has been covered.

Now the drive to decorate and the drive for colors.

How to satisfy the drive for colors and for decoration, especially in women?

# Notes

1. Pagination references are to J. G. Fichte, *Gesamtausgabe*, ed. Hans Gliwitzky and Reinhard Lauth (Fromann-Holzboog, 1994), II/10.377–426 with page number in brackets.
2. (FICHTE'S NOTE) Humanity means *sociability* . . . instrument of speech, a tool. Where there is order for the better, there it occurs. Where the organization itself leads to a worsening, there you can look the undeserving in the face to avoid being infected by them: there occurs merely the trial of the individual.
3. Phantasie
4. Klugheit
5. Unverständig und unwissend
6. Sich zu ermannen
7. Schwärmerei
8. (FICHTE'S NOTE) A more determinate plan: increasing carefulness, as the products of increasing age, and of the estate which in that generation must rise. The original devotion of the unusual instead of the youth . . . active. Instead of the spirit, how this bloom of youth falls away, sinks away, for the women, beauty, the dutiful activity, and the virtuous maxims and the thoughtful art; they are right thus far.
Jews, Greeks, and others stand under their education to war — and so many savages. Age and experience.
9. Protektor
10. Leere Tafel
11. (FICHTE'S NOTE) The following arrangement: The progeny of the protector until he lives to see the next member [as ruler], are princes, sacrosanct, and

under the special protection of the successor: and they can only be established by him, while the senate can indict them. They can do nothing, or everything, other than becoming *protector*. Only after the elimination of the princedom can they be elected. The state is heir of all public offices, [and] cares for them.

12. (FICHTE'S NOTE) This gives much to think about. What can the countryman, or someone from a small city know about the great men of the nations, who all have to be learned men? Also businessmen, warriors. I have to turn my gaze to the *assemblies*. It will be best to let the large council *present* and choose. The writers presented the provinces over all.

13. Statthalter

14. (FICHTE'S NOTE) In education one has to ensure discretion, which is achieved through the absolute lifelong prohibition on disclosing what transpires in the classes. *Censors*, to whom such infamies are reported, and who are covered by another's confession. One can appeal, but [that would] draw shame on oneself. Not reporting is itself infamy. Objects of censorship.

15. (FICHTE'S NOTE) Question: Should and can the protector himself go to war? I think yes: during deliberation with the senate about internal matters he leaves behind his ministers, who remain answerable to him. On the conduct of the war he is unconstrained after all. Only with [launching] new wars, or peace accords, would he have to appear in person in the senate.

16. Stuffe

17. Forterzieher

18. Persönlichen bürgerlichen Rechte

19. A matter for deeper investigation

20. "It is not clear." This phrase refers to the cases in which there is no clear law to be applied.

21. Hauptkommando

22. (FICHTE'S NOTE) *Jus agratiandi* [EDITOR'S NOTE: the right to pardon in criminal cases] — Clemency can be recommended by tribunal or executed by the protector himself: but it makes a law for the future.

23. Stadtbürger

24. Judgment of ignorance

25. Schmachhemd. Fichte appears to have coined the term; the more common expression would have been *Bußkleid*. First mention of the cilice is usually dated to the Vulgate translation of the Bible. [King James: "sackcloth."] The secularization of the term — dropping *Buß* (penance) for *Schmach* (disgrace, shame) — may be intentional.

26. abgebeten

27. (FICHTE'S NOTE) The soldiers are punished same as the citizens, [but] the rod will not be found anywhere. Also [the soldiers] have censors. [If they display] cowardice or theft, the thumb is cut off, and found unsuitable for foreign service.

Someone like that never lives long. Insubordination and desertion are punished by death without exceptions and for every rank. — [Then their] name is incinerated in the community.

28. Because of the role or position that is held.
29. censetur
30. die Wilden
31. (FICHTE'S NOTE) Will the other Europeans accept German refugees? No, because homesickness comes and they [would then] be good for nothing. That would be the question. It is not to be alleged.
32. Fabrikaten
33. Comptoire, an organization that regulates trade especially in a colonial setting.
34. Contrôle, an organization that ensures quality control in trade.
35. [In the margin of Fichte's text:] Figure of speech: His iron remains in hell.
36. Incomplete sentence
37. Konklusum, which is the name given to the decree of a Germanic council.
38. (FICHTE'S NOTE) Should I expel the poor Venetians? Will Trieste do? I think yes: Could one not unite these two oceans through a canal in Germany? No, this does not work. Gibraltar would have to be German. Certainly something that could be united with the Danube flows into the Adriatic Gulf. But the Danube is already united with the Rhine, and so this connection would exist.
39. (FICHTE'S NOTE) [In the] academy: speaking skill. Orthography. Prosody, the art of declamation, plus song.

Academy of the arts: the art of poetry and so on recruit by themselves. Every educated person gives the verse a try. This is part of education. Their realm is under the protection of the Germans.

—

Universities especially practice the art of acquiring new knowledge quickly. Without having mastered this, no one can get away [from them]. Appointments. Moving events.

—

Jews. Either blended in or emigrated. They possess a highly interesting state in *Palestine*. Other European nations followed them. The remaining ones are all members of the new church. What else distinguishes them? The urge to wander. Ambition.

40. See 53n62 in Patriotism Essay about Johann Heinrich Pestalozzi.
41. *Selbst*ständigkeit
42. Mariendienst
43. Fichte is quoting from an unknown source.
44. (FICHTE'S NOTE) To hit a maid or to curse at her [would] lead, in addition to the communal punishment, to the cilice. Generally [this violence] has bad consequences. How to suppress the urge to slap in the female sex? And nosiness? There is so much material in education [that can help one] know why someone is being punished, rewarded, and such things.

The one who has been abused by boys is no longer allowed to help boys and must dig on the farms in solitude. Only the abusive boy can redeem her by asking her hand in marriage. She too can mitigate [his circumstances], but not his shame. The boy is told: the maid is weaker in some ways, more sensitive in others; the maid is told that she insults herself when she insults a boy. The two sexes should not eat together, because one should not witness when a member of the other is punished. But they should pray together. Stop: gossiping with the other sex is infamy. With maids [it amounts to] undignified familiarity, with boys it [amounts to] casting [oneself] off. But now punishments do their work. Good: Maids do not watch during exercises.

45. It comes to be
46. (FICHTE'S NOTE) For the preface. If I had come to describe it three centuries earlier, I would not have been short on fictions. How Merciers dreamt, like Dante in a vision. [EDITOR'S NOTE: Mercier, Louis-Sebastien, 1740–1814, and Dante Alighieri, 1265–1321. Fichte may be thinking about Louis-Sebastien's "The Year 2440" and about "On Monarchy" or the *Divine Comedy* of Dante's] But I did not dream, but apprehended in a state of heightened waking. And I know that truth is what I say, even if it should never become actual. I am bound to believe and to hope that my testimony can contribute to it becoming complete and whole and it gives some beginning to its reality. In this belief and hope did I make my face public.
47. Näscherei
48. (FICHTE'S NOTE) Her sister, also a widow with a son and rich in food, goes to the sister to help her and share her poverty. All of their naivety in such actions.
A brother rescues the others from the hands of the savages. Dying for the officer [is] quite naive. He is probably worth a thousand of us.
The local city, district city, regional city, national city.
49. bürgerliche Taufformel
50. The word before and an entire line after *Protestant* are illegible in the original document.
51. (FICHTE'S NOTE) They have a clean slate and sketch of the entire human faculty of speech in which they easily enter the actual determinations.
52. Solidität
53. (FICHTE'S NOTE) Or in front of the tribunal of mankind. We will, in order to thereby make their legislation comprehensible for everyone, frequently use their own authentic interpretation.
Our purpose. We maintained this concept of the whole universal and its deduction in this last concept, except regarding [the fact] that several Germans . . . [consists in] the maintenance of the independence of the state from external influence . . .
54. (FICHTE'S NOTE) These had much support, exclusively had culture, and did not take part in the other [activities] to [accumulate] bigger riches of external religion. [These religious denominations were] in opposition of the state, which dealt with religion [in a way] that it did not even demand from its best citizens.
55. Fichte does not complete the sentence here. A clearer expression of the same idea on page 76 concludes "they believed it merely based on the word of a man mostly unfamiliar to them."
56. Christuße

57. Three unintelligible syllables in the manuscript here.
58. Illegible two words in the manuscript here.
59. Heerbahn
60. Fortbildung
61. Anschein
62. Schlechtigkeit
63. Volksklassen
64. Nahrungsstoffe
65. A red hat worn in Germany as a sign of the dignity of the prince, given by the emperor.
66. Galante Studien. Fichte is using the expression sarcastically here, referring to the frivolous 'education' of the ministers, e.g. feasting, drinking, whoring, and gambling.
67. Erziehung oder einer wissenschaftlichen Bildung
68. Reichsverband
69. i.e., France
70. That is, the Catholic, Lutheran, and Reform denominations.
71. Vorstellungen
72. Christuße
73. Christianismus. While the term usually has negative connotations today, e.g. the deployment of religion for ideological ends, it's unclear whether this is the sense Fichte has in mind. He may also just be helping himself to an earlier term for Christianity to distinguish the two groups.
74. Sklavengemütern
75. Taufformel
76. Vorwelt . . . Nachwelt
77. A reference to the French Revolutionary calendar, introduced in 1793.
78. Epoche
79. Entsündiger
80. This whole paragraph from "Meanwhile" to "thusly…" was crossed out in Fichte's text.
81. (FICHTE'S NOTE) With skirts there is a question about attaching them. They must not press into the body. Bulges on the hips are objectionable. Hence they are attached to the bodice, as well as the trousers, through buttons. The skirts can also be fastened from behind. Like on the [clothes of the] Levi [women].
Women hired to do field work wear trousers, skirts at home. For the former they are never needed in conditions of sickness.
82. (FICHTE'S NOTE) Why black? For the sake of the durability of the color. Leave it *gray* or *white*, as the felt is.
83. Praxis
84. (FICHTE'S NOTE) A new opportunity for the farmer to [exhibit] cleanliness. Saturday evening his beard is *cleaned*. He is also *bathed*.

# 4

# Lectures on the Vocation of the Scholar (1811)

*Translated by Anne C. Reitz*

## [313] First Lecture

It[1] is the intention of these lectures to answer the questions, *what is the scholar*, and the related one, if a scholar *comes to be* and gradually begets himself, how does he come to be a scholar? And then *this one*, how does his inner being express itself in appearance?

*The scholar*, we said: but the teaching or doctrine is not an end in itself and is not there just for the sake of being there. Its goal is *knowledge*. The goal of the teaching or doctrine must thus be accomplished in a scholar and the instructed through the doctrine; the scholar must have passed through doctrine to arrive at knowledge. Otherwise, he would not be a scholar, but rather one who is still very much being instructed and is to be instructed. The scholar is therefore without a doubt a knower.

Now, we presumably ascribe a *value* to such a person, and a not insignificant value, since we would certainly barely talk about what is completely worthless in our own good judgment, or, in this case, expect any attention for our remarks. So, then, the question is, above all else: does *knowledge*, in which the essence of the scholar is supposed to reside, thus have value, and does all knowledge have value? And if perhaps not all of it does, what is that knowledge which has value?

One can at first view knowledge as the mere likeness and copy[2] of being that is located external to knowledge and completely independent of knowledge. Every single person who has only just lived consciously on this earth has collected and taken in his portion of *this* kind of knowledge, without thus claiming the label scholar. Within *this* type of knowledge, the scholar could only distinguish himself from the uneducated in that he would have grasped a much greater amount of such knowledge than others. The scholar would thus be different from the uneducated absolutely not in the type of his knowledge, but only in the quantity of it. The differentiation [314] would be an infinite one, founded only on a fluid relationship, and not in any way a definite relationship. It could be that the same person who makes no secret of his ignorance now might have previously served as a competent scholar, if he had only come along a few hundred years earlier. On the other hand, the person who now might be one of the foremost knowers would not even advance to being good among the common men a millennium later. Here and there, the situation really has been seen in such a way.

Even without taking this into account, it is not easy in general to see what value such knowledge can have, and then what purpose it might serve — this mere repetition in just the dead image of that which is already there in being, and truly and powerfully at that, even supposing that it could ever be done completely.

In contrast, that knowledge, to which alone everyone might tend to attach value, is clarified by the antithesis and represents itself through it. Such knowledge would have to be not merely the likeness and copy of an already present being external to it and independent of it, and *inquire into*[3] this being, but rather it would much more have to be the model of a being, and be able to contain within itself the basis of such a being, and therefore precede the being belonging to it. Phrased in a more familiar way: this kind of knowledge would have to be practical, and active, and constitutive of a being.[4]

What was just said, that knowledge has a value only under the condition that it be active, is pretty much generally recognized in common sayings, such as "what good is knowledge, when you do not do anything with it; action, not knowing, shows a man's worth," etc. It is so frequently recognized that it has often enough been misused and turned to contempt for research whose practicable[5] goal cannot be understood by every common eye right on the spot. But what knowledge has to be in *itself,* if it is supposed to be practical, [315] is something those who use such phrases most often have *so* little considered that they go crazy as soon as you truly take their own principles seriously and they think precisely that which necessarily follows from that assumption and is a given with it, contradicts it. So then let's consider what the claim that knowledge needs to be practical actually means.

Knowledge is practical means: an *action is required* and outlined by it. As certainly as this action is just now *required*, it *does not exist*, since it is required; and just as little does that which would be *brought forth* by it, if it did exist, exist. A practical knowledge is thus one to which, in existing itself, its *object* does *not* correspond, and to which absolutely no object corresponds. It thus also does not determine any object, neither is it a likeness of any such thing, and thus it is a pure knowledge formed by itself, a copy solely of itself and not of anything else, an *a priori* knowledge, as people have phrased this concept.

How can the *same people* who talk about doing, often even at the wrong time, *overlook* the fact that according to their own words, if they should make any kind of sense, there would have to be an *a priori* knowledge per se in the meaning we established. You want to *produce*[6] — certainly not just what's there

— since in that case you would not in fact want to produce, but to leave everything just as it is. Therefore, you want to produce that which does not exist. But if you want to produce *with consciousness*, and according to a concept of what you want to produce, and according to a model for a being, whose being absolutely does not exist while you commence with the producing, and whose being will come to be only after your producing is complete. In all this you presume a concept of the absolutely not existing and a knowledge that is not a mere after-image of things, by presuming that an action in consciousness is possible. Whoever talks about action and denies *a priori* knowledge contradicts himself to his own face[7] and doesn't know what he's talking about.

Practical knowledge is knowledge *determined by itself*, or an uncovered *Gesicht*,[8] as the German language so aptly expresses the Greek word for idea. Such knowledge is one that announces itself clearly and articulates itself as that which does not correspond to reality [316] at all. It has no external existence, but only an inner one, and does not coincide with anything besides itself, but only with itself: an idea from the world that is not *there* at all, from the supersensory and spiritual world that can yet become real through our action and that should be introduced into the radius of the sensual world. Whoever talks about action and denies this type of second, supersensory world in our inner selves also contradicts himself to his own face and does not know what he is talking about. The outcome of what was just said is:

If knowledge is to have any value at all and be more than a mere repetition of that which is better off independent of it, then there must be something such as *practicable* knowledge. In contrast, whatever value knowledge that merely repeats could have, if there is such knowledge, cannot be seen at the present time.

Further, if a person is to have value through his knowledge, as we assume and seem to presuppose about the scholar, then his knowledge must be of this type: the scholar need not merely repeat the given being in itself, but rather he must see ideas from the supersensory being. Just as someone might throw his whole being and life into knowledge, immersing himself and submerged in it, and intending nothing else of knowledge other than that former type of knowledge, merely repetitive and reflecting of being, then so would that person in fact give up his own being and life entirely. He would release himself from it to become a mere shadow of that which already exists outside of himself, and is alive and powerful. His whole aspiration would in fact be the aspiration to become nothing, but we can't possibly be inclined to discuss nothing here.

So it must be, I said, there must be this type of pure knowledge, shaping itself by itself, if knowledge is to have any value at all, and in particular if it should be worth the effort of somebody devoting and sacrificing his whole life to it. Thus it is in fact what we have been claiming up to now based only on the outcome of others' research not to be used here. — Knowledge is certainly only determined by itself, never by things external to itself, whose mere reflection it would be. In this, its absoluteness, it is the image of the inner being and essence of the divine. God alone is truly supersensory and the actual object of all ideas. [317] Knowledge is *also only there* as the image of God, and by being this image, and it is *conveyed* solely by the appearance of God in it. This pure *a priori* knowledge, determined by itself, is also the only true knowledge, and whoever has not found his way into it knows nothing at all, in fact, but rather spends all the days of his earthly life in deep unconsciousness.

But then after that, where does the second type of knowledge, besides the one we claimed is the actual and only true knowledge, come from? The knowledge that represents itself only as a mere likeness[9] of the being present outside of itself and that indeed surely is, too?

The following is the answer: The idea must appear and must explicitly be seen precisely *as* an idea, as knowledge determined by itself and by no means alien or found outside itself. But it can only do that *contrary* to other knowledge that appears explicitly as *determined* by an *alien* being found *outside itself.* And thus, this entire field of knowledge,[10] and the sensual world that appears in it and as a representation of it, is then simply nothing other than the medium of recognizability of the first, true world as such, in contrast to another, untrue and not in fact existing world. It, the sensual world, is an image that means absolutely nothing more and has no other goal than that it come to the only true image that has content, to the image of God in the idea.

The idea is God's image, as I said, and the sensual knowledge of a given world is only there so that the first can appear as such. But a second question: How, then, does the ought,[11] the relationship to the act, its demand — in itself completely alien to the idea — join this idea, complete in itself, so that it might be expressed and represented in the world of the senses, the sensual world that we just conceived of as the mere medium of recognizability of the supersensory world? That image of God, bright, clear and definite, is already seen in the idea itself: why, then, should it be expressed once more and made visible in the sensual world? Obviously, that does not increase its visibility. So why does the sensual world not disappear utterly to whomever has finally raised himself to the intuition of the supersensory, since it was only the medium for gaining this intuition, after all? Is the purpose not achieved for that person, and consequently [318] the medium would seem to have no further meaning nor reason for its existence?

The answer to this question produces the following: That appearance of God in the idea becomes (according to a law not to be specified here) *an infinite one*. For that reason, a direct portrait of God will never step forward in time, but always only an image of its future image, which again is only an image of its future image every time, and so forth into infinity. But the actual original image never becomes real, but instead transcends all time as an eternally invisible reason and law and design of the infinite continual forming[12] in time. Now further, according to a law of knowledge likewise not to be developed here, *the appearance of every future, prospective expression of the supersensory is conditioned by the representation of the previous 'common' idea that has taken place in the sensual world*. Only thus, interrogated by the real fact, does the original appearance of the divine express itself further, and continue into infinity according to this law. Look at it again, like this: The appearance of God in knowledge is not somehow a solid and standing *image*, but rather an infinite forming. Within this eternal stream, the singular images and the *ideas* held in moments of time get their spirit from God, but they adopt their physical and metaphorical shaping from the sensual world, not by any means as if this shape in the sensual world is *given*, which contradicts the previous entirely, but that the shape attaches itself directly to the shape that is given, just as it finds it, and forms it further in the mere image. That is namely how you would have to conceive of a very first appearance of the divine image. But not so for the ones following — in their metaphorical formation, they do not join reality just as it is given to sensual intuition, but rather as it is given *in the previous idea* and by the real representation of this idea in reality. According to that, this representation must precede them, and they themselves are limited in their possibility by it. Thus are the sensual world and the supersensory completely united and indivisible, and form a single, complete and true knowledge only in this unity, never to be divided. The supersensory world continues to make itself visible in newer and newer forms, into infinity. A sensual world must thus oppose it and endure [319] to interpret it, into infinity. This sensual world must further be formed, into infinity, according to the image of God as it has really appeared and emerged in the idea. For only under this condition and only inasmuch as the character of the supersensory world that has appeared up to now has left its mark on the sensual world does the former emerge from its eternal invisibility in a new, visible form, and emerge only to an eye that is already transfigured at the sight of the renewed form of the sensual world. The divine image is *in itself* eternally creative out of itself, on and on, but it can be so in *reality* only under the condition that *subsequent to it*, the world will still be eternally created. And so, the sensual world keeps and eternally conveys the character that we settled on above, that it be merely the condition for the visibility of the supersensory world. Above, we understood it in such a way: only in this, its sensual character, is a supersensory world visible at all. Now we understand in this way: a supersensory world is only visible by way of its character as *one eternally developing itself*.

And *thus,* the demand that this appearance should be represented in the world attaches itself to each specific appearance of the divine image in a moment of time that obviously, clearly expresses itself as a singular and disjointed appearance, because the present appearance drives the following one. This requires that this following one is not possible without the representation of the first; and this representation is thus required to begin with. The ought is actually the requirement of the eternally constant, further development of the divine image, and only as this is not possible without the representation of what has already appeared in the sensual world, this ought transforms itself into the requirement of this representation. The ideas of a supersensory world become practical in this way, not as if the original image of God, absolutely not possible in any time, would be practical in itself, and should be represented at some time and the divinity be repeated, but rather because the possible image, determined in time, is itself only possible under the condition of the preceding action according to the *preceding* image. The image thus remains the last and highest in all eternity, and the practicable power of every single image is merely the *means* to the eternal image.

Hence, in this way the laws of which are familiar to several of you from the W.L.,[13] independent knowledge is possible, and becomes fundamentally practical in this way, further creating and continually formative for the sensual world.

[320] The scholar must have elevated himself through instruction all the way to this independent knowledge, if his knowledge and his life in knowledge is to have any kind of value. But if he has elevated himself to it, and, as this can never fail, if his knowledge has really become *active* and driving, then his life has value, and indeed the only possible value that there is at all and there can be. For precisely this, and this alone, is the goal of all being, that God be transfigured, that his image perpetually emerge in new clarity out of his eternal invisibility into the visible world. Only in this transformation of God does the world advance, and everything actually new that can occur in it is the appearance of the divine essence in new clarity. Without this, the world stands still, and nothing new under the sun happens. And thus does this knower become the actual vital force in the world and the driver of the continuation of creation through his knowledge that has become active. He should be just this precisely, and being this is his actual vocation. The assigned question has been answered, and whatever we say further about this subject can be nothing but a further development of that positive principle.

And so it is, dear gentlemen: such knowledge as described is possible in reality. This knowledge alone has value and the scholar has value only to the extent that he elevates himself to this knowledge. So it is: do not let your faith be shaken and be driven into the sad state of doubt by objections to the assembled claims that might sometimes be heard here and there. Believe nobody but yourself: first of all, your own sense of truth, then your own insight that you have to achieve yourself, and the achievement of which is limited in that for the time being you have to yield calmly to instruction. This is precisely the characteristic of our age,[14] that light and darkness no longer struggle only for the possession of this or that *field* as they have from the beginning of humanity onward, but for being itself, and neither of them even wants to suffer the other alongside it in the world. There is no question about how the struggle will finally turn out, but on the other hand everyone is given the certain question as to which side he wants to be on, since it is no longer at all possible to be on both sides and to hold to both parties.

And that contradiction, what of it? We not only admit, but also emphasize keenly at every opportunity that only the person who simply sees the supersensory world, sees it; and only with the inner eye and by absolutely no other means, not perhaps by poeticizing and rationalizing [321] does one become aware; and one is not by any means moved further into this intuition by physical birth, but that a new, spiritual rebirth through absolute freedom is needed, that last of which not everybody completes. And we are in no way of the mind to coerce those who simply do not see, to see, since we well know that we do not possess any sort of such logical means of coercion. We might as well tolerate them quietly managing their affairs and never getting the chance to hear of our affairs, because they are in a completely other world. Why do they not simply have the same attitude towards us? It is immediately clear that they cannot join in the conversation about the supersensory world at all — whether it exists or whether it does not exist and how it might be — because they are missing the vision[15] to which alone this world unfolds. Why then do they nevertheless insist on being involved and saying it doesn't exist, where they are really actually only able to say they do not see it, which is the truth? The physically blind see colors just as little as the former see the supersensory; however, we have never heard that the blind are so obstinate as to claim there are absolutely no colors and they who accept colors and pretend to have seen them are liars or dreamers and in fact, dangerous; however, in calm cognition of their blindness, they are all content that they are not able to talk about this subject. Why, then, will the spiritually blind in the exact same position simply not be content in the same way?

The situation is somewhat like this: to have to make do without one of the senses that does in fact *exist* and that others claim to have does indeed always seem belittling for the person, and maybe the physically blind, too, would prefer to claim there was no sight if they could only get some kind of approval for the claim rather than admitting it is just gone for them individually. But they will not get anywhere with that claim, and such an opinion could never take root even in themselves because they only very seldomly meet up with a blind person who alone could be taken in by their belief, but instead are far more generally with seeing persons who unanimously contradict them. In this respect, the situation is completely different for the spiritually blind. They find approval for the similar claim and validation of their opinion everywhere and it is only the rare exception when they are contradicted, since by far the larger majority is itself just as blind as they and they all have the same interest that preferably there would be no spiritual eye at all than that they would have to make do without it. And in this way, they persuade [322] themselves of the assumption that there is no spiritual light and no supersensory world at all, supported by the approval of the other blind people that lean on them in turn, yet still with the invariably persisting, secret objections of their conscience. There is an anxious fear that the situation might indeed be different and the good opinion about themselves that they want to keep upheld might go dim, such that they become embittered all the time and infuriated whenever the claim, apparently belittling to them, that there is indeed a spiritual light, is expressed and repeated anew. This should not even be heard, nor become known, and certainly not believed. For if it became commonplace, then they would really no longer matter, with their deep thoughtlessness, their inner dissolution, their superficiality in all things, and their entirely ungodly sense. But they want to matter in their worldly sense and have firmly resolved it; therefore, the divine is not allowed to matter.

We in no way claim that they are aware of this actual reason for their judgements and of their way of proceeding, or that they act with deliberate freedom according to that dictum. We would only do them too great an honor with the demand for such clarity about themselves. Obviously, that root of their whole being and life remains invisible to themselves because they are generally inwardly blind. But to everyone who sees, it is evident that they cannot have any other foundational being[16] at all.

But still, we want to let the utmost justice be done to them, we want to assume that it really, and thus honestly, seems to them as if grave danger and disadvantage for humankind resides in that claim and that belief, and that they warn us of the danger out of selfless goodwill. In this case, right at the very beginning we cannot let them skip altogether *the* observation that they are completely incorrect, and that in this, their own self-importance is already playing the first really bad trick on them by having something about similar such subjects appear to them and letting them presume a judgment about them. These subjects do not exist for them; they do not know whether they exist at all, or do not exist, and therefore know even less whether they are dangerous or not.

But let us hear what they put forward! From the very first, they fear the dangers of misunderstanding and the addled confusion that could be generated by them. Nothing more can follow from that but that we must apply all means in our power to avert misunderstanding; but only so far as that no damage happens to the highest and liveliest [323] *comprehension*, which might very much limit that carefulness. Or do they perhaps think otherwise? Do they perhaps want us, for the sake of possible misunderstanding, not even to work on comprehension, and prefer silence be completely and absolutely maintained about everything that can be misunderstood? I fear we would then have to stop speaking completely, and especially speaking in a new way. From time immemorial, everything that has come down from the supersensory world into the sphere of ideas in the sensual world has perpetrated misunderstanding — that much more, the bigger and holier it was and the more it spread — and has caused infinitely more foolishness and disaster than rightness and salvation, if you merely count people and events and yield to appearances. But whoever reverses the holy thing into evil does not just then *become* foolish, but was already. His inner foolishness only reveals itself and expresses itself in this object. But all that which appears to us as disaster is not truly present at all, but rather only salvation and the progress of salvation is actually present in the eternal world. From time immemorial, the majority was wrong and corrupt, and will remain so for a long time; from time immemorial, too, this corruption was nothing other than misunderstanding, antithesis, and its expression as opposed to the truth present in the world at the time. As this truth *increases* and develops itself to a higher clarity, corruption and nothingness develop simultaneously with it, precisely in an opposition to this *new shape* and clarity. Why indeed, then, are those apologists[17] for wretchedness — they who prove with their heartfelt participation what relationships they come from — still whining that they who simply cannot do otherwise but misunderstand, will misunderstand and reverse precisely that which we might have said, for instance, rather than something else? And then, what kind of grace could thus be won for those who just cannot be any good by any means in a sort of new, previously unseen way, if they just were not any good and were futile in the old, customary way? Nothingness is nothingness, and is its own equal all over. It is not a bit improved nor worsened by the accidental colors that it takes from the eras that wear it.

After that they say a person is ruined for action in the *real* world by inhabiting the *supersensory* world. How can these naysayers know that, since they themselves will surely have kept well isolated from inhabiting that world and therefore are completely unfamiliar with it and do not know how it affects the human being? But we who claim to know it will say, and [324] will also present in these lectures in a variety of ways, that there is absolutely no stronger impulse to action at all, and no clearer guide for it at all than the ideas of the supersensory world, and, in comparison to these, every sensual impulse disappears to nothing. Their claim can ground itself neither on their own insight, nor on their experience of those moved by the idea, since those so moved will contradict them every time. It would therefore be merely a randomly produced defamation. But, indeed, this is too harsh, and we simply may well not understand them correctly. They may perhaps, when they talk about action, only mean the action known *to them*, an action following mere sensual impulses and according to the plans of a mere worldly cleverness, and the distracted preoccupation and affected busy-ness and that fight for nothing and the various nothings that arise from such impulses and plans. If they say that type of thinking is disadvantageous in praxis, they might well mean only the practices. In that sense, then, they are completely right and pronounce instead of a criticism, as they intend it, one of the highest praises of this type of thinking.

We have considered it appropriate to say this for once and all, and thereby to rebut the possible opposition at the root. And from now on we will quietly continue on our way, as if such opposition is not even there at all.

## Second Lecture

In the previous lecture, we pronounced the vocation of the scholar as such: the ideas of the supersensory world appear to him, and the sensual world shall forevermore be further shaped according to them. In the scholar, ideas are *driving* towards the act. Therefore, he is the mainspring for the continuing creation of the world according to the divine image. Through *him* alone, the world moves further and obtains the concurrent determination that it can and should have in the time that has now arrived. Without him, the world would stand still and nothing actually new under the sun would occur. He is the actual meeting point between the supersensory and the sensual world, and that member and tool through which the first intervenes in the second.

Now, without a doubt we are discussing scholars as a *particular class* — as opposed to the unlearned — and as *the* class [325] that comprises the smaller number of people by far, while the greater majority is unlearned. But we have described the intuition of the supersensory as the only true and real knowledge that all other knowledge is based on, and only means for the representation of the supersensory. Whoever does not elevate himself to this intuition, we said, actually knows nothing at all, but spends all the days of his earthly existence in deep unconsciousness. So, are we then willing to make the scholarly education into the single and exclusive means for gaining true consciousness at all? And do we mean to sentence without exception the decisive majority of people, who have to remain excluded from this education, to deep unconsciousness? Just simple natural sensitivity would damn such a premise as the first sure sign that it cannot be true.

In order to remove the doubt without digression: the situation is like this. The supersensory world can appear to each and every one and is held out for and offered to everybody in the general education of human beings in our day, in the idea of God itself, as the basis of the entire supersensory world. This appearance, just as it is and formed without further additions, is the supersensory world itself, without further determination. It comes down to the insight *that* it is, purely and simply, but not at all in *how* it is.

It remains shapeless,[18] just as God Himself is shapeless. One mind,[19] possessed by this appearance and driven by it in doing, is called a *religious mind*, and this entire appearance *religion*. The sensual world is not shaped any *further* whatsoever by this idea, neither in its perspective nor through an action grounded in it. Rather, ordinary action is only permeated by this idea. The action remains the same according to its content; it simply gets another *inner spirit*. The person who is only religious lives a life that propels the world onward just as it is, but in no way intervenes creatively in the foundations of its further development. He does what even the most sensual person could do — but he does not do it with the same *frame of mind*[20] not only so that the act might happen and its result be there, but so that God's will might happen in him. In this respect, I would say: religion in its pure form does not further shape the sensual worldview[21] at all. Rather, in the view to God it is taken *just as it is*. But the inner world of the religious person, his will, is shaped [326] according to the will of God and fixed on it alone. For such a view,[22] the sensual world should be exactly as it is and remain so, in that it can certainly be there only by the will of God, and for this reason he puts up with it and lives forth his life in it, just as it has been given to him. He does it not so much for the sake of life and as though he loves it, but for the sake of the will of God, whom he loves above all else. That is why the religious person always comforts himself with another, future life, and directs his view toward it as the only true life. Even *he* cannot avoid generally attributing a shape to the supersensory world, but he is not able to reshape the given sensual world into it. Because of that, the present world becomes for him merely a preparatory and trial-world for eternity and nothing more, since for him both worlds are completely divided and a gulf is enforced between them. On this side of the grave, he finds himself not yet in eternity, but only at its gate, and breaking through this gate and being let out of a life that he bears only out of obedience drives him and distresses him.

Completely otherwise, and set in opposition, are *the* ideas that we have ascribed to the *scholar,* glimpsed from the supersensory world. The supersensory does not *just generally* reside in them, as it does in the religious, but rather also *shapes* itself into a solid image that attaches itself onto the given shape of the sensual world, and whose features can be impressed onto it. This person should not, like the former, abandon the world as it is and bear it for the sake of God, but should make it different, for God's sake, and should form it in the image of God. (For the religious, the idea of God is formal only; for the scholar, it's material and qualitative.) For him, too, there is not a single, future world, but an unending series of future worlds upon worlds that differ from the present first one overall not according to *type*, but only according to the order of gradation. For him, eternity is not only *prospective,* but has already approached him and he finds himself in the middle of it, since the supersensory already surrounds him ubiquitously here.

It is in itself not impossible that someone be moved by such an idea as described in that last bit, and, enthused by it, be swept up to act and to stream out into the environs without tracing this idea back to the source of all enthusiasm and without understanding it as the divine will within him. Such a person would surely be driven by God, but by [327] God as unknown to him. He would be a tool in God's hand, but he would not be religious. This, I say, is not impossible. But on the other hand it is not very possible that the true basis of his intuition and his life should conceal itself for long from the *scientific* person, who works towards clarity everywhere and context in his cognition. Even if he did not come into the world of his ideas with a religious mind, he certainly cannot *remain* in it for long this way, without being drawn to the *spirit* from which it streams forth. True scientific enthusiasm either comes from religion or leads to the same. Over the course of these lectures, we will find *evidence* for both claims.

And so, the unlearned and the scholar can be religious, and the latter, if only he is a true scholar, almost necessarily becomes it. In that, both are equal. Because, however, the whole worldview of the second is a different one, the religion in him must take on a different shape. Namely, the religion of the unlearned simply *permeates* the rest of his usual life, externally distinguished by nothing; the religion of the scholar *determines* and *shapes* his life beyond the usual and makes it into a new and creative way of life. Both live with their own good consciousness and with a complete devotion of their will *solely in God* and *they* desire nothing more, rather the divine desires in them. In this, they are the same: in the first, the divine will desires only to continue *preserving* the world further; in the second, the divine will desires to *create* it further — and in that, they are different.

After all this, our claim is now limited like so: the intuition of the supersensory world *as such* by no means requires a scholarly education, but only the common education. But the intuition of the supersensory world — *as forming the sensual* — and the actual formation of the sensual world by the supersensory world in fact *requires scholarly education*, and *only* by means of the passage through the latter does one arrive at the former.

Now, should the principle stand unconditionally with that latter limitation, or is it perhaps in need of another, new limitation also in this sense? Is it true that since the beginning of time, as long as there have been people, the passage to insight into the world-shaping power of the supersensory concept has *only* been scholarly education, and that it is necessary, or is it not true? It is necessary [328] to investigate this question first, in order not to stumble into the confusions that *always* arise when we have built up from assumptions that are only *half true* and not *completely* determined.

This much is already directly clear from the above: that the idea, according to which the world should be shaped in any time period, must connect itself directly to the actual shape of the world in the given time period, *that* this idea must be completely cultivated, from the point of its coming forth out of the supersensory to where it should intervene directly in the world just as it is, and that between these two points a continuous line of clarity and certainty has to be drawn without breaks or gaps. If the idea were not so solidly formed, all the way down to the ground of actual experience, then the germ of a truly spiritual one would reside in it in vain. No matter how one would go about implementing it, it would not take action; it would thus not establish any act and its intention would not be achieved. A dividing gulf would exist between it and the real world.

What should be shaped directly in the real world according to the idea is, as a rule, *present human society itself.* Either the idea itself aims to form the general manner of thinking or the social relationships and constitutions of people, or else, in case the nature surrounding us and the material world were the object of the spiritual concept, it too requires unifying the powers of many for the same end — at the very least, that they don't disturb our effectiveness — and thus [it always requires] the *general good will.* And *thus* does the principle just expressed establish itself with *significant* generality.

Of course, it has been the law of the supersensory world since time immemorial that it originally only came forth as ideas in a chosen few, and beyond that, those few were determined in the counsel of the divine. The large majority of the rest of the people were then to be educated by these few, who were simultaneously there as mediators between humankind and the supersensory. It was always thus and will remain so. But over the course of time, this majority of humankind has had, on the whole, a very varied and even opposing relationship to the (329) idea and to its immediate instruments, and humankind has thus *not* remained *the same*. It worked like this:

The life of our species[23] began with a natural and inherent eye for enthusiasm in others and with the ability to be immediately seized by and carried away by this enthusiasm. In those times it was easy for those visionaries to affect their surroundings — their enthusiasm itself stood as evidence of the truth of their idea and seized the inclination and the will of the masses that they *became,* according to their ability, what you wanted of them, at least doing what you desired. At the time, it was not necessary to ascertain one's action-oriented[24] idea all the way down to the ground of real experience. If it was only one idea and if only the hallmarks of enthusiasm, recognizable to all, were present, then the gaps were filled by the enthusiasm that seized everybody else. At the time, human nature was directly in contact with the spirit-world to some degree; a societal intuition of enthusiasm lived in everybody, just as a societal intuition of the sensual world lies in *us,* and that intuition became the drive and the determining power for communal life.

It had to have been so, and in this way humankind must have *begun.* The *most general* requirements of the idea for the world, such as that religion exist at all, that there be a society, and that these stand in a lawful relationship to one another, that the necessary arts be invented — through which alone it is possible for a person to stand against the forces of nature and to maintain himself and his species[25] in spite of them — these most general of requirements first had to be *set aside* in the world, even if only with the help of a blind instinct for reason. Partly, this was so humanity could even exist into a second time period, partly so that this second time period would find a model, in the same instant as in its intuition, *of that* which it itself should reproduce in freedom.

Humankind did not have to *remain* this way. The same thing is determined in each individual for making *himself,* in absolute freedom, into every self, whatever it should be, and to keep nothing left over in himself that is not the product of this freedom. It should be *spiritual,* and should freely raise itself precisely to this spirituality, above and away from its entire dimension through singular and individual power. *But then,* as soon as the capacity for such freedom, to which (330) mankind would have been raised in the first epoch, had developed the provision of spirituality through nature *had to* cease, so that everyone *would produce* his own share of it by himself. The natural enthusiasm raised by the enthusiasm of the original visionary would therefore have *to cease to exist,* and the ribbon that binds everybody among each other and binds them to those intermediary visionaries and through them to the supersensory world had to break so that everyone might find the entrance to that world, by themselves and without needing an intermediary.

*As* this situation emerges, and it emerges *at once* as a result of higher legislation of the supersensory world for the sensual one, needing no human work but rather effective in itself, as soon as humanity is capable of standing on its own feet, the relationship of humankind to the ongoing determination of the sensual through the supersensory changes completely. The originally enthusiastic visionaries who will be there and must be there until the end of days — they who, on account of the relationship of the rest of humanity to them in that first epoch, were *prophets* and miracle-workers — now cease completely to be this, because the relationship has changed so much and they transform themselves into another appearance that itself is *doubled,* opposed within itself depending on the extent that the ideas that they are viewing are opposed. They actually become poets and artists, insofar as their ideas don't aim to express *some kind of world-condition*[26] *actually to be brought about,* but only the general form of such ideas. Insofar, then, that these ideas do not require a *definite* shape at all but can be represented in any material their goal cannot be to drive a definite act but only to maintain the spirituality of the masses forever in movement and expose these masses on the ground to the idea. Their vocation is only to maintain in activity the general organ for the supersensory world, but not on any account to show a definite *idea* in this world. But only *now,* this organ has grown in the masses by the transformation that occurred, and has separated *internally* in their mere imagining: before, enthusiasm affected them like a force of nature, sweeping them away to action. Although [331] even in art there is still that immediate and incomprehensible propagation of enthusiasm, it is just no longer *external* but inner, in the imagination. In contrast, insofar as the visionaries' ideas require a *world-condition* actually to be brought about, these visionaries transform themselves into a scholarly and scientific community.

After the completed transformation of humankind, it is no longer enough for someone to have merely cast a glance into the supersensory world. Now the task of determining the idea *exactly,* down to the ground of actual experience and not leaving any gaps between this and that, crops up with all the rigorousness with which we have just expressed it. The point of the idea's intervention into the real world is, as of now, the *clear understanding* of at least the decisive majority of human society. Until the possibility of infallibly creating this [understanding], the idea has to be tuned down. You want to bring the people to where they shape themselves and act according to your will, as is in your good rights, since you know that they *should* shape themselves and act just so, in that your will is nothing other than your immediate intuition of the absolute ought for humanity and you are actually sent by God, as you of course know. If you could demonstrate this, your divine mission with a great *miracle* so that they would be compelled to submit to your will as by a force of nature, then nothing further would be needed. Your goal would already be reached. But the time for this miracle has passed. They do not have an *eye* for the sign of your divine mission, your enthusiasm. They want, as is their good rights, not to feel the will of God itself through a stranger any longer; but to feel it within themselves. They want clear insight for themselves. You therefore have to direct yourself towards this clear insight and gain it for yourself; and besides you will not get anywhere with them. I know very well that in great distress, as our species was seized by in the transition from the extinguished ability for enthusiasm to clear insight into what is right, we tried to shortcut the slow path of instruction with other, substitute means, through deceit and through coercion. But the deceit only lasted a short time, the coercion has but a very narrowly limited sphere, above or beyond which it is not applicable. After they have provided a short time of service, both leave behind an even greater evil.

[332] In this new condition of things, then, the *fundamental task* arises for him whom we have described here as the seer of the world-shaping ideas: to *educate downward,*[27] from his perspective, but without giving up any of its content, and to educate the people upward to himself until the gulf that lies between the clear insight of both is filled in, and the insight of the former intervenes directly into the *insight,* and through it the *life,* of the latter. There can be no question whether the work towards this goal would not have to be started as

soon as that condition of humanity and the clear concept of it emerges in the time period, so that accordingly, an education of the visionary must take place from that point on for the purposes that the people should have, and an education of the people must take place. But it is to be expected that a generation, and *several* generations will go by before the goal is reached. Yes, seeing the situation at its core, the goal will never be reached as long as humankind lives on earth, since the image of God will for evermore develop to new clarity in individual visionaries, and they will forevermore have the task of cultivating these new ideas to comprehensibility for the people and of cultivating the people into the ability to understand them. It follows from this that the life both of the visionary and of the people must be extended beyond the single generation to one, single, continuous and progressive life of them both until the end of the world. It follows also that the scholars of every age have to instruct scholars for the *subsequent age*, to whom they pass on their accomplished education, so that they further it for the assigned basic purpose and in this increase they pass on to those whom *they* instruct for *their* future age and further according to this rule until the end of days. With this, the scholarly community would first of all have to provide for their *own* preservation, for the progress of their life in eternal continuity and for the lasting growth of it. *Further*, the education of the people[28] of every age is bequeathed to the following one and, in this, will regularly be further built onto from the previous one and this will forever be increased in the same way until the end of days. The scholar-community will forever guide the supervision over that education of the people, since only they understand the actual purpose of it. And now the concept of a community of scholars lies within that just said.

(333) Gentlemen, in this lecture, we have once again expressed a fullness of deeply incisive cognition that might also spread light in many other contexts besides the one to which we are first applying it here. I therefore consider it appropriate to add a general and strictly ordered overview of what has been said, since I am speaking to a scientific gathering here:

1.) Knowledge of the *supersensible* is at the bottom of all knowledge. Without that first thing, absolutely no knowledge *exists*. Even actual knowledge that does not go back to that wellspring of its knowledge is not genuine, but the mere empty appearance and shadow of knowledge. And such a condition of the world in which no person at all might really know of the supersensory can also never emerge, since then the purpose of the world would fall away and it would have to founder in the abyss.

2.) The supersensory world expresses itself in a twofold way: either *in the general*, simply *that* an extra-sensual knowledge exists, without any further determination; or, in a further determination and shaped in a specific way.

3.) The first type should be immediately accessible to all humans as religion, and is accessible to all people in the present condition of humankind.

4.) That of the second type constantly shows itself as one according to *which the sensual world* should *be shaped*; and there is a constant law, according to which it does not appear to everybody directly, but only to some as determined by God. In contrast to them, we can call the majority, to whom it does not appear directly, the people.

5.) But now the actual world, which is at first the people, should be shaped according to those ideas. How is this possible?

6.) It is possible in both of these two different times in a twofold way, due to the relationship of the people to the idea, which (due to a law of the supersensory world) is a twofold one that is self-excluding in time. Namely, either:

a. the people have an eye for enthusiasm and are swept away by it, as if by a force of nature, directly to the intended action. In this situation of the people, the visionaries are prophets and miracle-workers, and a learned and scientific public does not occur.

[334] b. or this external eye for the spirit and its natural power disappears and visibility of the spirit withdraws internally, solely accessible to each person's own clear cognition.

The visionaries who have arisen in recent times assume a different form in a twofold manner. Namely, either

α). they represent the enthusiasm and the supersensory vision itself, as such, in this its form. They are then poets and artists.

b). or they do not represent enthusiasm itself, since they carry it invisibly and internally, but they strive only to represent a *specific idea* glimpsed *in* enthusiasm, and specifically to represent it in the actual world. They then become, necessitated by time, scientists and scholars, and in fact especially a community of scholars.

Even separating the poet from the scientific person, and especially from the philosopher, proves that the changed condition of the world has emerged and that humankind already struggles for clear insight. In the time of enthusiasm, all of these subjects reside together in the visionary.

The first task set for the scholar-society in this situation is that of educating *themselves and the people* reciprocally, until the end of days, for the exchange of clear insight. What resides in this education and upbringing is indeed that which we must call scholarship[29] in its actual sense, as will all come out more clearly in due time. It is nonetheless imperative that ideas be present in the scholar-community, and that all learned education is only considered as the means to shape the people and the world according to them. For only under this condition does the scholar-society even have the right to exist at all. Without it, it would itself certainly be the people and there would absolutely not be anything present in the world other than the people or actually, since the people would also not be meant to be educated up to anything, the mob.

The result of the previous lecture has therefore been limited in today's lecture in this way: only in that age when enthusiasm, as a force of nature driving to action, has disappeared and clear insight alone rules, does the scholar step up to the pinnacle of the further creation of the world. Earlier, nobody seized by the idea was in need of scholarly education. His enthusiasm seized the environment directly.

[335] The previous, more general concept of the scholar is thus also more clearly defined by this lecture. Not by any means the individual, but rather

only a tightly bound scholar-society that has grown up together, constitutes the meeting point between the supersensory world and the sensual one. The individual in his seclusion can do nothing and is nothing. Only with his power and his peculiar essence flowing through the whole and he himself in turn further forming himself for the whole is he anything. The dignity and the gains of the individual rest merely on him claiming the dignity of the place assigned to him.

## Third Lecture

We will proceed in the development of basic concepts set up in the previous [lectures] without a special preface.

It is an immediate given, in that which was just said, that in the new and second time period after enthusiasm stopped being the driving force of nature and instead the clear insight of the majority became the basis for the determination of general and public human life, the idea of the supersensory world has gotten a completely new and different type of immediate function than it had in the first time period. In that first time period, the idea streamed directly out into the act through the propagation of enthusiasm that filled in the gulf between it and real life; in the new time period it makes use of the general, clear insight for the time being, and intends general illumination first and foremost and then only as a result of that, an act. At the same time, a new *middle* world[30] has now arisen with the beginning of the new time period, a sensual world in the interior of the human being, the intuition of the given world that each person has, and his concepts of that which is desirable in it. This new world has emerged in between them, between the one, supersensory, eternally remaining identical to itself, and the external sensual world. Now people plan ahead before they act, and consider, and choose, and will, and their action is led by all this. Whoever wants to direct their action towards some kind of goal has above all to direct their thinking towards that goal. After that, the intended goal takes place easily, as if by itself. And so, from now on, the first task is to educate the worldview of every individual according to the supersensory order of things and to introduce this initially in his *eye,* from whence it will easily empower his *hand,* too.

[336] Indeed, this education of insight is, as we have just seen, a twofold one: in the scholarly community, education according to the known and *immediately beheld* idea, and among the people for the ability to someday represent in the real world an idea that is currently unknown and indeed unknowable. For the scholar, it is an educating downwards of his entire perspective to the people's perspective. For the people, it is an educating upwards of their insight to that of the scholar, continuing until they both meet in the middle. In any case, not counting this difference in direction, it is always an education of the same thing, of the general insight of human beings into the *same thing*, the supersensory world-order.

The activity for the supersensory world-order in the sensual world thus collapses into a doubled one, *first of all* into activity for *illumination*, be it of oneself, be it of the scholar class, be it of the people, and thereafter *activity* for the immediate education of the relationships of the real world, determined by insights taken up from the foundation of real experience, now sufficiently ripened. Those persons who make that first type of activity their occupation are generally called *educators*. For the second type of this activity, which from now on becomes a continuous action, taking the rule from the respective condition of the general education, a *community* that propagates itself and lives on until the end of days must be achieved, just as we in fact described the community of scholars in the last lecture. This institution is *government administration*, in the higher sense, namely in that through it, human society is not merely *maintained*, but also cultivated to ever higher perfection. It is immediately clear that the members of this government agency, who ought to make the idea from the supersensory world a real, apparent existence through scholarly education (without which, according to the assumption, such a representation is not at all possible), must have *passed through,* and they must either themselves be *visionaries* of those ideas or at least possess the final cultivation those ideas have obtained in scholarly treatments in the firm belief that something supersensory, and the ought-to-be as such,[31] underlies the basis of that scholarship. The state governing agency in our indicated sense is therefore absolutely the one, necessary component of the scholarly community, the final cultivation and the active body, one might say, of all scholarly education, as of the inherent spirit. It is the ultimate organ through which the idea, already gone through the entire scholarly education, *intervenes* in (337) the real shaping of general, public life and its relationships, the *member* of the supersensory world-order directly leading into the sensual and the true midpoint between the inward world — itself already turned supersensory by scholarly education — and the external one.

Accordingly, we find two main classes of a scholarly community, distinct in general through their distinct activity with regard to the supersensory: they who form it into insight, the educators, and they who form it in the real world, the government officials. Both are completely separated according to the sphere of their effectiveness. What still needs to be *taught* in the schools of scholars, as demanded by the supersensory world-order, is not yet *ripe* for implementation in life; and what is really implemented is no longer a mere proposition, but rather has come to light for all peoples and become human history.

This is not to say, as scholars frequently tend to say, that a perspective can be fully implementable, and the time completely ripe for it, and nonetheless not be implemented. For if any such person is right in that, in which he *can* be right, then the current unimplementability resides in the fact that *nobody can be found* who wants to implement it. Since an *implementer*, too, among other things, belongs with every implementation, and this is a very essential part of the implementation, then at *this time* the unimplementability resides in the fact that it is not possible to find such a person. Or perhaps you, (who teaches this perspective and in the absence of anyone better evidently very well do, when you teach it and continue teaching it incessantly), perhaps you say, I myself would implement it at once if they only put me in the right place. Then, if you should also be completely right in that, as we wish to assume in the meantime, *at this time* the unimplementability resides in the fact that those who could and should cannot make up their minds to put you in place. They may be wrong about that, as I want to presume with you. But the reason [why they are] wrong lies in nothing but the absence and insufficiency of the general education that should after all come from you and from the body you are a member of. If a wrong *were* here, then the wrong would be yours and your peers'. But maybe there is not even a wrong with you and your peers, maybe it resides not in the lack of your endeavors or in the applied means, that general education has not yet moved further on, but rather it is in the *nature of the thing*. Maybe education is absolutely too new and too young that it could already be so far advanced. The government officials collectively may not, then — if you are right — be members [338] of the scholarly community, but in part themselves members of the people, that is, the people in our sense, the masses incapable of the ideas, governing themselves through their representatives chosen according to the perspective of the people. If you are right, the scholarly community is, as a rule, still limited only to the class of *educators* and even between them and government administration there is still a gulf. And they, who should form the meeting point between the class of educators and the people, quite actually make the dividing *partition wall*. This might be, as history indisputably teaches that it has been so, and thus is certainly not as it should be. This condition of the average might also be very oppressive for humanity, but the class of scholars are in the last position to complain about it, just as there is no honor in an educator complaining about his pupil, and even less so, in that the latter could maybe have found a more fortunately gifted disposition to educate. The scholarly community's pupil, however, all of humanity, simply cannot be better than it is. If the world is not better, then you are the ones who have not made it better; maybe you are not to blame if with all the exertions in your capacity, let us say, you could not make it better. So, surrender to necessity and be patient and bear it and await the time not yet in sight. Your scolding, where it perchance does not itself belong among the pedagogical methods, and thus is not meant very seriously, is completely baseless, if it were ever meant seriously.

In short, a teaching that is not really implemented may be thought of as possibly implementable if we allow ourselves to think of another worldwide connectedness[32] than the actual one. But this is a veering off in our thinking — in real-world connectedness, it is certainly not implementable, as certain as it is not really implemented — and next on the agenda is not *its* implementation, but the obliteration of the obstacle that gets in the way of its implementation.

We divided the scholarly community according to the type of their effectiveness outwards from the idea into a class of educators and one of government administrators. Accordingly, it is, in all seriousness, our opinion that the *educator*, too, lead an active and effective life, one that further creates the sensual world modelled after the supersensory world order. Thus, we have not only the government official, even if he were what he should be, a real scholar and visionary. The expansion of general insight is the work of the educator and what is brought forth by him will become the source of new insight and sometime all of this will [339] intervene in life directly, having become an act.³³ But it is evidence of complete blindness, not only for the supersensory, but also for sensual notions and concepts as causing real action, if you deny the life-affecting activity of him who forms the general way of thinking, and through it the will. [It is evidence of complete blindness] if you want to recognize as an act only that which is visible to the eye, and sets down in the physical world a tangible product. That what is currently not yet implementable (in the stricter sense, that we have given this expression) should certainly nonetheless be *taught*, and precisely to teach it is what instructors are there for. Because it is kept on in the teachings and thus continues to educate, it will certainly come to implementation at some time. Were it to be lost from the teachings, then it would be completely expunged from humanity and the hope for its eventual implementation would be obliterated. Those who want to tolerate only whatever spiritual diversion is directly at hand for them and excites them are completely forgetting that once, when they, too, will be no more, humanity will still be here all the same, and generations will flourish over their graves. Those generations that will have completely different needs and different strengths befitting those needs than the meager and limited ones that have become their lot. The educator provides for these generations and accounts for the possibility, to the extent that it is up to him, that they will arise. When you and your act, which you want to see as the only act that counts, are forgotten, his teaching will still stand as an act and as the liveliest and most powerful being.

After all this, we have situated the actual *essence* of the scholarly community in the *possession of the ideas* from the supersensory world. But we have comprehended the special, scholarly *education* as the singular *means* of introducing those ideas to the world in the second time period of humankind. The previous lecture has marshalled *evidence* for the last proposition in excess. And by the way, those ideas reproduce themselves even in the second age of the world³⁴ by themselves, just as they can generally reproduce themselves alone in a supersensory way in the spirit of those who are determined for it in the eternal world order. And so our opinion appears to be thus: that *he* who obtains entrance into the higher world in this supernatural way must also gain access from then on to *scholarly* education as the means to make his idea effective in the world. *Such* a person, I say, and absolutely no other, in that surely only the *scholarly* education [340] can be regarded as the means to *this* end and nobody who is unable to set himself to this end can have any kind of reason to desire it.

Of course, it would be very good if things could be arranged such that absolutely nobody gains access to scholarly education who is not either already presently in possession of the ideas, or for whom it could at least be predicted with certainty that he will come into their possession at some time. But other needs create another necessity. The scholarly community must unconditionally provide for its uninterrupted continual preservation³⁵ in all its branches, and cannot allow that at any time it not be represented in its entirety or in any one of its branches. It cannot count on the *chance* that first hand, enthusiastic visionaries will attach themselves to it from time to time for this secure, continual preservation. If they do spontaneously generate, then they will doubtless unite with it and those will be its finest yield; but we may not build on this chance for that which plainly must be, the uninterrupted continuation of the scholarly community. People decide on *other* human modes of occupation[36] early. Those who are to remain left over for the occupation of the scholar therefore have to be singled out and sustained for this occupation equally early, even before they are receptive to the ideas and before anyone can know whether they will ever grow to be receptive to them. Besides that, there is an abundance of external reasons by which parents and guardians can be moved to dedicate those commended to their care to the class of scholars rather than to any other. So from now, a scholarly education will be offered to all of them before anyone can know whether their inner eye for the supersensory, for the sake of which alone scholarly education exists, will ever open. Will scholarly education, in this reversed relationship, perhaps now be regarded as the means to introduce them to the world of ideas, just as this education was previously regarded as *the* means for introducing ideas to the real world?

To begin with, if we *were* also to be of this opinion and also regard scholarly education as just *such* a means, then at least this much already is clear from the above: that we cannot regard it as the *only* means to introduce people to the world of ideas. In respect to the first age of the world, when a scholar-community is not possible at all, we [341] expressly claimed the opposite. In respect to the second age of the world, we expressly allowed for it as a poetic art, and for all the so-called fine arts, and for the special ideas calling for a continuing education of the world with propositions that assume this.

If, as a result of that, we cannot claim anything else at all in this consideration other than that the scholarly education also be one of the possible ways *among others* by which a person can come to ideas, then in what sense can we even claim this?

We know that the supersensory world simply appears by itself, determined by itself, and not in any way by the sensual one that should more likely be determined by it, after it has appeared. For that reason, the relationship between *scholarly education* — which at first is certainly nothing more than the education of the inner *sensual* world, i.e., our perspective on the given world — and the idea cannot be such that the latter emerges out of the former, as a conclusion to coherent and continuous thinking. It, scholarly education, cannot at all be the basis for insight into the supersensory world: at the most it could only be *that* which instigates the appearance of the idea and perhaps makes it easier. There is an absolute gap that nothing can pass through between all possible scholarly education and the supersensory. This can only be jumped over; in its own coherence and on its own basis, even the most extensive scholarly education only leads up to it, since it is also only sensual in its essence. — Even if the educator is really seized by an idea and the aim of his instruction is nothing other than sharing this idea, indeed even then he can never directly transmit this idea itself, but only comparisons and images of it adopted from sensual intuition, the mere bodily shape, that awaits its inspiration solely from the pupil's own inner intuition, as I have already very clearly proven in other lectures.

Now, how and in what way can scholarly education even become the opportunity and the initiation for catching sight of the supersensory idea? I answer this question thus: The scholarly education at least leads a person inward to himself, to the foundation of his inner sense and makes him at home there by teaching him to pursue knowledge and understanding,[37] and thinking as a free art, and his eye is always fixed on it. In contrast, the sense of the uneducated remains fixed outward, as a [342] rule, and never finds the actually *abiding* site in his inner person. Only at this foundation of the *inner* can the supersensory even unfold to a person; should it unfold to him, since his gaze is fixed that way and he simultaneously keeps watch over this foundation, then it will not easily pass him by unnoticed. *Beyond that*, since in his other affairs he is already used to shaping freely in this area, he will easily capture the fleeting flash and know how to give it shape, concept and word, which the *uneducated*, in his condition, would not be able to. This illuminates the relationship scholarly education actually has to ideas and how it can indeed manage that which we demand of it here. It watches over the area of the idea's appearances and keeps a constantly prepared ability for comprehension always at the ready for them. It simultaneously sets down a solid foreground for the ideas in which they refract and reflect themselves and can be understood. In contrast, one may imagine, that in the person who lacks scholarly education, the higher and spiritual world stirs itself just as powerfully but its appearance either passes by completely unnoticed or it remains as a mere stirring, since it cannot be caught in a solid shape due to a lack of proficiency of intellect.[38]

Add to this, that scholarly education should certainly always be accompanied by an education in the fine arts, at least in the most general, the art of poetry. As we have previously remarked, the poetic arts always keep the ground that is to germinate spiritual ideas in movement and life, while the fine arts constantly keep an eye on this ground.

At the same time, this secondary purpose of scholarly education clarifies the actual composition of it, and the character that it should inevitably convey can be indicated in one breath. It must develop and educate the inner person himself, from its very first step, keeping an eye on this goal only, and believing itself to have done nothing if it has not in some way accomplished that. The inner, sensual person, just like the outer, is made up of an active instrument and a receptive sense. The instrument is the intellect, the sense is the *vision*, always fixed on the inner appearances and especially on the products of the intellect. The instrument has to be educated in the practice of having oneself completely under control, and taking up the whole life of the person into oneself to understand everything that one is tasked with understanding, and forming everything in thought with freedom and ease that should be formed for any kind of [343] purpose. The vision must see everything that is in any way visible in its area, so that the world of the intellect[39] is further educated according to its specifications. This exercise of the intellect and the spiritual eye is obviously not undertaken for nothing, but rather is undertaken for some kind of substance on offer, and this substance constitutes the material of the scholarly education, which of course must at first be set in memory so that a practice can be made of it. This same scholarly education, and especially, too, the content of it, will later become the means again, after others have come to the idea, for introducing the idea to the real world. For this reason, too, the material of scholarly education has to be remembered. But if anyone might believe that merely memorizing the matter without the most complete education of the intellect and the inner sense constitutes scholarly education, then that person would find himself in piteous error. Even the highest cultivation of skill and sense within the world of the intellect is nothing and has not reached its goal if it has not brought the development of supersensory idea with it. Mere taking into memory, though, is even less than nothing, and he who has contemplated what is right lacks the words, almost, to communicate with a time that considers this, too, to be of value.

In this way, then, scholarly education can become the source of opportunity for the development of an eye for the supersensory world.

## Fourth Lecture

We have seen: the idea from the supersensory world that should further shape the world has to be further worked out in the second age of the world, until it intervenes in human beings' *general clear insight* and can become the basis for a reshaping of its real relationships from there. This further working out of the idea happens through *scholarly* education, and solely by dint of the passage *through it* does the visionary become a competent instrument of its idea in the real *world*. We then looked at this same scholarly education from yet another side and in a reversed relationship, as one of the possible *means* by whose initiation and use the inner eye can develop itself for the sight of the supersensory world.

[344] Insofar as scholarly education can be considered in this latter manner and as merely the means to an end that should really be achieved at some time, it must at some point be *concluded*. A human being is intended[40] for life and for active effectiveness[41] but merely having oneself educated is passive receiving, with which no human life will flourish.

A scholarly education could be *concluded* in two ways. Either its purpose is achieved, i.e., the pupil really has used the means and gained insight into the supersensory world, and he has gained for himself the *ability* to make his idea effective and active in the world in the way he intended through the education acquired. In *this* case, an education is concluded by success itself, and the pupil is set free by *it*. Or, the purpose is not achieved, and we also probably cannot expect, after so many vain attempts, that it very well could still be achieved, so then the education likewise must be concluded, since, as we have just seen, *real* life demands the strengths of every human being, often even (and this quite rightly) keeping him in the struggle for his earthly preservation. Nobody enters this world solely to be educated, but instead he should also make *his* contribution to the possibility of education for others.

The former transitions quite naturally after the conclusion of his education to activity with the idea he has achieved; from *apprentice* he becomes an *artist*. But the word *artist* can be understood in two ways, and we therefore first of all have to explain the sense in which we want it to be taken here. To begin with, it goes without saying that we are not talking here about the so-called fine arts that were previously strictly determined according to their essence. We are talking instead about what is attained by diligence and scholarly education. And now, as has already been indicated above, the *intellect* is cultivated to artistry, for which the ability for *language* is also needed, at least for the needs of the intellect; that is, the need for the ability for strictly and discerningly characterizing concepts according to the analogy of available language. Now *these* skills educate the mere intellect-artist and artist of words. But of course, this whole art is now there only to gain the supersensory entrance into the sensual world, and without that it is a useless and purposeless art. If such a mere intellect-artist can indeed educate others to his art, as long as they are applying themselves, (345) and if he can thus perhaps show them the way to the supersensory, in a certain sense sharing that which he himself does not possess, then the practice of his art *in the context of the whole* is thus not useless and empty, although it certainly remains empty for him. It *only attains its meaning* in the world order outside of him. In this case, then, the *world order* that adds what is true to his inadequate works would be the actual *artist*; it is in fact not him at all. The soul of the art of the intellect[42] is the idea; this gives it its real substance, meaning, value. We can thus only grant the designation of actual artist, consummate in himself, to the person who has taken part in the idea, and will use the word only with this meaning from *now* on. We can take it for granted, based on the above, that the visionary must have become an artist if his idea is to have any kind of effectiveness in the second age of the world. It is understood that the entire scholarly education really only exists to make either the already realized, or else the possibly future, visionary into an *artist*, too, which is something completely different. But that is to admit that even the non-visionary could at least be an intellect-artist.

In the second case, somebody's scholarly education now needs to be concluded but he has in no way come to the ideas of the supersensory world, whether he might otherwise be the most practiced intellect-artist or only might have filled up his memory with any kind of mass of scholarly substance. [For such people] there are fortunately enough a plethora of positions available, whether in school or in the state, where their industry can usefully be employed. Only under *this* condition, and in *this* situation of human affairs, it could be allowed that the scholarly community detain young people from the choice of other types of professions by accepting them into their education, on the off chance but without a guarantee that they will succeed in their actual purpose, since they can nonetheless assure those young people of an appropriate usefulness, even in the case of failure. All of these actually failed scholars for whom education did not achieve its true goal can be called *practitioners*, in contrast to the artist.

Because, purely and simply, all real education, both of public insight coming from the school and also of world relations from the state, moves towards the ideas of a higher world, the practitioners who do not themselves possess the idea (346) must receive the *rule* of their activity and the goal of it from outside, specifically from the artist, *who* in contrast carries the rule within himself. And this is the *actual* differentiating characteristic between the two classes. The practitioner is only the instrument of the artist and can only be a suitable member of the whole if he subordinates himself to the artist; the artist alone is the direct instrument of the supersensory law of the world.[43] The artist can evaluate the effectiveness of the practitioner; no human being can evaluate, or judge, the effectiveness of the artist. He is answerable to God and his conscience alone. *This*, I say, is the deciding *fundamental* character of both *classes*, even as very diverse among themselves as the individuals of the latter class of practitioners may be from one another (from the most adroit intellect- and word-artist down to the dull wannabes and mechanistic workers just going through the motions), and as many gradations as the *rule* may be capable of that therefore necessarily holds for them.

If he who has not reached the ideas did not want to accept any *rule* or admit to any subordination to something higher and inaccessible to him, then his effectiveness would not only be useless, but it would even be detrimental and become confusing for the higher plan. It follows from this that *everybody* who has entered the proximity of scholarly education has to be educated by it and before the conclusion of it, at least to the extent that even if he himself does not decipher the idea in a certain shape, he can nonetheless absolutely see that such a thing exists, and what a commanding status it has in the world order. If he has not even come this far, then the attempt on his behalf is not only a failure, but he would even become *corrupting* to himself and the affairs of humanity, and it would be far better if such a person had never entered the vicinity. This then is why it strikes us as an indispensable condition of all scholarly education that, in case it is not itself able to lead its pupil to the idea, it surely impresses on him unfeigned reverence and willing subordination to it, and it does not dismiss him without at least having reached this purpose. We will see further below that scholarly education possesses an infallible means to achieve this goal.

Therefore: the *fully trained person*, no matter which way he might be released, whether with the appearance of the divine within him or through the number of years he has put in, moves out of the mere reception of scholarly education and into the *active* rank of the artist or the practitioner. This is not to say that such a person learns nothing more from now on, and does not continue learning scholarly substance by himself or under others. [347] Much more, actually, since for the person who is caught up in just the right way, learning only now takes root in earnest, the learning of his *art* or his practice. But rather, it is only to say this: that from now on, learning is no longer his first or his actual occupation, but instead the art or the profession is now his actual occupation and learning just happens along the way, as the daily *means* for his actual occupation. In contrast, the apprentice's *actual* occupation — learning, in the sense indicated beforehand — is not merely the *taking in* of a substance, but also the practice of the art of the intellect in the free working out of this substance.

It goes without saying that the previous division of the whole community of scholars according to the two main types of their activity remains here, too, and that is why there are artists and mere practitioners, both in the teaching profession and in government administration.

We will therefore without a doubt answer the question being asked, 'how does the scholar appear at all,' exhaustively when we answer the two secondary questions: first, how does the *apprentice* appear to scholarly education and then how does the *artist* appear in his two relationships, as a teacher and as a government official. In answering the first, we will simultaneously give an account of how the scholar creates himself and becomes a scholar.

I have announced that I want to discuss the appearance of the artist only but not especially that of the practitioner. What there is to say about him can be said in few words and has for the most part already been said. He is to subordinate himself as a willing and obedient instrument, and allow himself to be given the guiding rule of his activity by the real artist. This artist will without a doubt give him that rule every time, appropriate to the conditions of the times and depending on the particular individual education of each practitioner, as often as any such individual will need it. Their variations go on into infinity, since every time they are based on the indicated, changeable conditions and we have no need to preempt the enthusiastic artist. A general comment can be made, however, in relation to this estate of practitioners, that has never been deemed superfluous and that we want to deal with here at once.

We are sticking to the generally stated principle, to which an exception has nowhere been found, that scholarly education actually exists only to lead the ideas in to the world, and that without this purpose, the scholarly community itself wouldn't have the least right to want to be in the world. Only in [348] him who will become an artist does the scholarly education have this influence on the world. Thus, only *in him* has scholarly education achieved its purpose. It intends this purpose of educating the artist accordingly, and should intend it absolutely, without exception, for everybody that it takes into its care and should give up on this purpose for nobody until it has sufficiently convinced itself that it cannot be achieved at all with an individual and until it releases such an individual to the class of practitioners in life. The calculation of the entire scholarly education — and especially of every institution that claims to be an institution for scholarly education — must always and ceaselessly and in all its institutes set out to educate for *art*, as the instrument of the ideas, and therefore not to educate in any way for the practice of any kind of subordinate learned trade. In case it might somehow fail in this purpose, it is the scholarly community's good fortune that the apprentice has gained quite a few other things on the way there that still make him a useful member of human society (since without that not so many would give themselves over at the risk that the actual purpose might not even be achieved), and it is the apprentice's good fortune. But to start right at the outset thinking that the attempt might fail and that you would be in need of comfort would be completely backwards. The scholars' school is definitely an art school, and not in any way a school for practical pursuits. All of its standards have to be established for the artist, and its arrangements must be set up for that; they must never limit themselves to the practitioner. The practitioners will not elude it anyway, if it only pursues the former honestly; but if it limits itself right from the outset to the practitioner, then as a rule the former evades it for certain. Because the entire scholarly education resides within scholars' schools, the needs of a practice can never be affirmative of, and calling for, something insufficient, if it is really the practice of scholarly education alone and not somehow that of a specific trade skill. Those needs could only be negative, and demand that everything that cannot be used for their practice's purpose alone be pushed aside, that anything seeming superfluous to them be disposed of, and the efforts wasted on that be directed to their practice's purpose. If it is really the practice of *scholarly* education alone, I said, the demands of practice can never be affirmative. But one characteristic is decisive as to whether or not it is: the scholar's instrument as such is, after all, the intellect, and absolutely nothing else, as the organ of the interior world in which alone he has his essence, and the word, as that through which he communicates. The substance in which he [349] educates these, and which he will in turn be in need of as a consummate artist is, as much as possible, a universal — and equally widespread in its parts — knowledge of the world. The scientific artist is in need of nothing more and as such, he has nothing to do with the field where more is needed. For the mere *practice* of any branch of scholarship, there might yet be a need for the artistry of other, perhaps external organs. To take an example from something that does not present itself as a science at all, but as a fine art: if somebody wants to attain mastery in music, he is first of all in need of that inner excitability by the form of the supersensory through which his art even becomes *art*, and only then is he in need of learning the rules of composition, and of a very educated intellect for their practice, in order to hold his inner emotions in a definite shape within the world of tones. And if beyond that he now wants, for example, to present his compositions perhaps on a stringed instrument in a masterly fashion, then neither inner spiritual intuition nor his educated intellect is enough, but he also has to educate his *fingers* artistically. But exactly for that reason people have to count the latter neither as his actual art nor as his science, but instead it is only a *mechanical* art. When the *practice* of any branch of scholarly education has such a mechanical component, we only recognize it in its essence and say clearly and openly what it is. If we single it out from the actual scholarly education as far as we can, all the better; and after the conclusion of the actual scholarly education, we will refer those for whom that purpose has not been achieved and who, simply through the acquisition of the mechanical art, can still make themselves useful, in that direction. Or also, since in no case can the real, scientific artist be prohibited from mechanical art, refer him, too, if that is what he desires. We only require that the really scholarly education not be issued laws out of the needs of the [350] mechanical trades and in doing that, exterminate all scholars' schools in order to find more space for the trade schools, which is completely the same. One therefore does not say, 'away with the theory of harmony and the basso continuo and with all the arrangements that could be conducive to the promotion of these studies,' since that would only waste precious time, which the pupils could have used to exercise their fingers.

The community of scholars cannot take those demands into account without giving up its existence. In fact it cannot allow itself to be given the law based on these needs, nor even allow itself to be given good advice. It will be very much more beneficial not to give the practitioners anything, and instead to make it perfectly clear to them at every opportunity by saying aloud that they are only *unsuccessful* scholars, that the scholarly institutions do not exist for them at all, but for a higher will that they have simply not become. They are not themselves its end, just as they will surely never in their practicing lives be able to become the end, but will always remain only the means and instrument in a foreign hand. When they yield to this, recognizing this as their vocation with humility, and fulfill it in good faith, they will become respectable again, and, in their person but not their effectiveness, [become] their own end [again]. But when they behave as though the world is there for their sake and should arrange itself for them, they who themselves should not actually be there and who would very much have cause to beg *pardon* for their existence, then they stir up indignation mixed with nausea, and every upright person must oppose them.

In this, nothing is more backwards than when they somehow think to base their claims on the grounds that they surely make up the majority, by far. With that, they only announce their *profound* crudeness. Only where a physical application of force is intended does the mass of arms decide. Does really no other concept of human value at all take place in their intellect than that of the force of nature? On the other hand, every single thing in the spirit-world is that much nobler the rarer it is, and that much less noble the larger the masses of it are available. One could name individual humans in world history who outweigh the value of millions of others. The divine expresses itself directly through extremely few and they are the ones in whom and for whose will the world is actually there. The masses are there to serve them as instruments, and this part, too, makes up by far the slighter number among the masses. The very decisive majority of these masses is only there to test those others, to alarm them, in every way to hinder them so that [351] their entire power will develop. In the general order of things, they are only the antithesis, and the negative powers that have a stunting effect, so that in the fight with them the positive and beneficial powers step into the light. Should these, who are there only to be fought and defeated, be taken up into the council that is held for no other intention than to expunge them? What a demand!

It is now fully understood, how, after humanity as a whole develops itself towards freedom and full self-consciousness, the supersensory world intervenes in the sensual world. Even the mere appearance of its original ideas in the spirit of human beings is no longer left to the dark and unfamiliar power, but has instead been brought under a law of freedom to the extent that was possible. The very ground of this appearance is continuously moved by fine *art* and preserved in life. Scholarly education, if it gets to them, presents them a solid foundation on which [the appearances] are refracted. With public education, the whole of humanity will be forevermore maintained in the ability to be educated according to them, and with the community of scholars, a society that undertakes and carries out this continuing education by every means that time presents it stands forevermore in readiness.

## Fifth Lecture

I begin this lecture with a general overview of what has been said so far.

The creation of the world by God is thus in no way, as we usually imagine, concluded, with God laid to rest. Rather, the creating continues perpetually and he remains the creator, since surely the immediate object of his creation is likewise not a *sluggish and stationary* physical world but *life,* free and itself eternally living from itself. The actual true world, for which alone the physical world exists, is the spiritual one, the life and thinking of humans, as of one *world*, that is, as of a whole and of a community. For the individual *exists* only in the whole, and has *meaning* only in relation to this whole. It is *this* world, then, that God directly is perpetually creating further in his image, since he always continues to develop his image to a new clarity in it.

[352] This spiritual, continuous creation goes along then in the following way. It commences directly with individual points of the spirit world, as a spiritual idea; completely *producing* itself within these individuals, as intuition, and allowing the human being no freedom nor self-sufficiency in this matter of the ideas. In this matter, a human being is simply nothing on his own accord, but everything through God. But direct, divine work concludes at this point, too, and from this point onwards, God makes use of the freedom and self-sufficiency of the human being to spread the work from the individual point where it burst forth outwards over the entire species.

The entire spiritual world, taken as one, *is free,* and its actual life, separated from God's, exists in that. As free, it is *located between a double being*, first of all, that being in which God directly works, and then that being which itself is to produce the spiritual world as the copy of that first being. There, where the real life of the entire spirit world has become the completed copy of that first being revealed in individual points, is where the second summoned being has emerged — and the continuing creation of the world can now process further, purely from God. I have said that it is the one freedom for everybody, for the entire community, by which the image of God, begun in individual points, is *expanded* to everybody. It *is* thus one communal freedom of the whole, and the freedom of individuals is not segregated and limited to itself. Instead, each freedom intervenes and affects the freedom of the others and a general, spiritual bond exists within everybody's freedom.

We have gathered this much in general.

The divine creation of the world especially *begins* by elevating to reality this freedom for everybody and its spiritual tools for binding, the thoughtfulness and consideration of everybody (which exists in spiritual life only as a possibility), because *this* is the condition for all further creating.

In the same way this freedom and the cognition, even if only a dim one, of this whole relationship of the spiritual world to God, first developed, so, too, does a *community of scholars* generate itself out of the spiritual nature of the matter, and is continually maintained by that same nature, partly as the spirit world's permanent faculty for perception of that continuous creation of the world, representing itself in ideas, that comes directly from God; partly as the ready instrument for introducing this continuous creation to the middle world[44] of [353] freedom per se, giving that spiritual nature a solid position in this middle world only for a time, until the general being forms itself from it.

The highest thing in the middle world is understanding — it is what the community of scholars actually has to form as its purpose. This community forms it expressly with the intention and for the purpose that it will grasp the spiritual ideas and form them further in *freedom* for universal communicability and comprehensibility. This is the actual character of intellect-education[45] in the scholarly community, and in that, this education of the intellect is different from every other that can be undertaken for various other reasons. But the *means of communication* is the *word*, and the scholarly community therefore also has to form it, since without it education of the intellect would remain unusable and without any influence on the rest of the spiritual world.

The scholarly community must elevate this use of the intellect, and of the word as the medium for that intellect, to a *free art*, always under the assumption that ideas are there that will be processed by the intellect and expressed in words. The one who has achieved this last purpose has the rule of the practice of his art in himself and is thus a self-sufficient artist. Whoever has not achieved that purpose has to adopt the rule from the self-sufficient artist, and is thus merely a practitioner of a higher *insight* not present in himself. If we now want to interpret the appearance of this scholarly community, educated in such way, then the first question is: How does it emerge and, since we have already *generally* grasped its emergence, how does the individual member of this community emerge? So, we first of all, we have to talk about the *pupil* of this scholarly community, as just such a member.

I think that this society cannot have its members forced upon it. Rather, the community is to select them, with deliberation and caution, during some kind of event, and I presume such a selection process. According to which principles should this selection of pupils for the scholarly community take place?

There are *two* points of view. First of all, the perspective on the content of the actual scholarly education itself, the cultivation of the intellect and the word, and of the inner world generally. Only those in whom a prevailing drive for constructing such an inner-world displays itself should be allowed into the scholarly education. But all, without exception, should be subjected to the test of whether such a drive shows itself in them. This drive shows up [354] very early wherever it is present. If the child does not only perceive the given things of the outer world, but instead strives to perceive his perceiving itself at the same time, by comparing singular and diverse perceptions and seeking to trace them back to unity and context, then a lively drive not to content oneself with the mere outer world, but to construct an inner world of concepts and their unity is certainly displaying itself. Whenever the boy interrupts the stream of mere perceiving with amazement and initiative and hard thinking — and solving such questions can be much more important to him than extending the stock of his sensual cognitions, and can completely divert him from them and drive him into himself — then an inner self is already beginning to grow within him. Not one of these boys should get past the community of scholars. In contrast, those who are constantly taken with the outer world and carried away by its advances and always open up in it should not be withdrawn from the immediate world, because they are completely made for it.

The other point of view as to the choice of pupils for the scholars' schools goes to the *purpose* of the scholarly education, the intuition of the supersensory. For this intuition, too, a predominant natural facility must be displayed. The general form of intuition of the supersensory is, as we have previously shown, religiosity. But we do not have to expect too much intellectual development before its time at all, and neither do formulas memorized without meaning, nor dim stirrings need to be presumed to be it. Instead, the development of understanding shows at first in the facility for justice and morality, the second of which, if properly cultivated, sooner or later develops into religiosity. The facility for morality exhibits itself in turn as selflessness and in the elevation over the self to any higher thing. This not being inborn in the sensual self, but instead being above it, is the genius for morality, and by means of morality, for religiosity, and by means of religiosity, for the intuition, if it be pleasing to God, of spiritual ideas. On the other hand, the early egoist,[46] whose first thought to develop to clarity would be his own self, and who would never forget himself and his own advantage, who would relate everything to it, and who would never give of himself impartially and without self-serving purposes — the boy who is shrewd from early on, if there be such a thing, would need the wisest and most conscientious discipline in order not to be corrupted for any position and [355] become harmful in it. And he is to be completely shut out of the scholarly class, whose actual vocation, after all, he would hardly be expected ever to achieve.

Luckily, by a law of nature, both of these requirements for the pupil of the scholars' school coincide. Where a real, natural drive to understand the issue and the context of things is present, this drive occupies the person completely and engages him, and he does not want anything more or anything other than to satisfy this drive. Everything else disappears for him, and thus the petty, narrow self disappears to him, too, and he has no time left to let his eyes, filled with other sights, linger on it. The drive to form the intellect leads to morality and thus equally to religiosity. If, in contrast, a boy overcomes the natural antagonism against learning, as can well also be the case, but learns, not without success, as can also occur, only to be praised or rewarded or even, perhaps, to become a respected and famous man — after being talked into this perspective by ignorant people from outside — then such a boy is obviously an early egoist, and he would just for that reason be excluded from scholarly education. But he also has no true inner drive; he seeks nothing but mere satisfaction for himself.

According to this, then, such persons, in whom intellect breaks through by itself, and strives and *works* within itself to expand itself, and on itself to construct itself, only so that it might exist, and who thereby simultaneously guarantee us their morality and their sense of religion, are to be chosen as pupils of scholarly upbringing. This upbringing[47] now has nothing more to do than to keep them in this innocence and ingenuousness.

The means for that are part purposeful instruction, part removal from contact with evil. First and foremost, purposeful instruction. The active and living drive to construct a coherent insight in himself is already in the pupil himself, as certain as he was rightfully accepted into this schooling. One only sets at hand for him the means for satisfying this drive in a regular and coherent way: the means closest to him and easiest for answering the question to be solved with his own work, only led by the educator, and continuing from there to the second, more difficult and so forth. Thus is his drive both satisfied and spurred on at the same time. Each clarity that opens up in him puts a new task to him, and every success that cheers him makes him [356] want to and hope that he will solve this new task, too. His life unfolds in this constant self-development of the spirit in pure joy, love and desire for the development of the spirit itself. He strengthens and revives flagging energy with the fine arts, the practice of which, as we were already reminded earlier, should be continuously combined with scholarly upbringing. And he is not at all in need of another and cannot even desire or get himself another unfolding. This whole unfolding of his life in the development of the spirit results that much *more surely* if all other excitements, and the sight of other ways of living that could lead that still inexperienced age into temptation, are kept completely removed from his gaze and he is kept in complete ignorance that there could be yet other ways to fill up and make use of his time.

This ongoing *direction* of the development of the spirit by means of the *order* of instruction and this removal of all contact with evil are called for at the *beginning* of scholarly schooling, which one can generally call the time of the *lower* scholars' school, and these duties are incumbent on the *teacher* at this school. We have thus described in total what he should do and how he appears if he is worthy of his position, but not at all what the pupil should do or can do. This pupil's whole life does not emerge even in the appearance, but rather its appearance is only the result of his natural facility along with the direction of the teacher, who attends to the actual, deepest life-principle[48] of his pupil and holds it in his hand.

Every human being should one day become self-sufficient, and take over for himself the principal direction of his life. That much more should the scholar, who, after all, if he comes to his true calling, should take over the highest direction of the whole of humanity and its highest relationships, that, when all is said and done, must always remain hidden to itself. The scholar therefore must be *raised* to self-sufficiency, and must test himself in the use of it and be able to be tested by others, *before* he emerges into life. He thus must receive the described, highest direction of his life itself, even during his training, actually. This constitutes a main phase[49] of scholarly-schooling, and the last part of it is at the higher [357] scholars' school, or the university. The single and far-reaching difference between it and the lower scholars' schools is that at the university, everything that was assigned to the educator, at once teacher and mentor[50] at the other school, *is assigned to the student himself* to do for himself. So then not the schooling so much as the external mentor falls away, in that only the instructor remains and the student becomes employed as his own mentor. From now on, precisely that which at the lower school the instructor managed for him, the purposeful direction of his spiritual development and removal of contact with evil, he now manages for himself.

Above all else, the *purposeful direction of his spiritual development* is transferred to him. Instruction continues at the university, only in a higher sphere and following through with the instruction of the lower school. The general scope of the sciences is drawn up, more according to the particular connections within science itself than according to any such connections that count on the mental powers and the continuous advancement of the individual. And at the university, there is no division into the lower and the upper classes, where one is not let out of the first without a satisfactory exam into instruction in the latter, as at school. Instead, the entire university curriculum is offered to everyone in the same way, the capable as well as the incapable, the more practiced as well as the more unpracticed. It falls to everyone to choose for himself what is appropriate right now, according to the education he has already attained earlier, from the entire curriculum offered. And although good advice about this choice might be available in part in the general tradition of the university, and can be sought out in part from the instructors, surely this advice can never suit the individual completely or exactly, for it is impossible to know the individual completely or exactly and it will instead always remain a generality to some extent. And even when this selection has been made and happily made, the instructor lectures as a rule more according to the context of his science and in the sequence that it calls for, as previously mentioned, than calculating his lecture to the specific mental powers of the individuals. This is because the instructor can never know them nor oversee them, nor, if he oversaw them even only partly, can he get a fixed rule about them, since with so many they are really very diverse. Thus, it remains up to the *student* to interpret for himself, in his way, to explain for himself, and to order, and in this way to assimilate himself what the instructor presents to a general and undetermined audience — and then again to digest the instructor's lecture and recite it to himself in the way that a very [358] skilled instructor would have lectured if he had him alone as listener and knew him completely. Of course, no student, unaware as he is of the execution of that business just described, believes that he really uses the university lecture for the purpose it is determined for, for the development of the intellect into artistry. At the most, namely if a student possesses a very fortunate memory (and not, as sort of happens most often, the copied-out, scholarly lecture only hangs around decorating the notebook), at the most, he perceives it in his memory, which, where it concerns facts, is really something, albeit the most negligible thing. But where it does not even concern any kind of perceivable result at all, perhaps as in philosophy, and instead concerns the education of the spirit in the skill of finding results for oneself, is nothing at all, and actually is not even possible at all.

Regarding separating the apprentice from contact with the world's corruption as the lower school should, the university cannot do it, and neither should it. At the university, the aspiring scholar should anyway be educated to live and to be effective in the world as it is. The student himself should therefore separate himself from contact with corruption and thus take over the second part, where up until then the schoolteacher looked after him. If he is now, as we assume, seized by a lively eagerness to train his spirit since earliest childhood, if this drive has been quite conscientiously nurtured and strengthened by the school upbringing up to now, if his thirst for knowledge received definite assignments, the solution of which he expects from the university curriculum alone, then just by himself, without any effort and further resolution, he will separate himself from what is bad. He is occupied, his whole spirit in filled with something higher. The base and ignoble repulses him by itself, it arouses in him a gnawing emptiness, it awakens disgust in him, he cannot bear it. But hopefully he will not be so cowardly and so disheartened that he would allow a way of life to be forced on him by the pretense that it is a part of a student's honor, or to go along with it a way of life that does not arouse the least joy, but instead the most inner repulsion and disgust because of the threatened contempt of the bad ones, who themselves are much too contemptible even to be contemptuous.

After all that has been said, the well-known saying that we hear put forward more and more often and from students, too, that the university is actually there for enjoying life at it, might make very good, correct sense. You cannot enjoy what you do not have. The student would therefore have to *live*, in the more exquisite [359] and higher sense of the word than he perhaps lived previously, at the lower school. And, indeed, so it is. There, not he, but his schoolteacher in his stead, lived the best and most noble part of his life, the inner life directing his outer life. From now on, he himself lives this inner life and will also *enjoy* it himself, if he lives it happily and with pleasure. He will become inward, so that he has a strong inner life and self, sublime above all else and omnipotent. He will learn to trust it and count on it with assurance, which is without a doubt life's highest pleasure.

If you take this saying in another sense, then you surely should not say "enjoy life and its activity," but instead "enjoy not living, suffering and death." [In this case] you want it understood [to mean] that the university years are destined for enjoying, for example, the lawlessness, liberties and lust that one can attain for oneself, and you conceive of the university merely as a *negation*, perhaps, of the orderliness of school, namely without being able to attach any kind of positive sense to it, and therefore assume the essence of university life to be the representation of this negation of the school order in all possible ways. If you take the saying in this sense, one only has to recall that the poor, misled adolescent who traded school for the university hoping for this, would find himself very much deceived in his calculations. Nowhere would he come across life's hoped-for pleasures during his university years, and he would understand at the end of them that he got himself a lot of worries and trouble in order to waste his time and not learn anything, and he could have had it much more comfortable and learned some things after all. So, first of all, as far as the famous lawlessness and freedoms are concerned, well, this might look one way from a distance to the pupil who knows his own troubles well and thinks those are the only troubles on earth. But once you get to the university, it turns out that here, too, various uncomfortable and constricting arrangements have been made. But as far as the enjoyment of life in this sense, that is, the enjoyment of sensual desires, is concerned the students at the university are in fact poorly cared for, since above all, only the very fewest of them are in the independent possession of such great wealth as it takes nowadays to enjoy life passably well. Instead, they are under parents or guardians who never want to spend as much as those in their custody could certainly use (360). And then they are also not very good at enjoyment. This part of the instruction was neglected in the schools or the private schooling they come from, and the schools where pleasure is studied as an artform are not accessible to them. So then, they have first to learn enjoyment, with very stinted powers, with attempts that mostly fail and, in the end, do not yield any pleasure at all. Once they have really enjoyed a day or so, then come austerity and privation, and after a little while, regret, chagrin, perhaps shame and responsibility. And so, you have to admit that if universities are there for enjoying life, they are extremely poorly set up for the purpose.

Such a perspective on university life is held, as I said, solely when a person does not bring along any definite, positive purpose at all to the university, and moves to it in utter emptiness and unconsciousness. There are always still plenty who come to universities with a certain purpose in mind, such as perhaps to solidify oneself in this or that science that they are already taken with, or to avail themselves well of this or that instructor, for example, whom they already know by his writings and the like. They know well that there is more to find at the university than enjoying life, and they look for it. But when the newly arrived student, who only knows that he wants to *study* but absolutely does not know how one begins, and gets shown the way by his nearest, best compatriot who was maybe himself already corrupted earlier, then such mistakes will surely arise. You can certainly well imagine how such a pupil — who went to school in obtuseness and unconsciousness and did nothing that he was not obliged to, and who thought it was the highest good and singular pleasure in life not to have to go to class — how this kind of student, I say, grasps concepts such as the pleasure of life at the university and academic liberty. But how old students, who would surely have had time to forget class and who can see every day of their life what the academic life can bestow, can persist in these mistakes and revel in an image that is only in their imagination has always been a puzzle to me.

We therefore certainly can gain a different, correct sense of this concept of the life-pleasures of a student. But this is harder with another equally very widespread idea: that university life is actually there so that an adolescent can vent whatever amount of crudeness and wildness he has been blessed with, and [361] get it out of himself, and that these years are really quite wisely used for this purpose, so that he is rid of this very bad endowment for the rest of his life. One can only imagine how more mature judges of human nature who are long past their university years look from their high place down onto student life in this way. How have they even taken this perspective on human life at all, namely, that to each is granted at birth, just like his portion of sleep or food, also his portion of stupid pranks that he can never escape, not by any freedom or consideration, and for which therefore the only possible intelligent measure to take *is to use up* the supply of them very early, in the years when it still does not matter so much? If these men are right, and since they know this so well, then of course they will have wisely used their own university years for this purpose, and will already have relieved themselves of all of their foolishness and crudeness, so that now no further trace of that kind of thing shows up in them. But precisely that is usually not the case in those who most often give voice to this doctrine. The way precisely this doctrine itself, for example, is preached particularly to young boys and is given to them as an endowment to take with them into life, is by itself gross crudeness. You should therefore conclude just from this consideration that those men could not be right. Even if they might be right in the circumstances that obviously exist, that the young student who is making his first attempt at the use of complete freedom will rush and make mistakes and show a lack of finesse and practice in life, errors that the more educated friend of youth does not perhaps consider right and approve of, but will certainly overlook them good-naturedly and not judge them with the sharpest strictness. Now, all of this is easy to imagine. But that students themselves, talking about themselves, attribute this character of crudeness and lack of education to themselves and should *surrender* themselves to it as if to their inevitable and unavoidable fate, even with a kind of satisfaction, and demand of us that we let this crudeness pass and recognize it as their lives' vocation and that we should resign ourselves to it — that is harder to explain. It was also, of course, not like that in earlier times that obviously also did not lack for crudeness but that claimed not to be merely crude. Rather, this point of view was reserved for our self-tolerant time, thoroughly enlightened and recognizing itself very well in each of its features as it is, but also with great self-satisfaction in everyone.

No, gentlemen, it is but a joke, and mockery of the great masses, when it has been said that to each human being his measure of foolishness is meted out, from which he [362] surely cannot escape, for the multitude surely has the appearance that no instruction or discipline has had an effect on them. Insipid minds have taken the joke seriously and made themselves more ridiculous than they might think. It depends on the freedom of each person, whether he belongs to the masses that will evidently never get beyond foolishness, or whether he wants to elevate himself above it. If he elevates himself above the masses, then even if he might not escape all foolishness, he can nonetheless reduce the measure of it as much as possible. And it is also a truly nonsensical claim that if one just completely gives oneself over to foolishness and crudeness for a time, one will be safe from it for the rest of one's life. The opposite occurs. Foolishness and crudeness grow the more one cultivates them and, in this respect, too, one will do in old age what one got used to in youth. The truth of the matter is that a person can destroy his health and so ruin his body that all his ability to sin further escapes him. Is this perhaps the actual meaning of the aforesaid wise-advice[51] to students, that they should completely ruin their health so that for the rest of their lives — as sicklies and half-corpses — they are assured against superficial sin. Then he will hardly be seductive and there is no need to warn anyone about him.

Summa summarum: all wise utilization of the university years, and with them morality and religiosity, and the student's true enjoyment of life depends on him being seized and completely possessed and fulfilled by an animated drive for knowledge and spiritual education.[52] Wherever this is, there all other virtues, and kindnesses, and the commencement of the inner, blessed life are produced completely on their own. Wherever this is missing, in otherwise upright and God-fearing natures, these can still be claimed only if the young man leaves the university as not appropriate for him and devotes himself to another way of life. If he remains at it, nothing else can occur but that he, not occupied with the scientific instruction of the educator who finds no point of engagement anywhere in him, and seized by the most oppressive boredom, is driven to relieve himself of it. Since access to the apparently respectable pastimes is mostly not open to him, he does it in a common and tasteless way. No human laws of morality or institutions help with this omnipotent law of nature to escape boredom; and I have pronounced in this breath the reason for the history of most universities. A completely well-mannered university [363] can only arise if we allow no one entrance who does not pass a convincing test that he is animated by the drive for knowledge. Until this happens anywhere, the majority even of students, like every majority in all of human life, will have to be seen as the antithesis and as the control group by which the virtue of the better ones appears and proves itself and steels itself. And with this, I want to recommend this viewpoint to the better ones with whom alone I wanted to put myself in conversation. Incidentally, everyone, without exception, who is attending here has permission to count themselves among the better ones, and, wherever your conscience perhaps makes a quiet objection to that, really has permission to join their ranks by means of powerful freedom.

# Notes

1. Pagination references are to J. G. Fichte, *Gesamtausgabe*, ed. Erich Fuchs, Reinhard Lauth, Ives Radrizzani, and Peter K. Schneider (Fromann-Holzboog, 1999), II/12.313–63, with page number in brackets. The first lecture took place on 11 May 1811.
2. *Abbild* und *Nachbild*. Here and throughout, Fichte employs the term *Bild* (image) and related terms *Abbild* (likeness), *Urbild* (original image), *Nachbild* (copy or after-image), and *Vorbild* (model or pre-image), whose relationship is difficult to capture in translation. In addition, Fichte will use the term *bilden* (to form), which is also related to the important term *Bildung* (formation, education) in his thought.
3. Nachgehen
4. (FICHTE'S NOTE): Such knowledge must thus not be determined — this is the first characteristic that we'll want to keep a good eye on for now — in relationship to itself and its content not be determined by something external to it, but instead only purely and simply by itself, just as it is; absolutely not because a being external to it is so, but instead because even by itself it is just so; it would have to be an absolute knowledge based on itself according to its entire content.
5. thatbegründender
6. machen
7. in sein eigenes Angesicht
8. The German term *Gesicht* has multiple meanings, including "face," "sight," or "something seen." Fichte means by the term *something seen by the intellect*, or an "idea," following Fichte's suggestion here that *Gesicht* translates the Greek term for idea.
9. Abbildung
10. Gebiet des Wissens
11. das Soll
12. Fortbilden
13. the *Wissenschaftslehre*
14. An echo of *Characteristics of the Present Age* (*Die Grundzüge des gegenwärtigen Zeitalters*), Fichte's 1806 book drawn from a previous lecture series.
15. die Sehe
16. Grundsein
17. Schuzredner
18. gestaltlos
19. Gemüth
20. Gesinnung
21. WeltAnschauung
22. Blick
23. Geschlechts
24. tatanstrebendes
25. sein Geschlecht
26. WeltZustand

27. sich herunterzubilden
28. die Volksbildung
29. Gelehrsamkeit
30. MittelWelt
31. das da seyn soll schlechthin
32. Weltverbindung
33. zur Tat geworden
34. WeltAlter
35. FortErhaltung
36. Berufsweisen
37. das Wissen / Verstehen
38. Fertigkeit des Verstandes
39. Verstandeswelt
40. bestimmt
41. thätigen Wirken
42. Verstandeskunst
43. des übersinnlichen Weltgesetzes
44. Mittelwelt
45. Verstandesbildung, could also be read as "formation of understanding."
46. Selbstler
47. In talking about teaching younger learners here, Fichte uses the words *Erziehung* and *Erzieher* rather than *Bildung*. I indicate this change by using the words upbringing and schooling.
48. LebensPrincip
49. HauptAbschnitt
50. Fichte makes the distinction in German between a *Lehrer*, a classroom teacher of content, and an *Erzieher*, a person responsible for generally raising a child in all other, nonacademic areas.
51. des erwähnten WeisheitsRathes
52. GeistesBildung

# 5

# The Doctrine of Right (1812)

*Translated by Jeffrey Church and Benjamin Hofmann*

## [Introduction]

(73)[1][197] First of all, about the lecture.[2] It will be purely analytic, following a single firm foundation, that of the concept of the relationship of right. Everything has to be contained within it. —

The method.

It is very easy, but nonetheless acquired through practice.

*In this concept*, we have to *establish ourselves*, especially since the analysis here is only carried out up to certain limits, and we should obtain the art of furthering it here.

Over and above the intended instruction, the *practice* is still needed for philosophy to come to be in general.

## [First Part]

### [Chapter 1][3]

Preambles.[4]

1) The doctrine of right is a pure true science.

2) Such a science is based on the absolutely self-originating idea of a cause of a certain phenomenon. (Insofar as we saw the matter previously, the deduction will be found.) The appearances exist for the empirical view, which declares *that the phenomenon exists*: the scientific (74) view sees the phenomenon coming into being, from its cause and according to its own law. This is the scientific view. *Take note*: here it is necessary under certain conditions, elsewhere it is factual.

3) Here we can find two opposing cases. The [first]: the phenomenon *exists*, without the idea of necessity; this [necessity] is recognized only later. After all, it is completely and immediately a law of factual being. A natural law.

4) Or, [in the second case,] the phenomenon expressed in the law does not *exist* at all, but it is to be produced only by freedom. / If it comes to exist — we will thus have to *find* it, and then will *be able to say* that it is to exist [198] *by* law, but not without a supplement, or rather, more precisely, mediated by a free decision. Hence: a) it is actually a law immediately for freedom: that becomes a phenomenon only through freedom, not through nature. b) Freedom acts only with clear consciousness and according to a concept of an end. The freedom through which the law becomes a phenomenon must therefore have known that law before the decision. — Cognition of the law precedes the phenomenon. In the first case above, it was not so, but rather the opposite. — Here we find a practical law: the practical consciousness is a scientific one. This is strictly so.

5) Practical [law]: such a law appears as twofold: *unconditional and categorical*. (The moral [law]). — [Or, there is a] *conditional* [law]: if one has this end, one must act this way, *pragmatically*. (Whoever desires to become scholarly or scientific must struggle and toil; whoever wants to build a solid house must lay a solid foundation.) Only through such an action can one arrive at the phenomenon, which one can arbitrarily posit as one's end and which is only possible through freedom. (75)

6) How about the law of right? — [How about] this, as the determining ground of a phenomenon? — I say, it does not fit into either of the two classes. Its phenomenon is: one such community[5] of several free beings, in which all can act and function freely; no one's freedom can disturb that of any other. — One wonders: *does it exist*, this phenomenon, *due to a law of nature*? In part, yes: no one can think the mind of another, no one can move the limbs of another through his will. (This applies to everyone through their mere *being*).[6] But then again, *not*. According to this side, the free decision takes place: to attack one another, to directly or indirectly hinder one another. Now, it is exactly the opposite: here the law of nature is a conflict of freedoms in perpetuity. — The constitution of right is thus not a phenomenon like the rest or movement of bodies.

It is not a law for *freedom*. This law is directed at freedom in an immediate consciousness, and this law is always *individual*. A command for individuals.[7] Now no one individual can introduce the law, since it is the same law for all. All must restrict their natural freedom if they are to respect the freedom of others. Everyone, all at once: all in the precisely determined, exclusively rightful manner. How should the law ever penetrate in this way into the shared consciousness of everyone?

It is therefore not at all clear who should execute the law.

Considered in a different way.[8] A *force* is having an effect here. This is either a natural force: which in general only *exists* and acts according to nature's laws (a thoroughly lawful force: its being and its lawfulness[9] are one). Or it is a *free force* — that is, *lawless* in itself: and it exists under the law only through itself: through itself, that is, with consciousness: thus the laws, which are found (76) in immediate consciousness. What one person can and should do, another can and should also do. In this, nature is not expressed; therefore freedom. And in fact, not the freedom of the individual [199] but the freedom of all. How this freedom of all should realize the law is incomprehensible. — This appears to suggest a unification of nature and freedom in the progress of history and education! In short: this seems to be the mediating term.[10] We want to leave the question behind for now. — (We will be able to make interesting observations about it in the end.) Yet it is necessary that we know this. Overlooking this principle has brought significant disadvantages to the doctrine of right. We will get to the bottom of this.

Having left this question aside for now, the conclusion remains: the doctrine of right is not a part of the doctrine of nature. (It was never considered to be so, although there was a *mixing* of it with the doctrine of ethics). Nor is it part of the doctrine of ethics. — [there is] no practical law. It has been confused with this, other than by *me*. "Neminem laede, suum cuique tribue."[11] "Quod tibi fieri non vis, alteri non feceris."[12] "The maxim of your will must be able to be the principle of universal legislation."[13] [etc.] . . . Since *Kant*, especially, we have been struggling [with this confusion]. (77)

My doctrine of right came before the Kantian.[14] *Towards Perpetual Peace*.[15] The book itself: overall a good introduction:[16] by the way, old journal issues are bereft of clarity.[17]

*Natural right*. 1) as opposed to right grounded in factual agreement, contract, or even the arbitrary force of the legislator. — as opposed to written law: "haec lex nata non scripta."[18] There are many errors here. 1) Natural right, that is, the *right of reason*. — should this not therefore mean: all right is founded on an a priori concept, a thought as such: it is intelligible, and knowledge itself the ground? Quite right: lex nata,[19] innate ideas. 2) but this is *wrong*, [namely:] the distinction [that] some right is grounded on this, some on [200] agreement. — But then what is the agreement itself grounded upon? — The contracted and written right is never right if it is not (78) grounded in reason. All right is the pure right of reason. 3) Many understand *nature still differently*. The natural feeling guides us into a certain company. However, in certain times, it does not persist.[20] Then the artificial state steps in along with its right. — It is true, and it has been done, [claim] the old Germanics. *Hobbes* disagreed with this, [asserting] "Bellum omnium contra omnes."[21] Only through force and coercion did rights make themselves valid. / And that is how it happened. Consider the South Sea islanders.[22] — What should we say about this? How does all of this concern the concept and scientific inquiry? That is indeed the historical side question we left aside above. — On the other hand, we will undertake a rigorous analysis of the concept.

It is demonstrated in this concept: through nature alone, in the above sense, without art and free will, without contract, a rightful condition will never emerge. The law of right states that the contract should be made, and only where (79) this is fulfilled is its form realized. — Natural right = a rightful condition external to the state does not exist. Right = the right of the state.[23] To also have elevated this point beyond all doubt is a distinctive feature of our work.

In short: the doctrine of right is a pure analysis of the concept of right a priori as an *ought*. It examines the content of this *ought* without wanting to decide *who* ought to.

The form remains in the *ought*, even though no freedom is found where this ought is directed.

Thus it is certain: an absolute law of reason according to which a condition of right should exist.

The first question reads: is there such an a priori concept in the system of knowledge? That is: 1) not, does everyone have this concept in perfect clarity? [For instance,] do we all have the concept of gravity or that of any other law in perfect clarity? — Another question that of course does not matter to us is whether it manifests itself? Certainly, even in children, in strong outbursts. You see far more misgivings in them about violations of right than about its advantages. It certainly exercises a natural and invisible force. [201]

But rather, [the first question means] 2) does someone who thinks all the way to the end have to think the concept? This would normally be determined through a deduction that belongs in the *Wissenschaftslehre*, and which the doctrine of right rightly leaves to it. / Every particular science assumes its foundational laws as a factum: wherever it comes from [is assumed to be] the final ground. As, for example, in mechanics. Where this ground is in turn explained is for *another* science (the *Wissenschaftslehre* as the ground for all). We thus rightfully, and for the purity of science, rise above this deduction.

## [Chapter 2: Discussion of the Concept of Right][24]

As a side note, we want to indicate the *place* of the concept of right: thus we offer a discussion of the concept

1) The concept rests on the fact that several free beings are in a communal sphere that reproduces everyone's efficacy. (It is based only on this. If one of these conditions is not met, the concept disappears. For example, where the free beings do not have such a communal sphere, everyone has his own understanding and his own will.)[25]

Why is this? Knowledge should understand itself as this and this (as the appearance of God). Hence it is a self for itself, an I.

It must comprehend itself as *one*, as it is in fact.

But it must in turn comprehend its comprehension of this unity: it must see this as a pulling together of thought into a unity out of the multiplicity. Before comprehending itself as one, and as a condition of this comprehension, knowledge must thus discover itself as a multitude of I's. This finding must be complete, that is, must be present as a closed world, a system of I's.

(This lies in knowledge's self-intuition[26] and self-understanding[27] of itself.)

These I's must be intuited as effective in a *communal sphere of effects*. — Proof: because it is to them as individuals that the moral command to realize the image of God is directed. But the command directed at each individual is only a part (81) of the image of the one [God] that everyone ought to generate with *communal* force; the image of the one [God] is connected visibly [202] in everyone and is only partially generated by each. Hence they necessarily have a communal object and communal sphere for this forming of the image of the one [God] by a communal force.

2) The second condition of the concept of right. Actually, the consequence [of the prior condition]. Now, in this communal sphere, the freedom of one person can disturb that of another. The law of right is only for remedying this disturbance: [if there is] no possibility of disturbance, [then there is] no law of right.

I say, with the matter thus established, a disturbance and interference of the freedom of one by the freedom of another is not even conceivable. The freedom of each arises in establishing his part of the image of the one [God]. Since this unity is an organic unity coming from the commands to all individuals, these commands can thus never contradict one another nor cause a conflict: what is required of one, is not [required] of the other, and the other way around. If everyone only does what is required of him, their freedoms will never come into contact. There is no disturbance and hence no law is required to negate the disturbance. There is no qualification on this, namely, the whole community of rational beings conceived under the moral law and with one will.

Thesis. In pure reason a law of right is not possible.

Antithesis. But the moral law can only address the individual after his *freedom* has developed. In order for the possibility of becoming seized by moral laws, the world of individuals must thus first be free, and act freely, to form itself. In this condition, they do not yet stand under the moral law, their freedom *can* be disturbed, then. If it is not to be disturbed in this condition, the law of right is required.

Synthesis. The law of right hence finds its application only insofar as the moral law does not yet (82) rule universally, and only as preparation for its rule. The *universal* rule of the latter abrogates the former (I say universal, and that the particular is of no help, which will become clear.)[28]

(Thus the conditions for the law of right are: 1) Multitude of free beings. 2) Commonality of the sphere and hence absolute possibility of disturbance. 3) That the disturbance not be negated by another, higher law.)

The limits of its validity.

We posit these premises:[29] a multitude of free beings, whose freedom can disturb each other in a communal sphere of efficacy. The law of right follows from this [203] by the mere principle of noncontradiction for everyone who conceives of this concept, and this is the place to construct it once more, with clarity. All those posited beings are *in essence*[30] *free*, and nothing else but free. They are to be thought of *as free* in all perpetuity and in all determinations of their lives. This applies to everyone *in the same way*: *their* freedom shall hence be conceived in the *synthetic* thought of everyone *together* and next to each other. Thus no one's freedom shall negate the freedom of another in this synthetic concept. — To free the first one, then a second in a way that negates the first's freedom, etc. It is not like this. Rather, however many are added, it should not negate the freedom of those previously posited.

The concept of right = the *necessity of thinking* of all as free in the synthetic unity of the concept of everyone. / The opposite would be a contradiction, that is, a *taking back* of what was posited, (83) *posited as free*, in thought. — (Get this quite clear for yourselves. The concept is easy: it would not be good if we failed with the merely formally logical [concept]. In the future, it will be of great significance for the clear insight that we intend.) Such a taking back would be a *contradiction* because, as remarked above, all possible time is contained at once in the concept of *freedom*. "Revoked at some point in the future" contradicts the first principle. Summing up in one thought the *freedom* of many means encompassing the future of all, because freedom posits the future. In this future, freedom becomes an *ought*, a *postulate*, because the opposite is naturally possible through the freedom of individuals.

(N.B. Form cannot give way: quantity has to give way.)

This is to be remarked at once, thereby introducing the analysis.

The concept of right is required by logical consistency and the truth of thought. — Nothing more is needed to require it, and it is also not more than simply this.

All should be free: no one should disturb the freedom of another. Insofar as the natural, reasonable being has already determined the boundaries [of freedom], these boundary determinations are merely sanctioned by the law of right and made into law for all time. Everyone owns *his* body, which no other will confuse with his own, as a free tool of the will.[31] It is contained within the law of right that he will not be prohibited through external influence from being this [free tool] in every manner he is capable of into the future. This [law of right] merely maintains and lends unconditional continuance to nature's instruction.[32] No one should infringe on another's body, hinder him, or cause him harm. In short, no immediate, violent contact in any manner whatsoever.

[204] But, where nature has not separated [individuals] in the world of the senses as the sphere that produces their efficacy, (84) how should the indirect disturbance be avoided here?

Answer. Through artifice. One would have to erect particular spheres and each of us would have to be assigned one of these that all others would have to refrain from. Similar to what is at the foundation of the moral law, [which holds that] what one person should do, no one else at all should do. Accordingly, it applies here: [the law of right holds that] what one person *may* do, no other may at all. Each should have his boundary, within which all others should leave him undisturbed, exclusive and particular. A sphere of free action = *property* / This is the *foundational concept* that protects you right from the start from an abundance of mistakes about this concept that have crept into theory and life.[33]

This sphere must be demarcated through free artifice, because nature has not separated [human beings]. Property in the body is ensured merely through the law of right. The property of a sphere is commanded as a condition.

## Chapter 3: [Realization of the Concept of Right]

Thus, when we think of any being, we think of the community of several free beings. This is how one must see it, how it should be, must be, if everyone's freedom is to persist. Where it is not so, *violence* will reign, the greater strength will decide.

This however is a mere empty thought, an image.

(85) The concept of right should not remain an empty thought, but demands its own realization. *How*? I say: if the concept of right were to become the law of the will of *everyone*:

1) I say, law of the will of everyone who are to be free and in proximity to one another. For we have already seen that the limitation of individuals does not help anything, but rather absolutely everyone has to lock themselves into their boundaries if the freedom of all is to emerge as the communal product. [205]

2) The concept of right should be the *law* of the will of all free beings. Law: that is, that it would be absolutely impossible for one to *will to harm* another. He *can*: nature has left him free to do this. The stars in their course cannot influence one another's orbit, but the free individual is not so fixed. It is simply not a law of nature. — Wherein lies his ability [to harm another]? Because he can *will*! What, then, must one bind of his, since his power is not bound? The will. It would have to be made impossible that someone wills a violation of right by a law akin to that of a mechanical law that commands the will.

(It is important you see here, where things are simple, that this is exactly what is required by the validity of the concept of right. We will infer conclusions from this later that are not familiar or have not been clearly seen until now.)

3) The concept of right: *it* alone, nothing else, would be *what moves the will*.[34] Merely for the sake of right, and *because of right*. Not love, favor, pity, morals (whose appearance is not assumed and must be carefully avoided), concepts of utility and general welfare; even less violence and the like, but merely and completely the concept of right. These lectures are only about the concept of right. Everything else is carefully avoided. (86)

4) Why[35] we hold so strictly to this becomes readily apparent through an important implication.

a) For the sake of right, and for absolutely no other reason, the freedom of each is inviolable in this imagined state of affairs under the rule of right. Complete freedom: the personal freedom indicated by nature, as well as the determined sphere of unobstructed functioning. What *each* person *under this rule* has of freedom is given to him not *by nature*, which merely indicates, but precisely by granting everyone the power to violate freedom, revokes its protection — *rather, each has freedom by right*, but only as his right.

b) But the *concept of right* is a concept that must be thought by everyone who wants to be included in it and to have a part in it. It is a condition of right only insofar as everyone submits themselves to it for the sake of right, for this is a condition not of individuals but of *everyone*. Those who do not submit themselves to such a condition do not belong among this "*everyone*," and thus have no right and no claim to freedom, since in this condition everyone's claim to freedom, without exception, can only be grounded in right.

For the sake *of right,* so that *this person* would be included in it: but this person is included only insofar as he includes *all others in it*. Right exists only insofar as the will of all [206] is subjected to the same thing. Whoever does not submit himself is not included in the "*everyone*," and not under this concept.

Hence: the right of the individual is conditional on his recognition of the rights of all others: and without this condition no one has rights.

A condition of right exists only through the subjection of *everyone*. Whoever does not subject himself does not belong among the "*everyone*" and has no right.

(87) *Remark*. It already becomes apparent here that for a scientific, that is, a clear and determined, perspective, the law of right must be neatly separated from the moral law.

And if then someone does not recognize right? Should I therefore treat him without mercy, as someone completely without right, as a thing? Who says: perhaps [he should be treated as] a moral being.[36] He is nonetheless a tool of the moral law, rough now, but he can form himself; [you should] carry him, and educate him. — Everything goes according to moral principles. — And that is what we will state in the doctrine of morals. — There the law is directed at me *alone* and is unconditional. — Not so the law of right: it is directed at *everyone* and the subjection of the individual is conditional on the subjection of all and of each individual. If the condition goes away, then so too does what is conditioned. Just the same with right. If I do it — carry and educate someone — I do it because it is my duty, but not because it is his *right*; and that [right] is what we are talking about. (So then, moral law and the law of right contradict each other. The latter ignores the former, the former negates the latter.) How the state, which, besides its rightfulness, is simultaneously moral, might unite these two claims, we will see.

The law of right binds *all*, and [it binds] individuals only insofar as it has bound *all*. No individual is bound through the law of right who does not belong to the "all."

Conclusions:

1) The constitution of right includes a determinate and closed community of individuals whose inclusion must be known by all, directly or indirectly, as they are the only ones authorized by this constitution.[37] (88)

2) A right as such is only obtained by adopting the obligation to preserve the rights of others, specifically, exclusively the rights of those with whom one is bound in this manner. Hence [there is] no right without obligation and the other way around: precisely by binding oneself, one proves oneself to be subject to the *concept* of right, [207] which is the condition under which one *has rights*. — As far as the obligation to persons extends is how far right also extends. One has rights insofar as one accords rights.

Simply put: 1) the law of right necessarily includes an *allness*.[38] 2) Only the individual who has subjected his will to the law of right belongs in this allness.

The formal condition of right: it is related to specific others and states: that one recognize the rights of these specific others and submit oneself to them as to a law; and thereby they too are subjected.

## Chapter 4

Continuation of the analysis. What does this mean: everyone submits to the rights of everyone, as to a law?

This encompasses two things.

I) The original conflict of freedom must be laid to rest. Within the *effect of freedom*. Each person thus has to be allocated his particular sphere. *Property.* Every individual receives this, his property, by right, simply from everyone, in that he recognize the right of all others. Whoever he has bound himself to is bound to him in turn. Outside and beyond this sphere there is no property right.

(89) How does this *resolution* [of the conflict] happen? Since nature has not done this by agreement, i.e. the unification of the will of everyone, each individual is thus to possess this by himself. This is the first point.

Now this agreement should not occur because of some other motive (that of violence, prudence, morality, utility) but merely because of right: because of the concept of the freedom of *everyone*. Everyone has the same claim to right. — There may be something arbitrary in such an agreement. The question arises how far this arbitrariness might extend, but also to what extent it is limited by the *law of right*.

For clarification.

Agreement = contract: here the property contract. Right itself demands this in general. It could be that the contract would be entered into and thereby completely satisfactory for the form of right in general. But if, as we conveyed earlier, [208] the demand for right is not only directed at the *form that* [it was entered into], but also at a certain content of the contract, then it is possible that while the former condition is met, the second is nonetheless not. A property contract has been agreed to and made in accordance with right. But if it was not entered into in a way that [its content] is in accordance with right, then right is not realized in it.

Accordingly, we certainly have to investigate whether the law of right exposes the content of the property contract, if we are satisfied *that it exists at all*, as arbitrary and imprecise, or whether it postulates something about it and, if so, what?

You see where this investigation is headed. One imagines (as you hypothetically certainly can) how things might actually occur (earlier, I postponed this investigation completely), so that those who want to enter the contract doubtless come with possessions (not (90) property). If the property contract is merely formal (everyone will want to keep his possessions and the contract should not harm them), it only adds in the missing form of right and that of property. So then its content is: everyone should keep, as a matter of right, what he has now. Whoever has plenty now [will keep] plenty, and whoever has nothing, shall get nothing for all eternity. — It would be *different* if the property contract has a rightful content. Then the title to possession could be subject to a critique, and one could ask, not what you possess, but what you possess rightfully. And a new distribution could commence.

The existing doctrines of right have remained far removed from approaching this investigation, but have always philosophized based on the first condition, often underhandedly giving it the title of right deceptively and as an embellishment. We will proceed honestly in this matter as well! The consequences are not even that dangerous, especially in our times. These times have an equalizing power. We can hear a lot now, because we have nothing more to fear.

So, next comes the investigation into the *property* contract.

The personal[39] freedom of the human being is not the subject matter of contracts: nature has already separated us in this matter. But, mind you, only by entering a contract of right at all, and first and foremost a property contract, does the individual receive this personal freedom as [a matter of] *right*, [thereby] binding others by entering a system of right, merely by expressing his will. Hence he has this freedom *in the form of right* only through the contract.[40] (Without it, whoever pleases may still protect his personal freedom perhaps out of duty, but he is not bound to that by right.) Although a study of the freedom of human beings everywhere [209] would thus belong in anthropology, (91) not in the doctrine of right, the doctrine of personal rights of human beings as such, insofar as others are thereby *bound*, very much belongs in the doctrine of right. What the laws about it in a rightful constitution should be, must be, grounded on this doctrine and derived from it. Hence the doctrine of personal rights cannot be left out. It has a designated spot in the doctrine of right, especially because it determines the content of the property contract and serves as its premise. Thus, we must consider this doctrine as such. And we must treat the personal rights of human beings as the foundation of the property contract. (The doctrines of right are all the more to blame for neglecting this inquiry, since they certainly include a chapter about personal rights, and extend it to the point of unseemliness (because they improperly saw it as a chapter from morality), yet they should have felt its connection with the property contract.)

This would be one main part of the doctrine of right, that is, the analysis of the concept of right, assumed to be valid, and all that is connected to it.

II)[41] A rightful condition does not arise just by everybody sharing a communal sphere of efficacy and promising not to disturb one another in it. They declare their will to be rightful through a signal, but there are two doubts about it: 1) whether the declaration [of rightfulness] conforms with the truth, or merely serves one party to earn the trust of the others so as to attack them with greater advantage. 2) Also, even setting this aside, the will is changeable: for now it is serious about something, later it may regret that. A mere avowal thus does not grant right, because it does not establish the condition for right in general. — Consider this: just as freedom, by being posited in a certain moment, (92) is posited for all time from this moment on, the same is true for right, which is nothing more than a further determination of freedom. What belongs to me now, but can be taken from me at any time, is my contingent possession, but not my right. It lies in [the nature of right] that it can never and at no point be taken from me. Right carries with it an eternal imperative.

To this end, it is required that the will of everyone declared in the property contract be serious in intent and unchangeable: according to *law*, according to absolute necessity. That is, it should be impossible that anyone have another will (at least an active will) other than the one he avows to have (what he wishes in his heart is of no concern to right[42]), and it should similarly be impossible that he ever change this will. (This is a key condition, as posited already above, but now posited authoritatively[43] in order to solidify the premises of the subsequent conclusions.) [210]

I say, a necessity, and even a natural necessity, a natural principle, and thus a power,[44] is therefore posited through the realization of right. — It cannot be comprehended how this could influence the inner will of the human being, which is absolutely free in every individual. But we are only speaking of the active will, which has causality in the world of the senses. This power would absolutely have to stop every will that is contrary to right from breaking through, from having causality, leaving only that freedom which is in conformity with right. Thereby the right of everyone would be secured by a law akin to the mechanistic necessity of nature. Just as there is nothing against the natural law, so there would be no will against the law of right.

The idea of this power: it is set in motion by the willing of right (that is, [the willing] of the determinate property contract that has been agreed to in this society), (93) and by the absolute not-willing of what is contrary to right.[45] Right alone is the content of this power's will.

Therefore, it must be bigger than any other power in this society and all-powerful. When all but one come to an agreement to attack this one person, it must be able to prevent this oppression. It must never *will* nor *move* unless right is to be violated. But in that case, it must move immediately and nothing must be able to resist it.

*Conclusion*: only insofar as such a power is constituted and everyone who is asked to be bound [by it] clearly sees that such a power has been constituted — only then can someone bind himself to it. Because he only binds himself to right: but right is eternal and necessary, whereas this [society] is not eternal and necessary and it cannot be conceived as such except through the power just described.

Further: such a power, now, is not given by nature (as has been extensively shown, since the entire concept of right with a view to the possibility of conflicts of freedom is grounded on its absence). Accordingly, power would have to be constituted through *art*, according to a concept of *an end*.

Power is the expression of the concept of right in a powerful will. Whoever would therefore constitute it would have to think of right and its introduction in society as his concept of purpose.

The bound community conceives of this concept according to the conditions and wills its execution.[46] Accordingly, the community would have to constitute such a power as certainly as it wills right, since as shown it is only possible through such a power.

Right rules only through the power described.

(94) Now, everyone wills right.

[211] Everyone must therefore will this community and they must actually establish it; however, they do not will right, since they do not will its necessary condition.

There[47] are actually two principles, both significant. 1) Only through a community that wills right can a rightful power (let us call it by its name, a government) be generated rightfully. 2) The government must be generated necessarily by this community, as certainly as it wills right.

Principle 1) rests on the principle that only such a community can will right for right's sake. This is a shared concept that only emerges through the communal insight of everyone.

One could say against this — and I deliberately already prepare for it here, where the simplicity of the matter can still be seen very clearly — that the individual too can will right simply for right's sake, or that many can will it, but not everyone.

I answer: yes, just not for the sake of *his* right, because when he has accepted right and has the force to establish a power of right, he therefore also has the power not just to protect his right, but even to become an oppressor. That he is not an oppressor is due to moral reasons, which are higher than those of right.

For the sake of *their* right, everyone can only will such a power together as one, because each sees that he is only secure under this condition. The impetus for one's own right is only realized as a union. When a supreme power[48] is created in the first manner, through a naturally powerful individual, then, even when the substance of right emerges purely, the form of right will nonetheless always be absent, (95) since some will be *forced* to enter the rightful condition against their will and without their insight. They are forced to become free according to the law. If this coercion is to be avoided, everyone without exception must will right and a government for the sake of right. The meaning of our claim is therefore the following: in keeping with the form of right, the government can only be established by everyone. Explaining its establishment by one or many requires higher, namely moral, principles, which we do not deal with here.[49]

[212] (Everything that is a right in humanity today came about in the first manner, i.e. against the form [of right], not in the second [manner].[50] In the future, this may provide us with a standard for judging the reality of the ideal of right against claims to it.)

On principle 2). [That] this production of government is necessary is basically clear and proven. Power is the *condition* of right, the exclusive condition. I only make this point because of an important implication.

How does an individual prove his rightfulness and become receptive of rights in general, a *subject of right*?[51] Initially by agreeing to a property contract. — But the mere declaration of one's will does not secure right! Each person must make it impossible for himself to have another will. This impossibility only comes about through the establishment of the government. — So it is not by declaring that one wants to limit one's will with regard to the freedom of the others. This will is not unchangeable, or at least not everyone must be (96) necessarily convinced of its unchangeability. — Then, once an all-powerful will exists that wills right only, it will take over the declaring of property by itself and show everyone their boundaries, not through subjection to this power — which if it is as powerful as it should be it will indubitably subject everyone on its own without consulting the free will of the individual — but through everyone's contribution to the establishment of such a power. This contribution is the only unambiguous act of the will, that it only wills to live according to right, in that it is the annihilation of the possibility of every other [manner of] willing through his own activity: the self-destruction of the possibility of an unjust will. Its utter eradication.

[Hence, we have reached this] *principle*: only through his contribution to the establishment of a government does someone show himself unambiguously as a legal subject and receive rights, both property rights and his personal rights. Fulfilling this contribution is, by itself, the acquisition of right. Without this contribution, on the sheer terrain of the doctrine of right, each and every person remains without rights.

Of course, *everyone* who unites in [a condition of] right must make this contribution and all in the same way, in that everyone wills right in the same manner and for the same reason. According to this, the government emerges through a contract of everyone, which is unlike the property contract, a contract of pure omission, but is rather a positive performance contract.[52] Everyone pledges part of his freedom to receive the remainder as a right, and one can only receive it as a right through such a pledge. [213] This is thus the civil contract,[53] basically the last and complete condition for the capacity for right.

Outside of the state there is no right. No one has a right other than a citizen, but a citizen is only he who contributes to establishing the government. (There is no natural right, only the right of the state.)

(97) Hence we would have to speak of *the civil contract* in a second part.

It goes without saying that these two investigations [about property contract and civil contract] have to be preceded by an investigation into the *contract as such* and into its relation to right. / The doctrine of contracts and their bindingness in the area of right — basically the source of obligation in contracts — has become contested and it deserves a very determinate scientific pronouncement, whose premises are of course already contained in the previous discussion.

The subsections especially in the doctrine of the civil contract will emerge there and then [during the discussion of the civil contract].

*Final remark*: In the last principle — someone only earns rights by establishing the state along with others, and there is no other determinate ground of right than this — what is distinctive about [my doctrine] of right, and hence that it depends on the *Wissenschaftslehre*, has become starkly apparent, and it is important to ground it carefully.[54]

Consider the following [argument]:

Right is freedom according to a law. Whoever claims a right expects it not as a favor but as a debt and as another's obligation according to a law ruling over and known to both of them. — He invokes against him this [law] which limits his will.

Does such a law exist? Of course: the moral law. According to it, everyone should respect the freedom of everyone else. This law thus gives everyone the right to be free, because it imposes the obligation on everyone to let all others be free.[55]

Does this law also determine the boundaries of freedom and the right of everyone? With regard to personality: (98) yes,[56] but one could say, not so in the sphere of freedom. Here, law still requires a contract. (I said as much myself.) The answer to this is the one I gave earlier: the moral law cannot [214] *contradict* itself in its commands to individuals, in its tasks. What is commanded to one is certainly never commanded to another. Thus, if everyone only stands under the command of the moral law as its tool, they will never encounter one another without intention and will and by themselves. Their paths are separated as if by an inviolable law of nature.

Where the moral law is valid, no separate law of right is required.

But how is the moral law to become valid? A proposition [from the doctrine of ethics] that will play an important role in our theory. — The moral law only pertains to the will that is freed of all external ends, and equally released from nature and idle by nature. The external ends, however, that nature places in us as preconditions of the higher end, are *our preservation and our security*. These must therefore be achieved, and achieved universally, before the moral law can appear universally.

Hence there must be a means independent of morality to secure the freedom of all, which is the condition for morality as appearance and in the series of appearances. Precisely this question, about the law of freedom independent of morality, must be answered. (The principle of the doctrines of right completely missed this [question]).

Hence you see where those others went wrong. They thought in general terms that there should be right, but not how it should come about, or at least not how it should become what it did become according to them — morality. Their insight was not genetic all the way down, and so not actually (99) scientific. Right comes before the rights of the moral law as the condition of its appearance.

Now the principle: freedom as a right, according to a *law*. According to which [kind of law]: A physical one.[57] Hence whoever wills right before morality wills this physical force, and merely by actively willing it — that is, contributing to its establishment — does he confirm this will. But only he who wills right has rights. Only thereby does he confirm himself as a legal subject.

Right, as an artificial institution, hence as the object of a scientific construction, is found only outside the moral realm. Inside the moral realm, it arises by itself and is a mere accident of moral appearance that we do not attend to any further, because the essence of moral appearance consists in something else altogether. [215]

# [Second Part]
## [Chapter 1]

About[58] the contract in general, as an introduction to the two main sections, and on its obligatoriness according to the law of right.

Genetic [analysis]. Is a contract possible under the rule of the moral law? Someone wills to do something for the sake of another and for the other's advantage: also promises to him that he will do something so that the other relies on this support in his own actions. For what reason? To further morality as such, to help the other get by in this regard, and for no other reason. (Since everyone is (100) only animated by the moral law and its tools.) If this reason disappears, then that which it justified also disappears. [In this case,] if he can no longer do it without endangering general morality, his or the other's morality, if he cannot keep his promise without this risk, then he will necessarily not give [his word], for this law alone commands. Further, the other will not demand [it of him], for he too only wills the rule of the moral law.

In this area no one does anything for another, just as no one does anything for himself either. The individuals are not there at all. Everyone exists only for the common purpose. And then everyone does for others all that is contained in this common purpose, absolutely and without further [ado], without explicitly promising it, or binding himself to it without asking for something in exchange. Thus, far from the idea that the contract only applies in the arena of the moral law; [rather,] there isn't a contract at all.

The essence of the contract consists in doing or refraining from something for another only so the other can do the same in turn for him (I will make use of the words that first present themselves, and more about it further below), such that everyone actually acts not for the other but for himself, and for the other only because he cannot otherwise act for himself. Restraint for the sake of restraining, performance for the sake of performing.

Further analysis.

Any contract arises from two wills that conflict with one another because each desires one and the same thing for the sphere of efficacy of his freedom. The sphere of efficacy is universal: everyone has a claim to everything. [216]

But this freedom does not persist, so they each have to surrender some of their part until their will is no longer in conflict. The result is a communal will of both. A (101) standing together[59] without contradiction. They *contract*. Or rather, their wills contract.

Must such a contracting exist on the basis of any reason? Yes, for the rightful reason of the standing together of free beings. Freedom *should* exist. — but it cannot without unifying their opposing wills: thus, they *should*. The contract as such [is thus] for the sake of right.

Through mere declaration, however, nothing is yet achieved. Thus they must uphold it: they have to make it impossible for themselves to break it. Why? For the sake of right.

Right cannot contradict itself. It cannot demand as a matter of right its own opposite. Only contracts that are in conformity with the law of right should thus be entered into, not others. Only these are contracts and should be upheld. Others are void. The content of the contract, in relation to its conformity with right, decides its form.

A contract is binding only insofar as it conforms with right.[60] Wherever the following principle is found, and in whichever way of thinking, is of no concern to us here: *I want to keep my word and bind myself to it, even if it is unfair.* This principle does not rest on the foundation of right. *I do not bind and contract myself by your right, but by my precious word of honor.* This principle does not rest on the foundation of the moral law either, where everything occurs merely for the sake of morality: but where error has to be taken back and excused by the other. No one there will acknowledge such holding to a rash promise. For [this] has no application. Often the moral person falls back on the ground of right, and then he must abide by the contract. Thus, right comes before morality and is its condition. — I (102) can however indicate where they are located: at the midpoint of the will's preparation for morality. The commandment here is to keep one's word with oneself and others, to accustom one's will to unchangeability and inviolability.[61]

From this principle, we have no dangerous consequences to fear. Not that someone will make himself judge, a bribed and partial judge, of the rightful validity of the contracts he entered. If one conceives of it in the context in which it is presented, this is impossible, since the will of right is laid down and established in the state. The state ensures that there should be contracts and how they should be. It determines the conditions of their validity. In concreto, therefore, the question about the rightful validity of every contract always has to be answered in a generally valid way. [217] It is rightfully valid and binding to the extent that it conforms to the state's rules about contracts. If it does not conform to them, then it is void. It should not have been agreed to and should not be abided by. Both [agreement and performance] are punishable and prohibited.

Accordingly, it goes without saying that we claimed to speak only in general about the form of the contract here. The material legitimacy of contracts of all kinds — that is, what should be legal concerning contracts in a legitimate state — we will have to cover separately along with the matters which belong to it.

The *nature of the contract* emerges here. It is agreed to in order to obtain one's right: thus for a selfish reason. — It is the unification of conflicting wills. The basis of its bindingness: the law of right itself.

The contract in its general form has been described here as a merely negative contract of omission: (103) the limitation of two wills that each lay claim to the same sphere of efficacy. [Hence,] the distribution [of the sphere] and reciprocal abstention [from interference]. [This is the] *property* contract. We mentioned a positive performance contract earlier, the unification of all for the establishment of a government. That it has the same basis of right has become clear. Individuals do not enter the contract with other individuals, but each individual with everyone. Therefore, its form has completely different laws that will have to be investigated in their place. The property contract is merely a negative contract of omission. If no one interferes with the sphere of another, it is of no concern to him what everyone does or does not do in his own sphere. Nobody need snoop in another's sphere.

This is also contradicted by the common view, and it is good for us to treat it here where everything is still very simple. This view puts property contracts about mine and thine into formulas, in which they are regarded as positive performance contracts: "facio ut facias," "do ut des," facio ut des," "do ut facias."[62]

These designations are not meaningless, because 1) science benefits from the simplicity of its formulas. If the property contract remains only a negative one, then it can be comprehended with only one designation, 2) this precision even leads to important conclusions that are otherwise lost in inexactness, as will become clear soon.

I will therefore remind you of the following regarding these formulas, first: they can be traced back, admitting the affirmative form [of the contract] in the meantime, to a single formula. Namely, the *giving* which the three formulas also speak of, is it not really also a *doing*? "Facio ut facias." All the same, whether this doing, mine or yours, consists in an ongoing actual creating and effecting, or in a one-time completed giving and transferring [218] of a previously created and finished product of my or your labor. The reason for this empty distinction is that property was not (104) determined correctly right from the very beginning as a private sphere for free functioning, but only, foolishly, through the objects of this free functioning. Hence "do."[63] Later, it could not be concealed from them, [those who hold this common view,] that the object itself does not act but requires labor, i.e. being worked upon, and that therefore labor certainly also has a value. And now they come up with two kinds of property, property in things and property of powers. But here there is [in fact] only one kind of property, that of the free use of one's powers. If this free use of one's powers is determined, then of course it directs its objects with it, because it cannot be determined otherwise except through them.[64]

Secondly, I say that the affirmative expression [of the property contract] is false overall and can be traced back to the negative formula: "Non facio, ne facias."[65] In all these cases, I have an indubitable right, granted to me by the original property contract, to keep my property. The other person wants me to renounce this right, not keep it. He similarly has something that it is important to me for him not to keep. If we come to an agreement, we trade. I do not insist on my right, so that he does not insist on his.

Consider it from this side: does this contract provide either of us with an original acquisition or loss of property? Does the property of one of us become larger, that of the other smaller? According to right, I do not think so. Hence it is merely a *trade of objects* of property, after which each person's property keeps its previous value, so has not been changed.

Everyone should [be able to] keep his property without loss, as it was granted to him by the original property contract. The foundation of all right wills it thus. Can this grant that one party in this trade gains an advantage? (105) And could a contract that has this consequence be valid? Absolutely not.

All these exchange contracts are then based on the mere negative omission contract, as a higher law and as the boundary within which they can be agreed to. The negative omission contract prohibits the violation of others' property and preserves the status quo for everybody.

Precisely this has been neglected by conceiving of these contracts as absolute and overlooking their actual foundation. If I am cheated, am I by right bound to let the contract stand as valid? How could I, as the original contract of right is violated in my [case]? "Volenti non fit injuria."[66] "Open your eyes!" and so forth. What does this mean? Protect your right yourself, for in this regard you remained in the lawless state of nature and the realm of cunning and fraud! I did not know about that, since of course I have surrendered my self-protection by subjecting myself to the state and contributed to the protective power. And that [power] is obligated to secure all my right.

Things may be different in practice, but this is what right wills. All exchange and commercial contracts have a condition and are only binding if this condition is met: that everyone retains the value of his property. [Even though] trade continues on forever, no one gets richer or poorer. How to legislate this, and where such a standard of value comes from, is a whole other investigation, which we will undertake in its own time. (106)

*\*\*\**

## Chapter 2: On[67] personal right (formally, without limitation)

[Fichte reads here ¶10 from his 1796–1797 text *Foundations of Natural Right* (FNR), "Definition of Original Right," 102–3 in Baur translation][68]

(107) Addition to ¶10: Freedom as such: the right to be only the cause, absolutely not something caused, so just the first, the principle, not the second, the outcome.

[Fichte reads here the first two paragraphs of ¶11 from FNR, "Analysis of Original Right," 103-104]

Addition to ¶11: In the concept of an effect lie 1) and 2).[69]

NB. Freedom begins with the freedom of the body. (108)

[Fichte reads here ¶11, I) from FNR 104]

Addition to ¶11, I) Very rigorous and correct. One's body may not be attacked.

[Fichte reads here ¶11, II) from FNR 104]

Addition to ¶11, II) Similarly, one's effectiveness may not be directly opposed.

[Fichte reads here ¶11, III) from FNR 104–6] (109–11)

Addition to ¶11, III) A concept of an end posits cognition of the objects of the efficacy: a particular concept assumes particular cognition. (It counts on this enduring being, which should lead through causal efficacy to that which is intended). Its business is to acquire these objects. But when the acquired objects to which he subjected his purposes in this way are changed, his freedom is disrupted.

What he has *subjected* to his *ends*, he thus conceives of as permanent, and has resolved that they should remain so.

Without limitation through the contract: no one can modify what I have subjected to my ends, without limiting my freedom.

(112) [220] His efficacy [also] *not indirectly* opposed (by modification, through his effectiveness, of the objects useful to me).

[Fichte reads here ¶11, IV) from FNR 106–7] (113)

Addition to ¶11, IV) Every concept of an end contains a *future*. Every use of freedom (for the sake of a being in the future) therefore necessarily includes willing a future. The success in the use of freedom of everyone is a right and is secured for everyone through the right of each, which means that his intended future — that is, his self-preservation — is protected for each and belongs to his personal right. The success of his future is a universal one. His efficacy contains his future within itself. I allow him the former, (114) which means that I allow him the latter. We thereby secure our future.

Nature might bring about his demise, just as it created him. Only others' freedom should not kill him, for then freedom would be cancelled by freedom and would not exist.

One could think that this freedom is secured through the inviolability and untouchability of the body. Certainly, [it is secured] against direct acts of violence, but not against indirect [violations of] the property contract. We are concerned about these consequences, and here we reach the point mentioned above.

[Fichte reads here ¶11, V) from FNR 107–8] (115–16)

***

Chapter 3:[70] [Analysis of the property contract]

**First section**
1) The original right: to be understood as an ongoing reciprocal interaction between the person and the sensible world that is determined solely by the person's concept of an end. No one may oppose him, neither directly nor indirectly. In this world everyone is free like a God. [221]

2) The property contract assigns each his sphere, his *quantum of exclusive use of freedom*. This, and nothing else. Namely, [it assigns] rights, or better described, exclusive rights, or still better, property. Natural objects are by themselves without conflict. Only when the human being includes them in his higher concept of an end do they conflict. That is the place of the conflict, and there [lies the] separation. — The reason for the confusion is the not very precise comprehension[71] of the concept of right; the means against [the confusion], on the other hand, is precise [comprehension]. (They were apparently talking about God's right to nature, about the right of the isolated human being to it. Why not also talk about the human being's right to his thoughts and his will?). Right is a reciprocal concept[72] of the freedom of several individuals, its synthesis that reconciles them. It exists only where there is conflict about this freedom.

Principle: the freedom [we just] granted is the first precondition[73] determining the object in the property contract, not the other way around. Property of an object extends as far as this granted freedom, not the other way around, the freedom extending as far as the object. (117)

"To subject something *to my ends*," [states this principle.] "To which ends?" asks the contract. This is the *foundation*, hence the *standard* of right. — If a farmer farms, one should not therefore forbid him from animal husbandry or mining. — If someone makes a living from fishing, one should not therefore forbid him from ship-faring, and so on.

My right to actions and to objects only exists insofar as they are required for the completion of the allowed action. — This is more important than one thinks and fundamentally shatters old prejudices and wrong views. So let us look into this more closely.

3) An *ongoing* determinate reciprocal interaction.[74] The property contract is entered into for all time as a just contract — concerning the property each is due in this community:

Hence all those conflicts that could later arise as a result of changing situations and the inadequacy of the words that were said are obviated by this contract. The formulas taken from the present time are not valid (the contract is indeed an eternal one, and for all time), but rather the spirit that everyone receive what is *his* (in this community) and be [his] at all times. All future contracts about acquisition and dereliction are contained in this spirit. They only appear [to involve the exchange of objects]; actually only a change in the remaining sphere of freedom in objects occurs.

Hence this contract is actually one about the law that is always to structure and maintain reciprocal property rights: it does not determine the spheres, as much as the fundamental law that determines the spheres.[75]

Since, as we know, a rightful will must be established as a state, this structuring fundamental law is laid down for all times in the state. [222]

What was once *just* in regard to property does not always remain so. Hence even when it *was* just, it was (118) only conditionally just for this situation of the whole. But *absolute* right should rule, that is, the right that changes in its objects over time. They conceive of the concept of right as a dead concept; we conceive of it as a living one, a forming one, and one to be formed. The important differences in application will become apparent.

4) The ends of freedom can be different. If there is one that all must have, that they necessarily have, that therefore must be assured to each person without exception, then certainly it should be assumed that we have thought of his freedom in general. This is the inquiry (promised above) about the necessary content of the property contract.

There is one such goal that is accorded to absolutely everyone as his absolutely personal right, which no distributive contract can take from him, and to which he himself is bound. Thus we must pursue an even deeper analysis of personal right — through a synthesis.

5) Everyone has the right to self-preservation. Nature has made this self-preservation conditioned on activity, and as a way to be sure, has linked present pain to future threats to it.

Whoever has the right to something conditioned also has the right to the condition; in this respect, *therefore,* everyone must be accorded *the sphere* of activity, property, which assures *its preservation*.

In general, nothing more: only just right to a possible action preserving himself. — For example, *pastoral peoples, hunting peoples*. — "I want this piece of land!" "No way. Agriculture is going on here." Nature crammed human beings together because that is the only way their education is possible, by means that we will see. — What might be found in a pastoral state is not to be found in an agricultural one. How did it become this agricultural state and not a pastoral one? By the cramming together of so many (119) in this space. (Originally human beings do not want this. They also do not want to work in a factory. But nature drives [us], and right, as the boundary of the property contract affirms.) Conclusion: the determinate manner of this unification determines the possible work in general — and this is the sphere for it: so that each can live and endure.

Conclusion I. Whoever has not had this guaranteed, has no right. As soon as this disappears, every condition of right concerning him stops. As soon as someone cannot live, there is no contract regarding him.

*Quality*: the nature of labor must be such that one could live on it in this context.

The tailor among the naked. We will purchase your work and thus grant you the right to practice your trade. (This will have an important implication.) [223]

*Quantity*: It has to be left up to each person to make his living in any particular sphere.[76]

[Fichte reads here from "Pages 30–32" of FNR, III) and IV) pp. 185–87] (120–21)

The condition for according [this to everyone] is *that* he work. Work thus becomes an *obligation* of right, because it is complemented by the state's obligation to feed the one who is starving. — The right of supervision.

Thus, in this respect, the property contract provides an activity that has been forced upon it by nature and state. This is the first point.[77]

Now we read from V). In this regard, it is determined by this.

[Fichte reads here from FNR, V) p. 187] (122)

Conclusion II.⁷⁸ Everyone has rights in general only in that he contributes his share to the establishment and eternal preservation of the state. This is an absolute obligation, on which all other right is grounded. (123)

What this contribution will consist of is now clear: those who *order* and protect must *live* not through their labor — they have something else — but through the *labor of others*. Labor for their subsistence is thus the rightful obligation of everyone, without which their rightful status ceases.

Yesterday I introduced the term, *labor*. Labor, in the sense of civil right, is the use of freedom for the necessities of life. Tax = work as substitute for the work that is not done by others.

This power must arise through the contribution of *everyone* without exception, as each is a member of the union of right[79] only on this condition. Everyone for the *same reason*, hence in the *same manner*. (Each has to do as much work as the other, not for himself but for the goals of the state.)

(Surely not pre-empted. On the manner of *levying* taxes and on the different systems of taxation, nothing has been settled here yet.)

Just as supervision of labor belongs among the tasks of the state for the purpose of everyone's *preservation*, so, too, is taxation for the aim of the state's preservation. It is also accorded the supervision of the financial situation of everyone in this dual sense. (With regard to *the latter*, the state levies the taxes.)

[Conclusion] III. In these two respects, the freedom of the human being is subordinated to the law of necessity, both natural and rightful.

The human being has no freedom at all under these conditions. Proof: he should design the concept of an end with absolute freedom: it must not be imposed on [him], since otherwise the will becomes a second, material, and qualitative result[80] and product of necessity. Here the *doubling* [of the will]. Consider this from another side. The condition of right is a condition for *moral freedom*. (124) This has a purpose [224] that is not located in nature nor in facticity at all, but in a higher world. According to that, this is true freedom: the capacity for supersensible ends.[81]

(According to the principle: that by establishing a government, the will is bound to right, such that it is absolutely impossible to have a will contrary to right in this area. To the extent that it encompasses the human being, the will is a *consequence* of the mechanism, as will become increasingly clear.)

Now the entire property contract is concluded, and the condition of Right is entered into, only for the sake of freedom. But with the precautions we take to protect it, we see the exact opposite produced, freedom's destruction.

Contradiction. — *Solution*: after satisfying his own basic needs and fulfilling his civic duties, *everyone must therefore* retain enough freedom for freely designed ends, freedom within *his* sphere, within which he does not disturb that of another. The property contract must be entered into according to this fundamental principle.

This freedom for freely designed ends (initially for freedom of education, and education to freedom, actually) is the absolute personal right that no contract may abridge that the entire contract of right exists to secure.

The property absolutely accorded to each person is thereby determined completely. Everyone must keep such a sphere for freedom, in which, after the satisfaction of his basic needs and his civic duty, freedom, power, time, and space remain for him, and thus the right for freely self-given ends.

*Whoever has not received this has not received right at all, and he also is not bound to the right of others.*[82] The (125) constitution under which he stands is *not a constitution of right, but* a mere institution of coercion.[83]

With this,[84] I said, the concept of necessary property rights is *complete*. Whoever has this, quite simply has his property, but also, only he. The quantity of the sphere cannot be settled. The *quantity* turns back once again into the *form* from which it originated: the form of *freedom*, as a sign that the inquiry has led back to itself and is therefore concluded. Freedom is invisible, goes back again into the internal, and reproduces itself into the infinite. All further necessary labor and tasks can be formed through freedom. And thus, both labor and tasks thereby unite internally. The *educated* person *farms* the *field* differently when he *farms*, and with a different sense, than the uneducated person. [225]

In this area, freedom prevails everywhere, and thus also *no supervision*, as in the expressions of the freedom of the first type. That it originates in one's own internal decision and not in *external necessity* belongs to the essence of freedom. He can form himself, but does not have to. — [He can have] as much direction and instruction as he wants, but [there can be] no institution of coercion, which would become an external motivator of the will.[85]

An example. This freedom should really pervade all human affairs and not be limited in time and to certain activities. But until we get to this pervasiveness, a sensuous limitation and special circumstances might be necessary.

The giver of the Commandments for the Jews[86] introduced one such limitation, also obeyed later by the Christian Church, the commandment to keep holy the Sabbath.[87] — That which need only be a permission, he raised to a *commandment* given the crudeness and sensuality [of the people]. The higher freedom is limited during (126) a certain time. What is the meaning of this limitation? Left to yourselves, your greed will drive you to work all the time, or, if you are pack animals under herders, they will yoke you without breaks or rest. Thus, you should be *forced* to be free and your herders should be forced to let you free. (In this respect, the state really must hold on to the Sunday day-off). In this resting of your body, God willing, boredom will force you to think about your spirit and notice that you have a spirit until these speculations alone will do what they are supposed to, take in and sanctify your whole workaday life.

[Consider] pagan peoples. They had their festivals. Among them, however, there was no such order and periodic recurrence. [By contrast,] Moses, even further, ordered the seventh year for this.[88] Much good came from this. I do not want to ascribe my reasoning to him, but this side of his legislation unmistakably displays a deep sense of that higher freedom and the true vocation of the human being.

We have reached an important point. We want to deal with it more closely here and through some general remarks and overviews.

1) The human being is claimed by the state and is its *tool*. His will is *secondary* to and the *product* of the will of the state, which is primary. So it should be; to the extent that it is so, right is assured. Where is the actually free human being for whose sake the state was established? Every human being goes through the state, but does not originate in it. [226]

He is claimed now in part and namely by those who belong there. We must indicate the limit precisely: the claim extends to a certain (127) negative and positive product of his freedom. The negative: to disturb no property rights. The positive: the labor for the preservation of himself and the state. The spirit, with which he delivers this product and with which he himself permeates it, remains completely free for him.

This limit can even be visualized.[89] He contributes and must contribute, and he cannot be spared of this. But it is up to him whether he contributes with *some reluctance* of his will, or indeed out of coercion, or with a *good rightful* will, from an insight into right and morality. It is up to him whether his will be an alien will also in its form, or whether he desires to be his own will even though the product corresponds to an alien will and is qualitatively thought through. Result: The first product of freedom from the state is the creation of freedom from the state. Freedom, in this sense as everywhere, posits *itself*.[90]

It is thus clear: the *spirit* in which he delivers this product is up to each individual. Everyone will obey and will get no thanks for it. But whether he obeys the entire institution as a coerced slave, or freely, according to his own will, this is the spirit of obedience, which is left to him.

2) This freedom is the absolute right of the human being. He has no right at all, and the contract of right is not even concluded with him, if this right is not secured for him. The state is not the will of right, and is not a state at all if this right is not secured for everyone in it. The state therefore has two completely different sides and perspectives. (It is important to distinguish and unite these.) The neglect [of this difference] has had dire consequences: It is an absolutely coercive and obligatory institution; it has strictly speaking turned right itself into a coercive natural force. But it only has this right on the condition of an obligation: to secure the higher freedom of all, independence from the state for all. If this is not afforded in the state, then it cannot speak of right, because it (128) violates the central point of right and is itself contrary to right. It is mere coercion and oppression.

As with the individual right, so too, with the state. Right only exists through obligation. — Without this, there is no right at all.

You subject all powers to a shared, alien will. So then, what is the final end that should be achieved by the entire institution? I can well imagine that someone has set for himself an arbitrary and discretionary end — for example, raw violence, revenge, hatred, or generally the absolute rule [227] of his arbitrary will. He believes united powers are a secure means to these ends and that it should find and apply the right bond of order and peace of all amongst all. But what is everyone then but slaves to his arbitrary will? What is the purpose even of peace and rightfulness among them but the means to render them more suitable slaves? What is the final end? There is no possible *end* but morality, the absolutely necessary purpose of everyone. But this end can be furthered by external and sensuous means only up to the point at which they acquire the freedom to set *a moral end* for themselves. But they cannot maintain this freedom except through liberation and release from all sensuous ends, as we have seen earlier.

The rightful *form* of the state that lies in the entire previous discussion therefore does not prove anything about the rightfulness of a given state. The only proving condition is that moral freedom be its final end. Thus, we again find right connected to the entire system of knowledge, and also to be in reality what it is in the idea, the factual condition of morality.

I deliberately wanted to take up, rigorously, the state's basis of obligation just now. (129)

3) The absolute freedom of everyone must be secured by the state, because only under this condition is it a state. This freedom must be secured in a visible manner, because only the *obviousness* of this security indicates that it is a state and obligates the subjects. But how can it do that? On the point about the transition to this freedom, we saw that freedom necessarily creates itself in every individual. It cannot be created [for him].

Answer. The state can do this only through institutions for *the education of everyone* to freedom. For the following reason: this freedom is not *explicitly demanded* while entering into the original civil contract, because one only reaches moral freedom through the constitution of right. Hence, those we assumed are just now entering into the constitution of right have neither that freedom nor its concept. (Freedom for them means lawless arbitrary will). However, he who ventures to bring them *under right* — whenever this occurs — knows this freedom, because right is freedom's condition and is only properly understood as right in this way. He therefore must make this demand of himself, in accordance with his concept, after which the law [shall become] right. Now he cannot secure a freedom that *does not exist*. He can only secure the [228] possibility of its emergence.[91] [This] happens through institutions for the education of freedom for everyone and by creating the possibility of using them.

The latter represents in sensuous [form] the release from other labor and other sensuous ends. Time, freedom, space, and right.

This applies to *all without exception*, because this is not the particular right of some individual, but the (130) absolute personal right of each as a human being, for whose sake alone he can take on civil obligations.

Someone might respond to him who wants to bring him under the force of right: "But we just want to devour and annihilate one another. It may well be true that this means the demise of us all, but how is that your business? Who cares if a race such as ours exists or not?" Of course, he is right that the existence of the merely sensuous human race does not matter at all, and this is a game of nothing with no purpose.

The only thorough answer that can be given to him is: "But you should exist there, be preserved, because morality absolutely should exist, the realization of the divine image, and this cannot be brought about except through you." But if this is the final end of the union of right, it must also be possible to achieve this end through the union. And it must be possible to make clear before the eyes of everyone who can understand it that the intention is to achieve the union of right.

Therefore, [there must be] *general educational institutions for everyone*. If the state has particular institutions, it has particular ends for these. These are the absolutely common property of everyone as a *matter of right*, the pinnacle and ultimate end of all other property. I ask not to omit this "as a matter of right."

Educational institutions for freedom: for the ability to have a will as a first and initiating [cause], to set ends for oneself beyond the state, supersensible ones. Not by any means some sort of institutions for breaking and training[92], that is, for the capacity and skill to be the tools of an alien will. The despot and tyrant will indeed take after the latter. The former is undertaken only by the state.

There: breaking and training for the capacity to act according to a law not understood and to act for an unfamiliar final end, to be a skilled second instrument. Here: (131) education for the capacity to devise ends for oneself and to understand clearly the laws, according to which one achieves these ends.

Thus this is the criterion of the state to distinguish itself from despotism: whether education reigns in it or breaking and training.

The first development of freedom is that the state ceases to be a principle that moves the will. Hence it sets out to dissolve[93] itself, as it is completely in order. [229] After all, morality dissolves it. The despot can never do this, because he has a goal that can never become the goal of everyone. This, however, the necessary goal of everyone, would be their freedom. The despot's goal, by contrast, is slavery and oppression.

[Application of the Property Contract to the State]

Expansion[94] of the *perspective* in *particular*.

We want to apply the property contract wholly to a community of right, conceived generally. We will not return to it and thereby will settle it here. — With the aim of providing the foundation for all possible civil legislation about mine and thine.

1) The absolute property right of everyone is the free leisure to pursue discretionary ends after they have completed the work required for their self-preservation and the preservation of the state. Only then does everyone have property and right.

Now let us summarize this idea as follows. Everyone considered together as a sum (subtracting those who administer the state) has the absolute task (132) constantly to preserve themselves as individuals and as a whole (the individual members and the state). *Everyone*, I say, not everyone for themselves. Everyone jointly must just constantly stand up for the preservation of each who is included in the civil contract. Everyone in the same manner and with the same considerations, thus to the same extent. This mass of work *must* be completed; only under this condition is there *right*. These labors should not consume their entire time and power, otherwise they would have no right; they would have no higher freedom. — Out of the time and power of the whole of the working estates, a certain amount pertains to the state's ends. This [is a] fractional part of their whole powers, [with] a certain amount left over.

2) This relationship of the work of the whole to its leisure can be quite different in different states. Take farming as the fundamental activity: An unproductive soil will require more toil than a fruitful one. [Additionally, it will become] even more productive through the external powers of animals and machines. [230] Also a reserve supply for all sorts of needs — such that one can always choose the best time — saves work.

This relationship thus described determines what one means when one speaks of national resources, poverty, or riches. Also *state* resources. The distinction one had wanted to make between them is hopeless. It is based on an unfamiliarity with the state. No community except in the state and through the state. They imagine the state merely as a despot, or at least they think of it as a justified coercive force, but not simultaneously as an obligatory, liberating force. (About this at the right time).

It is clear that I have to bring up this relationship here. I want to speak about the rules [for] the distribution among individuals. But then I have to know the *whole* that is to be distributed. (133) This is naturally the property of the whole; that is, the leisure that remains for everyone after their labor is finished. (That it has not been determined in this way before only proves that they did not start from the depths of the concept, but superficially drew from appearances, causing quite enough confusion.).

The less leisure left over after the labor required by the state's ends, the poorer the whole. The more leisure it leaves, the richer. Does everyone have to devote 6/7 [days of the week to labor], 5/7, 4/7, and so forth.

3) The final end, secured by the state, of all associations for right for human beings is freedom, that is, first of all, leisure. This is therefore the actual goal, and labor is only the compulsory means. It falls under freedom to diminish the means continually. We take it for granted that the final end will be reached: Hence it is the state's goal continually to make the ratio of the work of the whole to its leisure more favorable (and to increase the nation's wealth).[95]

4) What other obligations this places on the state [we will deal with at] another time. Only one observation belongs here. A principle based in experience: Labor is saved when its different branches are divided. Everyone develops practice and capabilities in one branch. If everyone does exclusively what he has learned, it takes less work and efforts by the individual to yield a larger result of products of labor for the whole. Leisure is gained.

Since the state is plainly bound to produce leisure and education for freedom and since at least initially no other means to artificial and calculated leisure can be imagined other than this division [of labor], one can say that the state is bound to introduce this division of the branches of labor established by the state's ends. [231] (134)

According to this perspective, following the standard of the division of the shared work, the working classes as such (that is, those who do not belong to the civil service) in a state that conforms with reason will split up into different working estates, which gain exclusive property rights through the division. We will be able to see how these relationships are to be structured according to right and thereby comprehend the civil law from a higher point of view.

[Laboring for the State's Ends]

Task: *to apprehend the shared labor for the state's ends, according to its reasons for division among the particular working estates.*

[The Productive Estate]

A) [Agriculture]

1) The fundamental end is first of all *preservation*. Physical [preservation] simply of the *human being*. (Also of the civil servants, they must *live* and feed themselves without working for [their] nourishment.)

The human being feeds on organized matter from the plant and animal kingdoms.

It is to be expected that when, by using artifice and according to a free concept, more human beings cluster in a space than nature by itself would have gathered there, nature on its own will also not feed them, but the organization will likewise have to be brought into accordance with the conceptual artifice.

There will thus be a need to facilitate vegetation with artifice and calculation for our ends. — Nature generates plants all mixed up together. We must *separate* them. Nature's workings maintain a *balance*, we (135) prefer nourishing plants, and those to be kept safe, etc., while suppressing others. This is how it goes before *agriculture*.

Nature must deliver sustenance, which is the condition without which there would be no survival. Also meat: but in the end, this meat also comes from the plant kingdom that perhaps also requires a special care [because of its role] for animal husbandry. And this is why animal husbandry should appropriately be united with farming.

Hence farming is always the first and foundational labor and the condition for all others. This estate is the first estate.

I want to put the strictly rightful determination right at the top. The state perpetually guarantees to all its citizens their physical preservation as their right, and thus, too, the availability of the food they require. [232]

Since it is in a particular state that this nourishment can be earned exclusively through farming, the state [must] guarantee that farming always be in a condition to deliver this nourishment.

The state thus has the coercive right against everyone, that he dedicate himself to this first work of the state if his hands are required for it. And no one else has the right to settle into other branches of labor than those spared from this foundational work. The first meaning of the commandment: "you shall work" in an agricultural state: "you should toil the field." This can mean that [one may do] something else only insofar as this [need] ceases. (136)

Deduction[96] of the Property Right of the Farmers

[The following discussion] overturns pp. 36–37 [of the FNR].[97] (137)

Principle: the right of the farmer to the ground and soil is that of building on them, to subject the ground to the declared goals of his labor, as granted to him. — There is no other right of the individual to the ground and soil. — Everywhere there is discussion about property in *land*.[98] The source of that backwards perspective and backwards practice lies precisely in it, and we will certainly not eradicate it all at once through our philosophy, but just not want to embellish it, like so many.

Direct proof: Right, [as the] resolution of the conflict among free actions. Such a conflict can only be imagined in relation to the soil, insofar as several people want to toil on it for some exclusive end, and nowhere else. To walk on it, e.g. to move over it, is not an exclusive end. That everyone has ownership of his own body goes without saying. — *Excluding* through a certain use of the soil. Annihilating claim to property: this would be the opposite system, *to exclude a right without using the soil yourself.* This [opposite] system must claim this. Where should such a right *come* from? Clearly only through a contract with others. This is given: [But] what end should it serve? — To place those who want to toil on it under conditions in which they simply must toil on it along with us, or most especially, for us. — If these persons are considered in the contract, they can then be regarded as *equal* to us. They have this place and this relationship through a contract (amongst themselves) in which the others did not play a part, to which they never would have agreed, because it is based on inequality.[99] (138) [233]

Regarding the setup, they thus took on no obligations by placing some obligations on others. [In this case,] the absolute nullity of a contract. — Those who obligate and those who are obligated. What is this, their favorable standing and their privilege, based on? (That they are privileged, advantaged, is plainly evident.) They like to say: "we were there first!" But you did not in fact acquire [property], since only labor completes the acquisition. Therefore, the acquisition is only based on *power*. They can chase everyone off the land who does not want to accept their conditions. This too they are only able to do because of their union with one another.[100]

But might does not make right at all.

The latter, their *power*, provides a justifying perspective, which we mention not to embellish but to be complete. Through this power, they become protectors of this land against foreign forces. Their own interest drives them to this. This same thing also drives them to maintain order and lawfulness among their subjects as well as among all subordinates. Through the former, the protectors of the land, the products of the land diminish. Through the latter, keeping the order, their own rights, the reciprocal rights of the privileged, are infringed on. They have guaranteed their land reciprocally and no one [lord]'s subject can therefore infringe upon the land of another without simultaneously infringing on that lord himself. They therefore become the regents, the government. If they become this, they are due: 1) ownership in the land, which, as I will show shortly, accrues to the state; 2) the right to have others work for oneself, and to allow labor only in exchange for the costs to be borne for the state's ends.

— So, with regard to the quality of the relationship, everything would pretty much come back to that which is required by the law of right. With regard to the form, however, we should note: 1) this already existing government has not actually (139) been constituted by the community, but it has established and constituted itself. 2) They subordinate the subjects under the law not for the sake of right but for their advantage, while they themselves have no laws at all over them. (Among themselves they have the law of the original contract). (Thus two alliances: the alliance of the privileged among themselves, and the contract of each of them with their subjects.) 3) Because the advantage comes first and is the guiding concept, right is introduced only insofar as it advocates for the advantage of the privileged.

Remarks. 1) It is true that the states of modern Europe came about this way. Through *conquest*. (The documented power to drive everyone off the land.) The bond of agreement by their leader was fortunate.[101] [234]

2) It is true that they cannot appropriately develop in another way, so that right must develop in such a state of emergency.[102]

3) It is also true, to be sure, that this is of no concern to us. We develop the concept of right as an *ought*, without asking the empirical question, how *is it*, or how *can* it come to be? This concept of right absolutely does not contain the possibility of property in the land for the individual. It recognizes only the right to the exclusive use [of the land] for cultivation.

The state. It alone possesses the right to *property in the land*: 1) above all, as the right to distribute it for cultivation according to its end of everyone's preservation: [that is, the right] to confer in order to invest individuals with [a fiefdom]. 2) as the right to defend it against all foreigners and to exclude them from its advantages and from its use. — [This discussion] does not belong here, but rather in the [section on] international right.

Negative boundary markers on the land, etc. [is treated on] pp. 37, 38, etc. [of the FNR].[103] (140)

1)[104] Thus the right to farm is not property in the land.

2) Whoever is entrusted with the land has no right to prevent another from a harmless use of it.[105]

B) Mining

The state. Rules of ownership. Wage laborers. — a law about this is necessary; nothing may remain undetermined; (141) furthermore, the property contract is not comprehensive. Everything useful should have its master or a rule as to how it could acquire one.[106]

C) Animals

1) The *proof* of exclusive property is required here. According to rule and law. Property cannot wander. (142)

2) Difficulty with this:
1. generally, what could be property in this respect? Breeding cattle.
2.
3.[107]

Producers[108] is not the right word here. *To bring about, to process.*

[The Processing Estate]

[235] All we have discussed right here is *generative* work, gaining products, whether by agriculture, like farming, animal husbandry, or through mere prospecting, such as mining, wild fishing, hunting. This is the one main class of work for the state's ends.

The second would be: *further processing* of those products for human ends.[109]

Making such a distinction into two main classes has been criticized.

1) It is, when it has been recognized, the duty of the state and the right of the citizen, that this work be transferred exclusively to a *particular basic estate*.[110] Because with that, freedom and leisure will be obtained, and this ought to be *obtained*.

The farmer is fully dedicated to working his field, at every hour. The processing worker[111] is dedicated to his own labor. No one is disrupted in his activity by the other. a) Should the farmer make his own wooden shoes, since of course so much time remains after farming? That is a waste [of time]. *Spinning* however is good. b) Should the artisans in the countryside do their work, and cultivate fields in farm towns at the same time? The assumption would be that every human being be a farmer, and really and truly be one. This subsistence farmer[112] should only earn for himself, while (143) the actual countryman[113] should reap for others, too. But then agriculture will never become an *art*, because it is a side matter. Both go against the rule of a state educating itself to a higher level, against the rule of frugality and of gaining leisure.

2) This basic estate of artisans does not process merely for itself, but for *everyone*: just as they do not live from their *products of art* but also from products of nature. The artisan has to be able to do this with the guarantee from the state and its responsibility, a guarantee to work, life, and the portion of leisure that is due to each.

The *condition* for this is that there be a quantity of products above the life necessities of the farmer and the civil servant, that the processing estate requires for life's necessities.

Outcome: *thus, in no state may there be more processing of the raw products of nature than agriculture can sustain and pay for. Otherwise, the processing estate could not live.*

Such a state of production according to the measure of original fertility — of the number of hands dedicated to it, their power supported by machines and working animals — makes possible this level of processing of the raw material that requires so much time (of disuse of the material during the work) and so much manpower: since the material has to be delivered from the production, we have to be able to set it aside, the workers have to receive their sustenance from it.

The antithesis is not inadvisable or unpolitical — this does not concern us, and others say that too — but is *contrary to right*. [236] In this case, the original human right of the processing estate — to be able to live from its work — is not secured. It would be lacking in food and exchange.

Such a state of production, I have said, makes *possible* this level of processing. [It does] not also [make it] in any way (144) *necessary*. If a certain number of hands, x, occupied working in production suffice to feed the civil servants and a certain number of other people, y, then should they not feed them? Should they rather work *less* instead? But it is an assumption that they are not overworked (since otherwise there would be a different result). So, no, they should feed them! But free of charge, so that they are thereby idle? This is absolutely no human's right but an insolent demand. They should thus also work for their food and according to their measure. How? Further processing of the products. Hence, such a state of production therefore makes due that level of processing.[114]

The state's obligation to this basic estate of processors is best described as a contract of the producers with the artisans, under this guarantee: you provide them to us and the labor in the requisite quality; we on the other hand deliver you your food, the products. As one is provided for, so is the other provided for: but not *without* working, you may not demand this, but certainly demand work: you shall be able to live.

The artisans can be divided into two types: [first,] those who do not own the materials. We call their work opera[115] and them operarii,[116] and they are given work and wages. [Second,] those who own the materials and therefore their goods in entirely (we call their work opus[117] and the worker opifices[118]), and they are assured the selling of their work.

The contract contains 1) the necessity that the state grant benefits to each individual to dedicate himself to processing. (above: separation from the fundamental estate of the producer.). The state has to permit everyone what he should live from, because only he can oversee whether he could live from it.[119] (145) 2) the guarantee to which it is obligated.[120]

This [view can be] expressed simply. This [view] is opposed to the common views and leads to conclusions that are even more opposed. The sales of the factory owner are [claimed to be] of no concern to us, since he can see to it how he will get rid of his products. He did not ask us when he made his products. — [But,] first of all, this is not true in most cases. You have supported factories, and done so foolishly. Then if it were so, should you have suffered the cost? Nothing may be done without your permission. But then are the people among you like the wild forest birds whose doings are of no concern to anyone, but who are therefore outside the law?[121] The life of every citizen is guaranteed, and hence the manner in which he earns it stands under the guaranteeing power. *Citizens*: that's the crux of it; there are amongst you *wild ones* who are not even citizens. But within a state no one bearing a human face can live without being a citizen, without causing the highest disorder contrary to right. If it does not violate [the state's] right, then it violates that of the citizens. [237]

It[122] is always our assumption here that the whole of mankind forms a state, that the processing worker can expect sustenance and exchange from nowhere else but from his farming fellow citizens, because elsewhere the land is not cultivated. This assumption is necessary for the pure doctrine of right. We will see how the relationship may be changed by the participation of several states in the exchange of manufactured articles for products. The absolute obligation, however, (146) of each specific state to guarantee its fellow citizens in exchange for their work, that life and the portion of leisure owed to him does not change thereby and does not disappear. In no way does the guarantee devolve into a blind balance of trade (that as long as wares are just there, buyers will be found and whenever there are buyers, wares will be found) as they thought of it in the past, however much reason and experience contradict it.

Thus [this is] in general the relationship of the *productive* estate to the *processing* estate.

It follows that the most highly diverse processing of the mass of products, conceived as a whole, is then once again divided into specialized branches of processing, into subordinate estates of that one fundamental estate: according to differences in material (laborers in gold, silver, wool, and linen), according to the relationship of the [type of] *skill*, and so forth. Overall, it is divided according to the same principle by which the first division was undertaken: to gain leisure for everyone while reaching the same sum of labor and according to the same rules. The more productive the yield in leisure and savings in power, the better the division. — The state is obligated to make the best division, but not obligated to know that best division. It takes its cue from its own cognition [at the time]. [Sometimes it goes by] what just works.

1) In no class should there be more members than the entire farming estate and the other fabricating classes require. It goes without saying that every individual is assured [the right to] sell to other citizens. But the sales cannot be larger than the *needs* of everyone: hence the selling is only (147) assured according to this measure. Thus only according to this measure can workers be hired in each branch.

Just as no one may devote himself to art in general, so too no one may devote himself to a particular art without informing the state and without its permission.

2) Just as the entire processing estate is always closed, so too is each particular class (guild) necessarily closed. (No increasing in an unconditional or arbitrary sense without calculation and permission from the state). [238]

Their relationship [is accordingly] the following: all citizens enter into the contract under the guarantee of the state: you provide this work to us, each of you according to the share belonging to you, well and competently. We, on the other hand, take it from you in exchange for the appropriate equivalent.

But is this work competent? [There must be a] *test* administered by the state, the guild and the civil servants commissioned for this. The guild however will maintain the old abuses and will of course resist the progress of the arts. — Hence [it is necessary for the state] to give the commission to these other [officials].

[The Commercial Estate]

As a result of the division of the entirety of labor, through which leisure should be gained, a new burden has emerged for the entire citizenry. That which each person needs is distributed among the producers and the various types of artisans. Each has only what he himself cultivates, or locates, or fabricates. But after the division, this is only a small component of all our needs. (The complete civil service [for example] has nothing at all.) Hence each may look around on the surface of the state to see whether he might become whole, find an equivalent, and so forth. (148)

Brought up by this: a third estate must be established that provides for exchange. More strictly, the concept is: an estate, in which, for each person, the entire product of the work of the state in all its parts is expertly united again. A unification of the distribution created by the division of the branches of labor. [This is] the commercial estate.

Application of the already familiar concepts to it.

1) The breadth of the estate is set by the breadth of necessary trade. The more the specialization of the extraction of production, the greater the treatment of the raw materials, then the larger the breadth of the estate of artisans, and the wider the distribution, that much greater the commercial estate. The more modest the former, the smaller the latter. It also goes without saying that the estate of the producers must live off the commercial estate, since the commercial estate lives off the products. Calculation by the state is therefore necessary: without the state's permission, no one may dedicate himself to this estate.

2) Trade is its exclusive property. It has a right to attend to it exclusively. All who sell must be bound to sell to it, and all who buy must buy from it. Thus there exists here a reciprocal obligation. The commercial estate must buy and sell at any time.

But this exclusive right to trade is conditioned by the fundamental law of time saving. Where this end is not present, its mediating link disappears, and the builder or producer himself can trade. The commercial estate is not to complain about this, because it is not employed in this part of the exchange. [239] It is not at all included in its calculation: it would reach beyond the circle of its rights if it made a claim to this. — But from this it follows that a law must determine exactly (149) to what extent the trade should be provided by the first possessor or through the intermediary of the merchant. — The basic principle is this: time saving, in large and small, and [thereby] gaining power.

You claim that trade in grains and in victuals generally should be undertaken by the farmer on his own, so that it would be quite inexpensive. [You would do this] because you do not value the farmer's time.[123] — Otherwise [you would see that] there are losses everywhere when something that can be undertaken by one is undertaken by many, and if what is accomplished in a short time is undertaken over a long time. — This may serve the end of certain producers, gold- and silverworkers.

3) The merchant must be able to live from his trade. Therefore, he has to sell for more than he buys for, [which determines the] price value.[124] The share of

everything that is due to him remains in his hands, for his use. How the price is to be determined requires a deeper investigation into the value of all things.

4) So, in sum and overall. It is clear that trade can be divided, partially according to its wares, partially according to its locations.

This division must follow the fundamental principle of the knowledge available about it, through the law of the state, which must guarantee for everyone and must be responsible for the many [members] of each class. Here too assessment is necessary.

The second: in every area in which a merchant can sustain himself with certain goods, there should be one. (Because everyone has the right to acquire the goods he needs as much as the situation of the whole permits.) [This means that the state ought] not cram all trade into the large cities.

So the state must have certain trade laws that determine the universal right about this matter: as (150) a necessary component of civil law about mine and thine.

[Fundamental Measure of the Value of All Things][125]

*In a trade, everyone has to maintain his property.* What does that [mean]? The task thus involves: to find a fundamental measure of the value of all things!

1) Today we only want to introduce and to prepare. [I hope] you remember these principles, so that after the holiday[126] we can build the rest on it.

2) This is for many the most confusing of all investigations because they lack [an understanding of] what is simple. I hope to have provided you with it and recommend abstaining from further thoughts and ideas. We will touch on everything step by step. — Everyone talks of price increases and saving money without realizing that [in doing so] they assumed a basic price that is not expensive or cheap. These are *reciprocal concepts*. And also, finally, the eternal bias of money disturbs all healthy insight into these matters. Are the goods expensive or the money cheap? What is the actual standard? The value, which remains absolute. They [say]: money. But that is outrageous. All these investigations have to be undertaken without consideration of money. Money is nothing in itself. It is only the empty reflex and the sign of the value in all such relationships.

One might posit the following condition of things as the standard, one in which everyone who works would be able to live off of his work, so long as he works. In this condition, the *price* (151) *and value* of work, or of the product that was laid down, would be life during the time of manufacture. — If he can live, he thus has the price. Only when he has to die has it been denied to him.

The value of work thus is: the life for that time, which is required for its manufacture.

Kant.[127]

In this order, 1) *everyone* without exception must always work, because each individual only has a single human life; 2) everyone must work *all the time.* Whoever rests here eats no longer.

I will not hold back here. Such a condition is not possible because in it there would be no reproduction, no passing on to children, of the sick and the weak — no state [is possible] because those who govern could not be carried on. Let us name the essential at the start: in such a condition, human life itself would have no value, determination, or validity or independent being at all. Because it constantly dissolves into itself. [241] It does so to preserve itself. But why should it preserve itself? Then it is said: to preserve itself, which is obviously circular.[128] (152)

Hence it cannot be this way: life that merely preserves itself through labor must gain freedom beyond work, to express itself independently. Furthermore, life has no reason to be, nor does the living [have reason] to give themselves to the state. In the state it has to be thus, and the latter is the condition of the state.

But how it has to be otherwise: everyone must be able to live from intermittent work. If everyone works for some amount of time, for example half a year, with the effort assumed as the shared standard for effort, the product of this labor [provides for] their life necessities not just for this half year, but for the whole one. They earn through half a year of labor a living for the whole year, therefore [earning] half a year of leisure.

This sum of leisure must first be given to the state for the foremost and most necessary of life's demands, which the state meets: the security of all. This has two consequences: first, civil servants themselves do not work (for the immediate preservation of the material life — they surely do work for the preservation of legal and spiritual life.) Hence that which fell to them in the initial result, that of labor for everyone's preservation, the others must divide amongst themselves. If one assumes in this case that an additional quarter year of work falls to each, this quarter year would be the tax due to the state and this would be completely equally distributed. Now a quarter year of rest remains for everyone.

Now, what is the reward for everyone's work? Answer: *life*, in two respects. In part, that life be preserved, and in part that it be able to move freely (from work to leisure). This reward is earned through the work of everyone and is their guaranteed property: they all have the same legal claim to it. The same share in life is therefore the property of each individual. (153)

Because the leisure that everyone rightfully earns can be viewed concretely as the ability to live without work, we can posit the reward of all work in the ability to live.[129] The value of working for a determinate time is that of a determinate time of life, quite correctly according to the Kantian formula:[130] but not the *same* [time], because then life itself would be assessed no value, but [only] a longer [time]. In the case presented, 3 timeshares of work are worth four shares of life, and thus the value of pure life is ¼ of that of time. Therefore in this state, 3 hours of work, understood according to the standard provided, [242] are worth 4 hours of life. The fact that they are worth this is each person's property, absolutely guaranteed by the state. And if they are not worth this for him, then his property has been taken. This is thus the fundamental price of all things: the first factor [of this price is], how much time did the processing and acquisition of the thing cost according to the standard assumed? The second factor [is], how much time of the ability to live does this time provide in this situation of the state? From these factors one may determine the result.

Whence the surplus? It is the gain of the *pure rational life*, of the understanding, in its advantageous application to labor. The unwise application of power can hardly feed the human being. The understanding wins out. [It does so] by making other powers *subservient* to it.

1) First, the land: here, [the understanding] can put the entire organizing *force of nature* into service. Including the animals. This land works and enables one human power to produce the livelihood of several, who can therefore divide the work and take turns working. — His *life*, his *product* [are increased], because this is cheap. The land yielded the surplus, serving the rational and reasonable life that knows how to command it intelligently. To whom should this surplus belong? To that person to whom the land belongs. This is how the (154) ostensible landowners thought. But the land actually belongs to no one, but rather to reason and freedom, which have united into a state here, to assert their right. So the organizing force of nature belongs to *everyone*, and has to be distributed equally among everyone, not to the *farmer* alone, because cultivation of the land has been granted to him only under the condition that he throw his surplus into the common stock. [So too there are] many other sources of this surplus. — They constitute national wealth, or state wealth.

[The Value of Work and the Products of Work. The National Wealth and the Share in It][131]

Setting aside the details, the main sections once again. Property contract. What property actually means: freedom — leisure, through work. From this is derived the value of one's labor. This should be secured for everyone by the state. — The value of each product of labor = livelihood in this particular state, rendered for as much time as the labor time that was expended on this product. In the *particular* state, the value or price is therefore determined by the state, that is, by [243] the national wealth of the state, evaluated according to the time of rest that is earned through work. — It can be different in many states. It should be noted that we consider right only in one state and that all human beings who we take into consideration are [considered] as citizens of this one. Every exit from the unity of the state would destroy a reliable standard (155) of value. It is due to this that these investigations are usually so uncertain and meandering. For example, [if] this ratio is three quarters — so in this state, 3 hours of labor constitute 4 hours of livelihood. And a work product of 3 hours is worth the livelihood of 4.

*Remark.* On the value of the product of labor. Only the labor, the deliberate human work on it, may be factored in, which, assuming a certain basic standard of effort, can only be measured in time. Of course [we mean here] all work. For example, in the case of manufacturers, [we must take into account] not just the work of the manufacturer, but also the work gaining the materials, which the manufacturer has to transform after all. Where there are years of training, and training costs, these too [are to be] distributed over the work time, to be calculated [as] an average. As much human labor [as is necessary for a product] (the first factor), is how much it is worth in this state. Only the labor [is taken into account], not the favors of nature, such as the location of the state. This after all yields the surplus and is applied to all in the same manner. This is the standard whereby the state orders the relationships of the farmer, the laborer in material, and in trade.

This standard is simpler for the citizens in relation to one another. The deserved gain of rest is, as a consequence of the establishment of the state, attached to each work product in the same way, and it is transferred without loss from every owner to another. All our work has the same absolute value. We therefore measure according to relative value. However you work for me is how long I work for you. 3 hours of my work are worth 3 hours of yours. In both cases, the life possibilities resulting [from this labor] are 4 hours. Thus, an hour of each is worth the hour of all others without exception. (156)

All work for all. Each should be able to get the value of his work in the work of any other that he requires, because only in this way is his property secured. In this way in particular, the disadvantage of the required division of the branches of labor is cancelled.

Which measures should the state take to guarantee this exchange without diminishing the value?

To begin with: the absolute value of labor's products in a state *produces* itself; because it is based on the national wealth, which produces itself (which [244] the state should support, but cannot enforce), the state can only *find* and declare the value.

Solution. Some product of labor is to be fixed as the enduring standard of all value, and the value of all other products of labor should be related back to it. It must be that this product of labor is food, and in particular the most universal and ordinary food, for example, a quantum of grain (a bushel), because life possibilities is the ideal standard of all value of labor. (It is clear that this quantum for the basic measure of all value, e.g. the bushel, itself has to be preserved unchanged.) One has to accept a [certain] time [in which] this value is fixed, even if it is just in thought. During this time, it must be found that the basic measure, e.g. the bushel of grain, really must be worth that, its value determined by the national wealth rather than arbitrarily. The bushel of grain feeds a single human being for a certain length of time. Let us posit 4 timeshares: these are in the given state *worth* 3 equal timeshares of labor. It must cost this much and no more, but also no less work for the farmer. If it costs him more, he did not receive his property. If it costs him less, the other working estates did not receive theirs. One of the two must work for the leisure of the other without gaining the same leisure. (157)

Thus it must cost him a particular amount of his time; obviously after subtracting the tax that is due to the state, which everywhere is the first thing the citizen has to deliver. (It will become clear that in such a state the taxes can only be taken directly from the farmers, and solely in this way do we find the means of having every citizen without exception carry the burden of the state in the same manner.) It is clear that the state should collect exactly as much taxes as it requires for its end. Further, that it know what it requires and what it actually takes. From this it follows that, at every moment, it is able to have the overview as to which time[share] of life sustenance a specific labor time yields, initially to the farmer, as the basic estate, inasmuch as it always knows the three factors: the entire agricultural production in the state's territory, how much it takes from this sum as a tax, and the number of farming citizens.[132]

The natural price[133] of all other labor products, and other foods and products can be *found* and fixed according to this basic standard. [245] What is earned in the territory for the state through labor has to be estimated in its value in grain, for example, in a quart[134] [of grain], not in pennies. It costs a certain part of a bushel, a quart, or a certain number of quarts. [It is also possible to estimate based on] a pound of meat, the wages of labor on a waistcoat, because according to the usual standard, the cattle owner or the tailor has expended precisely as much time as the grain farmer.

This is shown more clearly in the following.

Divide the number of inhabitants of a state into 400 equal parts. Then, given the assumed yield of the land, the agricultural work of ¾ of a year will have to produce 400 annual shares of food. (158)

Further, assume that of these 400 parts, 100 are civil servants and 100 are artisans. Thus, 200 remain left over for farming. Out of the 400 shares, which are generated and which remain in their hands, these farmers retain 200 for their own preservation, 100 they give to the civil servants without any apparent recompense. Until this point, no actual exchange has occurred. But continue. For these 400 shares, all products of artisanal work ordered in this state through the law, which the artisans must have labored on with an effort of about three-quarters of a year, are to be exchanged, and must be exchanged, because the class of artisans is to receive food for its work as a matter of right. Because there are 100 artisans, one-hundredth of their entire product is worth one year's share of food, and the other way around, no more and no less. Should the one-hundredth be worth more, the artisan would gain leisure at the expense of the farmers. In the opposite case, the farmers [would gain] at the expense of the artisan, and always the property of one of the two would be diminished.

Divide the annual share of food into equal parts, e.g. bushels, and these in turn into their parts. Thus, [divide as well] the portions of the artisan's annual work, as for example the textiles of the clothmaker, [divide these] into equal parts, e.g. yards. Thus it will be found that the labor of the clothmaker [that went into] a yard of cloth is worth a certain number of quarts of grain, and that the farmer must pay out neither more nor less, lest injustice be done to either of them.

How should this fourth 100 get into the hands of the artisans? First of all, the civil servants should not merely eat. They too have a claim to their due portion of the products of artisanal work. They can only obtain this from the artisan commensurate with the requisite portion of food, which they can only gain from the hands of the farmer and without recompense. (159) He would furthermore have to give them this medium of exchange as a tax. [246]

Whatever then remains in this manner of the fourth 100 is theirs to exchange. It goes without saying that no single artisan lives on food alone, but also needs the other products of artisanal work, and that therefore not just his life but also the life of all who work for him have to be compensated.

This can be shown more clearly in the external change in value, because the inner [value] remains. Assume that the wealth of the country increases, partially through the higher productivity of agriculture, partially through the expansion of artisanal work. Thereby, more hands will be removed from farming and could be dedicated to artisanal work, and even that part [who remain farmers] will produce more than would have been produced previously in the same amount of time. But the sum of their labor is not worth more than the shares of livelihood that they are due. Furthermore, a bushel of grain remains what it was, partially [with regard to] external [exchange], partially [with regard to] internal [exchange]. But because more products of the artisanal industry can be had for the same portion of grain, these products become cheaper, reduced in price by *as much as what is right* based on the division [of labor and estates]. Does the farmer now have a part of the commonwealth? Does his grain actually retain the same price? No, it gets more expensive, for he receives more goods [in exchange] for it. Both are thus comparatively more *expensive*, that is, they possess more value, notwithstanding that neither of them gains an advantage [over the other].

As the wealth in a state increases, so too does the wealth of all individuals rise in such an institution of exchange. Everyone works less and receives for their work more of the other's work, because nature, transformed by rationality and the understanding, is also at work for everyone. (160)

This is the place to undertake in a simple way the proof promised yesterday that in the same constitution, although only the farmer pays direct taxes, all citizens nonetheless pay them indirectly just the same. The tax is actually a subtraction from the surplus of the common labor, and because the surplus is distributed equally according to the order of reciprocal value, the subtraction is equally distributed as well, that is, everyone receives less of his share. The sum of the products is always worth the *remainder* of the sustenance after the farmers' own consumption, and then that of the civil servants. If the civil servants took no taxes, the products would still be worth that along with what they take, which, however, they would immediately have to share with the agricultural estate for the sake of justice — as is clear in our example, instead of being worth *100*, the products would now be worth the *200* remaining shares. [247] But 50 of these must remain for the farmer, who would have to work less (for now, this is easiest to assume). In short, for the manufacturer,[135] that which is worth 200 would be worth 300, and for the farmer, who now would not have to work as much, his labor would be worth more by the same amount. They shared equal parts of the tax that was set aside; they now share the reduction in equal parts, and this with the strictest precision, in which the general equality of the increase in rest is the basic measure of calculation. Thus, [this is asked of] the farmer and the manufacturer. The civil servant pays no taxes: he only takes less for his person and supports himself with his share. If the wealth of the state were to increase, then he would without a doubt also have to take a share in it for his person. His salary would be calculated to increase based on his share of it, and so taxes would be increased, which is indeed very possible given the rising prosperity of everyone. They can all (161) give more and yet still keep more, because nature gives more.

In a state in which everyone is guaranteed the value of their labor, and primary sustenance is taken as the basic measurement, it cannot just happen to be this way; in fact, it *must* be this way. Because primary sustenance is precisely the *basic measure*, the nation's wealth has to be calculated according to it, and hence the deduction has to be made from it, because tax is a deduction from the yield of the national wealth that is simply not distributed. This is the simplest manner in which to regard all this and to orient oneself in every way on this. — The perspectives that our ordinary states take on it (to let everyone together pay taxes, to hide them in an excise [tax], also to let the taxes be given to the civil servants) that are quite incomprehensible from such a standpoint, nonetheless have solid ground in a source, which we will touch on further below.

Result: the state will find and declare the prices of all products of labor that have been produced in its territory and entered into commerce, and at any moment, each will be able to have the desired good for *this* price in exchange for the equivalent of any kind he holds in his hands.

How should it secure this? There remains no means other than that it takes on commerce itself, that it makes itself [into] the third estate described above, the commercial estate. Furthermore, there is [the need for] supervision, [as there are] countless opportunities for embezzlement. [For the state to] do it itself thus means that the merchants are civil servants who buy on behalf of the state everything that is offered to them without exception at the set price and also sell in this manner, on behalf of the state, in exchange for a salary. (The price calculations are very simple: at every moment the conversion[136] and the inventory have to be overseen). [248]

The state raises and calculates this salary as a tax. (162) This way, everyone cedes the appropriate trade gains.

How to necessitate someone to sell? We do not have to fear that the manufacturer will not want to sell once his goods are finished, because in this we should expect that the product of his labor will get cheaper, not more expensive. It would get more expensive only through a reduction in wealth, and *cheaper* through an increase in wealth, usually every year, since the harvest, considered the basic factor, can be used for an overall calculation. For the manufacturer, therefore [the price] *now* is always the best price. Concerning the farmers, we could fear this, because their goods conversely become externally more expensive for the same reason. It is to be expected that he can trade his bushel of grain for more products in subsequent years, since it is to be expected that wealth will increase, thus raising his interest in the harvest.

*Remedy* [for trade imbalances]: every year, the state demands payment of an appropriate share of taxes in grain and natural [products]. The state must have silos — and well-stocked silos — for reasons that will only become properly clear further below. If the farmer does not want to sell for a whole year, then of course the manufacturer would not get his food. But the state sells from its silos [in this case]. These [silos] will of course become emptier than the state would like, whereas the manufactured goods, whose sale to the farmer had been expected, remains with the manufacturer. After the next harvest, therefore, the state will order the deliveries of natural products as taxes to be increased by as much as this forced sale extracted from its silos. And so the farmer is surely forced to sacrifice the grain now that it should have given up before, at the right price. But as far as the manufactured goods are concerned that lie with the state's merchants, even if the situation requires that their price be lowered, the state will not do this until what could have been sold earlier (163) is sold and equilibrium has thereby been established. The farmer's stash will be depleted in the meantime and if he does not want to go without clothes, for example, he will finally have to buy something. And in this way, it is finally in the state's power to enforce not just prices, but also the required circulations of wares.

Further, I spoke of deliveries of natural products for taxes. I therefore assume another sign of value. Furthermore, undoubtedly it is not my opinion that all commerce will occur through the mere exchange of goods. (It is for this reason that all goods of the country are transported to the merchant [249] to be stored with him for a while.) *However*, first and foremost, there should be a sign of the *basic value*, and therefore of all value, e.g. of the bushel of grain, in its divisions, its quarts, and so forth: *money*.

[Basic Requirements of Money]

Requirements: 1) the sign itself must have as little value as possible in relation to the *material*, otherwise the state loses something. It also is, in virtue of being a sign, a *commodity* — the hopeless [state of affairs] this creates [is covered] further below. 2) The preparation of the money should not cost much. These costs would have to be covered by a *tax*. 3) If at all possible, it should not be liable to counterfeiting. (The counterfeiter usurps the work of others without [providing] equivalent [value in return]. This disadvantages the national wealth, [such that it is] partially a crime, partially universally damaging. But the temptation is great.) So leather, *paper* would be options. (164)

Here, in our [current] constitutions, one gets scared, and rightfully, for the reasons [explained] further below. In the constitution sketched here this all disappears.

Thus such a sign means, e.g. a bushel of grain. And at any moment, an actual bushel of grain is to be exchanged for this sign. If nowhere else, then most certainly at the closest state storehouse. And then, the farmer, if he wants to get rid of his grain, will surely have to sell it for this [sign].

Precisely *for this*, one must be able to receive *everything else* that is considered equivalent in the state's price index or in a fractional part of it, at every moment at this [price] through the storehouses managed by civil servants.

— The state, which orders the payment of taxes in bushels of grain, takes this sign as the surplus of what it did not order for payment as deliveries of natural products. With this, the state salaries all its civil servants and undertakes all its tasks. There can be no question as to whether the sign is valid, since the state as the biggest businessman with the highest demand accepts it and accepts it exclusively and nothing else. (For this is the tacit precondition.) The advantage of the sign is indeed that it always applies for everything, that everyone accepts it.

Those[137] who are accustomed to ordinary conditions say: "The state will perpetually multiply such money, as it is not bound in any way with regard to this. Afterwards it will lose its value!" They are correct, under ordinary conditions: [250] states have done this and therefore the fear when one speaks about paper money. That explains the reputation of France.[138] I would like to discuss [this]. (165)

About all of this I say: the state that we have been describing up to now cannot will this. [If it did so,] it would thereby destroy itself, renounce order and draw all the misery of disorder around its neck.

How much should money be [worth?] A sign = that which it signifies. As many bushels of grain as the harvest usually yields, this many bushels of grain, and neither more nor less, should be in circulation. Not less, since strictly speaking the bushel that is not represented [in the count] cannot be purchased. But this could be covered by quick circulation: a paper does not represent [anything] from one harvest to another. *Not more*: the sign above it represents nothing: whether it be the state or an individual who makes it, he is a forger.[139] — This sign for a bushel of grain can now be circulated and converted into meat and fish, into peas and cabbage, into cloth and linen, into brick and chalk, and so on, until it has completed its circuit through all appearances of value, has completed the metamorphoses required of it. — If the state spends more, the last owner finds [himself with] no sustenance, [and so] he must perish. He may have been cheated out of a year (166) of work: that would be the gain for the state. But then he, this individual, also perishes: this is the loss, the injustice. What should lead the state, which has the ability to increase taxes, to such an embarrassment: to stick it to the individual, when it can take from the whole without doing damage?

In this proof, it is the explicit assumption, and in the prior investigation it has been the tacit assumption that at least the initial food be consumed from one harvest to the next. While the state's storehouse [251] has been discussed, this was done only in passing, without the proper deduction of its rightful necessity. Yet this cannot be, because the acquisition and multiplication of national wealth would thereby be made impossible. (Notwithstanding that this is the case, the proof we offered is nonetheless not overturned by this, but rather, as will become clear, strengthened.) This is only possible through *capital*.[140] Hence we will conclude our doctrine of the securing of property with exchange through an investigation of capital. This doctrine gains clarity if we preface it with a theory of metal money and of its influence on the state's power over property, and hence over the property of all.

[On Metal Money][141]

All metal has through its permanence and malleability a great inner value as a good. This is true in (167) the highest degree with the precious metals, gold and silver. Nearly indestructible, as they are not damaged by air and they form a chemical process with it — hence their purity, as well as their divisibility and pliability.

Further, to obtain them costs time and power: however, it must have been worth it until now, as no state would continue to mine if it would be more advantageous to obtain the gold and silver it needs through commerce with its labor products, which it could produce with the same time and power. The external value of these metals is therefore worth at least the livelihood of those who obtain the metal, as is the case with everyone else's labor. But there is a very big and significant difference here, that the demands of every other labor to the human race can be fulfilled at the time when the product disappears: the food is eaten, the good is used up. The demands of those who obtain these metals, however, are almost irredeemable, because metal endures. — Whether it simply lies there, always when it circulates, or if it is transformed into various shapes, it never diminishes very visibly. The owner [252] of precious metals therefore has a nearly non-dischargeable debt demand to humankind and transfers such demand to every person to whom he transfers those metals. The owner may change, but the debt demand remains.

The durability and the divisibility into any number of parts without a loss turn these precious metals into world *money* without state action, through a naturally occurring agreement. — At the same time, it has an internal value contrary to the first attribute we ascribed to money, it is a good, and a very valuable good. It would thus very well be suitable as the basic measure of the value of all things, even if not also as money, as we have discussed with grain. (And this is in fact the felicitous practice of commerce at large. Transcribing, (168) ascribing in their books, according to the letter — that is their medium of exchange, [and] the metal is represented in it. This is also the prevalent opinion of statesmen about paper money. There must be exchange banks[142] where one can always exchange it for metal money. Just as in my theory, where the grain storehouses and product inventories of the state are the ongoing and continually utilized exchange banks.) So what does the precious metal lack for it to be an appropriate basic measure of value? The same thing that makes it possible to be money and that diminishes the display of it as such: the universal need for it as a good. — Everyone needs bread, but we can go our whole lives without gold and silver cutlery, and only a few get to possess them. It is almost never needed directly as a good and its use as one remains in the furthest removed background for everybody. It is sought after as money, as a means of exchange for all kinds of needs, notwithstanding the fact that it acquires and maintains its validity as money only through its background value as a good. It is not an appropriate standard, because its value as a good does not impose itself, and hence it can be a sign. We do not miss the lack of material. At the same time, it is not an appropriate sign because it conversely gets its validity as a sign from its internal value. It is a half-thing[143] that constantly fluctuates between its meaning as a sign and its internal value.[144]

This is shown by its success. 1) Its true value is quite undetermined and unknown. The actual value and price of life is leisure. (Hence it was important for me to find such an absolute value, which is missing in these investigations.) How much leisure — that is, what timespan (169) of livelihood — I will obtain for an ounce of gold or silver, I will never know, and the state cannot guarantee anything about this to me, because on this point everyone is as dependent as the lowest of the state's citizens, as we will shortly see. [253] Actually, in this system, all gold and silver present in the world is worth the same as all the present goods in it, and a fractional part of the former is equivalent to a fractional part of the latter. But there is no human knowledge which oversees both facts and could draw that conclusion. (Whereas by contrast, the given state always oversees both factors.) In this uncertainty, both those with money and those with goods fear coming up short. Everyone hopes for a better price for himself, and so the trade will never come to a conclusion other than through the need for one of the two. Those with money must have goods and those with goods must have money. (Hence trading: this is a polite survey of the needs of the other.) Thus, need creates the sale and thereby the price. But this need is quite changeable, therefore the prices are changeable. Here there is *force*, but certainly not right. Everyone wants to sell what he has for as much as possible, but buy what the other has for as little as possible. If it works, it works. Furthermore, we cannot hold this against anyone, since no one knows whether he is doing an injustice, because something completely unknown, money, eternally enters into the trade. So, everyone will act in this way, even those with the most honest of dispositions: if the other could not give it, he would not give it.

Needs change = when the value of money increases, more goods enter the market. Now if it decreases, if the value of goods increases, then everyone hides their money (except for food, which is subject to coercive right. If its transport is achieved, however, then import occurs with free commerce). Then, the owner of goods is in need and the situation changes once again. (170)

What is a penny[145] worth [according to this]? The need of those with goods at the time at which I spend it. Who wins in this and forces the prices? Who makes them? Whoever knows how to calculate the need of others. All commercial speculations, what are they but anticipations of such need, and even the artificial creation of need through purchasing.

Just as[146] the value of all money is undetermined, so too is the value of the state's money. Just as the individual gets poorer or richer in relation to everyone's coffers, so too does the state. Thus, 1) It must first come upon the money and look out for where it can find it. 2) Next, it must take as much as it can, because it nonetheless never really knows what it acquires and now has. 3) Thus, it must have the opposite *financial principle* as the one established by us. With mine, it should acquire what it needs — but it may never use the subsistence and all the leisure of its citizens. Otherwise, it would not be a state at all, and would not come to be a state in this condition of humanity. — In that case, it takes whatever it can get, because it never knows what it has, therefore also does not know what it needs and it has to make sure. [254]

Another consideration: why is there a call for the freedom of trade, the freedom of commerce? What will be the result? The market is overlooked, and money thus becomes more expensive. Advantage for those with money. Almost all proposals point beyond that. An advantage for the buyer? One should say, of course, because the proposals come from those with money, with a salary, and the like. But this is only for a time. About a generation sacrificed: then *comes the repayment*. "Well, then, we will not be alive anymore."[147] (171)

"d. 15x.[148] [This] provides savings for the public [through freedom of trade]." Who is this public? The clothmakers have surely been forgotten; these perish. — And what about their earnings? The baker of the village, the brewer, the butcher might well pay dearly for their cloth. I do not see that anyone will win in all this other than Mr. Civil Servant[149] who does not have anything to sell. This man takes advantage of his salary more [than others]. This man, in short the salaried and those with capital — would be the public, in the end.

Of course, a state can be in a position where it must pass such laws. The value of money attracts the money-holding foreigner. Where goods are cheap, the foreigner goes, and there he can use his money, since his money is more expensive. But the state wants to have money, because it can only assert its value and its power among other states in this way. Thus — there is a need if it legislates such laws with perhaps better insight. Thus all this need emerges from a single source, metal money.

In summary, in every state in which precious metals, the world money, that arose independently outside of the state, is [accepted as] money, citizens' property is secured only in the crudest sense, in that physical objects cannot be taken from them with violence. Their true property, however, the value of their labor, depends on blind chance, an incomprehensible force of nature, and they remain in the state of nature regarding this. (172) But the human being possesses reason in order to destroy the blind force of nature, to bring all his relations under a clear concept, and to organize [everything] with reflective art in accordance with this concept. This clear concept and this reflective art, in regard to securing property, are described above, and the [securing of property] is the state's responsibility. This is our opinion. And here it should well be said: this task has not been completed until now, and so far it cannot be completed. Here the actually existing [255] states are not to blame. We ourselves are of this opinion. But we should not conclude that because blind chance has ruled until now it should rule in perpetuity, while reason [should] never [rule]. And reason also should not speak and spread the clear concept, without which the reflective art could never have come about.

Given all that this political economy can do in a state that carries metal money, the mere doctrine of right has nothing to accomplish, because such a state is not a fully formed one, but maintains, by means of world money, the old state of nature, from which all attempts of the states began, as an ingredient remaining in itself. This is true even though it appears that such a political economy would be the true means for bringing about the true state, and in such a way, and [even though] the doctrine of political economy, in its place, has great merit.[150] (173) So did metal money have no advantage at all, and do the captivated admirers of its effects invoke advantages without any grounds? This will become apparent when we speak of capital.

First of all, it is always assumed in our theory that from the beginning of the year to the harvest, the civil servant, farmer, and manufacturer can live decently and with certainty during the time when the latter two toil the field and manufacture their goods, until the next exchange, which starts with the harvest. [256] [But] where do they get their livelihood during this time? From an earlier harvest and [from] there from an earlier one, and so forth. Since we must have a beginning, where does this end? So, the beginning of the state and the ordering of the industries we described assumes that everyone can live until the next (174) collection, have reserves for the year. Originally, food for everyone, whose emergence in the state we cannot inquire into, is thus the absolute condition for the emergence of a state. This is its foundational capital.[151] — The absolute capital.

But further, the wealth of the nation (the surplus of its labor products over labor [time]) should be gained and continually increased. How does this happen? By subjecting nature to the immediate ends of the human being through labors that are not *immediately*, but only *indirectly*, purposeful. So it happens that there is obviously a loss of power to [achieve] the subsequent end of preservation in the future, [but] it should of course be replaced at a future time at a profit. [For example,] if swamps are to be dried out and made arable, during the time in which this happens, nothing useful for the human being is created by this power. If machines are created that are devised and tried out in possibly fruitless attempts in which the task is not solved, then the intention is not to sell this machine, and no buyer could be found for it [anyway].

How is this interruption of present business in favor of future and distant [business] conceivable and possible? Clearly such preparatory labor required *working hands*, but these [in turn] required *available* food, which have *to be set aside* from immediate purchasing. If food is available, workers will be found. But this food must exist. It is the second part of the capital required for the end of the state, as a surplus over calculated consumption.

We will cover later what follows from this part of the end of the state for our end of the state. Now [we will see] how this end has been obtained until now, as a digression. (175)

The only known and surest means to entice human beings to labor for ends not present or not even comprehended by them was *metal money*. In it, a creative power was *set down* to rule *as far over all* human powers and the exercise of these powers as the sum of money would reach, and *this* at every moment. — Now only through such preparatory work [257] are all improvements of the human condition achieved and will be achieved in this manner in the future. Here is money's true, honest win for the human race.[152] Furthermore, I want to add this: only through this progress does human labor gain dignity and decency and becomes human, expressing the absolute creative power[153] of the concept. If after a generation, human beings still cultivate the land in the same way, still manufacture in the same way as before, then their actual humanity in these activities has stood still, and they can better be compared to a colony of beavers or bees than be recognized as human beings. — The incentive to this higher happiness and this higher dignity appeared to be the *inert money*, which contains in itself all the national well-being and national wealth to be earned. (Hence the cash capital resting in a nation's hands is frequently called the national wealth.) Where the coffers grow a little richer, we can see everyone rush in and hurry to acquire as large a share as possible for themselves. Thus [developed] the admiration and deification that even intelligent and thinking human beings evince for money, as the founder of all industry and, if you want, as that power which first turned the human being from the Promethean clay form into this richly inventive and (176) refined being. For them, money is simply the heavenly flame of Prometheus. *In being so captivated, they have overlooked only one consideration* that is nonetheless obvious. Money does *not immediately* and *unconditionally* cause these wonders, but indirectly and under certain conditions. When they come running, it is not about the money, which they cannot eat, and initially about the food that they intend to buy with it. If these are not there, they will surely perish despite your money, and they will not make vain efforts even to work for this money that cannot nourish them.

Hence it *remains the case* that not *money* but the *livelihood* it achieves is the incentive for activity, and for all improvements in the trades. Hence also, national capital is not the *money* that is in the hands of the nation, but the *food* that is present on their ground. Money is merely the means to tie the preservation of food that still [258] must be present to a particular [kind of] work. With my money, I put myself in possession of the food that is for sale, if I am the only one who wants to spend money. Whoever must buy, he must [also] help work, for example, at drying out swamps. Without that, he does not have anything to live on, and so he will surely be (177) forced to work at it, as ridiculous and perverse as the whole undertaking might seem to him.[154]

[On Interest]

At[155] this point, where it is the most comprehensible, [let us consider] as a mere side note the doctrine of interest. The person who undertakes the kind of labor that has no immediate utility, but that promises great gains in the future, has no money to preserve himself and the other forces he wants to set in motion for it, until then. And he turns to someone who has money; he does not need for any undertaking. (Money sits idly in his coffers). 1) This is the case, or something similar, with the student, the apprentice (if it is simply to eat, one can gift [money to them], but not lend [it]). When he has carried out this undertaking, what will be the result? He will work at a very great advantage, producing with disproportionately little labor many labor products in the state, because he has subjected a natural power to himself. Will he keep this profit in the state? Initially, without a doubt (what could happen in the future, we will see in due time), (178) since the state sets its prices according to the usual standard. Such a person therefore profits through 3 hours of work about 8 hours of life, when he should have gained only 4. Subjugated nature labors for these [additional] 4 hours. With which power [does it do so]? With the result of both invention and money. The money *labors*. Of course, [it labors] only as a result of the life of the invention where it was put to use. In the coffers it was dead. Both [invention and money] [259] work in tandem. Would it be unfair if those with money said: "what my money earns is mine. I thought we would divide the 4 hours that were gained — [you may] keep 2 for your invention, and 2 goes to me for my money." I do not think so. These 2 hours therefore would be his interest. Thus 1) Interest is rightful; 2) No standard for it can be prescribed. — But I want to advise the capitalists not to set capital in stone and expect an eternal interest, but rather to demand it back again at the right time. Otherwise, it will dissolve into nothing and he will lose both capital and interest for the following reason.

The improvement thereby gained will be imitated by others, and thereby the matter will become easier and easier until it finally becomes the common, basic measure. Then the matter will enter into the basic calculation of prices and nothing will be gained anymore. The private capital and the private and exclusive wealth earned thereby is absorbed into the common [wealth]. This is how it should be. (For example, arable soil that has been created from swamps has to be exempt for some time from taxation, thereby substituting capital for the invention and the utilized labor. This has an average that can be roughly calculated and which can be set higher or lower, according to the standard of whether there is more or less undeveloped land in the periphery of the state's territory, to encourage development. Only through this (179) freedom from taxation will he earn a higher price for his labor. After this time has expired, it joins the general condition of all lives — and this can happen all at once or gradually — and then the profit is equal again. — The same goes for artisanal labor with machines. As already described above, but gradually the invention spreads. It must be prohibited to conduct this art other than with machines, and those who do not make use of them will dwindle and die off. From this point on, the prices are to be determined by this calculation.)

In summary, through labor private capital becomes private wealth and after a fixed time it shifts into the public wealth, when the private capital may complete the same cycle in a different place.

Thus for the state, there arises the obligation to have food and goods in surplus, and to have taken into account labor that is not immediately useful for these food and goods, because without them the monetary capital[156] has no value. This means not distributing everything according to the most common and lasting condition of things. The surplus serves this end with its storehouses, which arise from the common natural tax (from the common tax, minus the correction mentioned earlier). This surplus in turn has no value if there are not workers who consume it in exchange for whatever work is imposed on them. Hence [260] in the state's calculation, it has to set aside some human hands from farming and from the other regular trades for this free and incalculable provision. So the matter is very simple. Besides those two, the farmer and the artisan, there is a third: workers that free invention can direct, and food [must be provided] for them.

Given this, the following cases are possible. First case: there is no private person here who needs them. Hence the state itself employs them in public construction and other (180) institutions, canals, bridges, streets, and the like, things that belong very much to the public wealth. As a matter of right, such things are only undertaken by the state, which can best oversee from its standpoint the order of their relative necessity. — It follows from this that these free laborers stand in fact in service to the state, which already must provide work for them and, in exchange for this labor, the appropriate livelihood (since it has not allocated work to them in the general distribution), [all as part of] the state's general obligations toward them as citizens. — A private business can now be found, undertaken with the metal money of a capitalist. One turns to the state; the state gives a salary to the desired workers, pays them the usual [rate], or what is desired, and, in exchange, the state receives the metal money that was designated for this. In this manner it gradually comes [into possession] of the precious metal. The determination of value will be found further below. (Do not forget this, as it is an important point. As I absorb metal money into the state, I must be curing it from its defect of indeterminacy). In time, the entrepreneur pays the capital back in national currency,[157] the only thing he brings in for his work, also the interest, which goes without saying. The debtor can take [national currency] without concern, because it has the same use. If he insists on it, he can also exchange metal money with the state. This is in conformity with strict justice and occurs without disadvantage to the state.

Second case: a private entrepreneur without metal money but with national currency can be found. [This case] is quite similar. Someone can earn capital in the national currency through the already described private advantages, greater industriousness, skill, and so forth, for his retirement. This has to be permitted to him, and public justice requires that his money be valid. The process with the national currency is entirely that of metal money, also in regards to possible interest. The (181) only thing that has to be considered here is if the national currency disappears and goes out of circulation. It must always be represented and it is also always represented in the state's storehouses. Except, it could be necessary to replace it by printing new money, if it does not reenter circulation in ways such as the one indicated earlier. In all events, the state, [261] which itself certainly conducts trade and thus oversees it, can oversee this necessity and must force [this exchange]. — The money that disappeared is to be counted now as not existing at all. But as soon as it returns, the state withdraws the replacement [printed money] and the principle abides: every piece of money in circulation is represented through its bushel of grain.

The third case: there are entrepreneurs and inventors, but no private capital, neither in national currency nor in coin. The capital of the state immediately steps in. The state can provide credit to the entrepreneur under the same conditions as in an *audit*. The capitalist can also issue an audit and if he does not do it, he does not act very prudently. You risk your capital, but the state can risk much less. We can hardly speak about interest. For what reason should the state charge interest? But we can speak about the shortening of the time period for exclusive profits.[158] This will be agreed to in a contract that is well-deliberated by both sides.

There is a certain sequence in the improvement of farming and artisanal industries. First, we need enough pure and healthy grain before cultivating the exotic herbs and fine vegetables. At first, we need solid and durable cloth before producing fine silks interwoven with gold and silver, and so much more that may be mentioned here and that everyone, in his knowledge, could easily add. The state must have this as a key consideration in facilitating such enterprises: it will reject projects that are not part of the order of the day and facilitate those that the order of the day makes quite popular. (182)

The state cannot just directly intervene. Public works are left to it, [while] the farmland and the trades are divided up. (Domains are a remnant of the conditions from where the state was an alliance among landowners and the regent was the largest estate owner). It can maintain agricultural schools which both present the normal economy and also have delegations for the mechanical arts that accomplish the same things in that field, and carry out its projects through them. — Furthermore, it can also lead, especially from these departments, and with their light, through instruction, through requirements,[159] through set prices — everything according to the basic rule mentioned. Without this, it would produce greenhouse fruits, and we get the most precious pineapple, but not a healthy potato; ornate garments, but not a sturdy shirt.

In summary, everything rests on the fact that the state 1) is to have a concept of human welfare, of the means to increase it, and of the right sequence of these means, and 2) that it is to know the actual and true condition of its nation, and its viewpoint exactly in every regard, at any moment. The former, as a priori, can be undoubtedly expected from the state. The second follows from the constitution, as the state oversees the condition of agriculture and the trades and their results, business, [262] which it continually manages and oversees. From time to time, it is necessary that the state give a precise accounting of business, since it has to set the prices of goods. The state by no means lacks power in directing national industry, since no hand in the state will move to this purpose without the state's will, and it always has a sum of powers at its free disposal that it can also increase or decrease at will. One need not fear an army of officials and their work and bookkeeping that would bring this about: (183) it would depend on the calculation to show that in this regard, too, it would save money as compared to ordinary states. For any work that moves forward labor that occurs in order and sequence and does not take any steps back, delivers a completely different product in a shorter time than labor that is always stagnating, that always has to take back and change things until in the end, one does not know what remains.

[Foreign trade]

Now[160] on trade with foreign countries (since until now we have only discussed trade among citizens of the same state. Because of the ongoing focus on metal money, we have put this off.)

Principles for judging foreign trade.

1) Whatever one does not need is too expensive even [when it is] for free.[161] No goods from foreign countries should come into circulation, and the state at this stage of culture should not profit and should not have profited off these. Not entirely independent of the fact that the goods are abroad, these goods would have to enter the calculation of necessary trades. Everything has to develop according to nature: to need something, because one hears that others have this need, is a desire contrary to reason — showing off, vanity, in short, nothing respectable. 2) This foreign trade, traced back, must be an *exchange*. What else but trade with money? If a country were to become void of [paper] money, [then] metal money is to be distributed on average, unless it has earnings from mining above the usual average, then it would indeed [involve] an exchange trade, [namely,] product trade. 3) According to our standard, the goods that both sides receive in an exchange (184) thereby must become cheaper through it, i.e. must be produced with less effort and time in the selling state than in the buying one. [263] This must be the case for both sides. (It can occur through advantages in climate, through a nation's special facility with a certain artisanal skill,[162] and the like.) It goes without saying, even with the additional transport deducted [from the total in the exchange]. Also, another disadvantage is deducted (more about this soon), the idea of this trade, the concern for it, has to justify and pay for itself.

Conclusion: For both trading states, this lesser effort in labor means national wealth. They now exchange this lesser effort in labor for a higher national wealth with a profit for both, since this is their trade profit: an increase in *global wealth* through trade among states and the distribution of national wealth.[163] [This increase occurs] according to the same law by which national wealth arose from the division of branches of labor in the state. — This is a highly significant idea *under this condition* (otherwise an empty thought), hence the excitement. I, it is said, am an enemy of the idea. You have heard this. 4) These requisite calculations — as to whether [goods are] necessary, whether [they are] cheaper — can only be made by the state, which oversees the whole. Therefore foreign trade falls fully on it, as does all trade. — It goes without saying that the state is not in need of profits, and so it has to set prices to conform to its other calculations. 5) However, with foreign trade, the trading state and its nation become dependent on a power that they do not control in a dual sense: partially in procuring the goods that it accepts, partially in selling those goods that it gives in return. What if trade stops? One measure against the former would be: have every good with a price be produced domestically, [while] prohibiting any branch of labor relevant to the system coming in. a) For determining the true price. b) if the situation occurs, then this branch can simply be staffed more robustly. c) the higher prices can be avoided (185) in two ways. Either that the state, selling at around the price in the foreign country, purchases them [at a] more expensive [price] than it sells for. (A remnant of the old way of thinking: here the state loses. Is our state really so poor and beleaguered, on the brink of bankruptcy? I think it will retrieve it in taxes.) Or, what I would find better, it sells it for the price that would be obtained domestically. [This must happen] if smuggling is to be prevented, as I believe [it should be]. Then, in case of foreign trade halting, this requires no change in price — "[But what if] it receives trade gains?" What should it do with them? It will not therefore probably allow taxation decreases, and in this way, an increase in national wealth will have occurred through trade. [In case of] *stagnating sales*, it has to let these branches diminish by this amount. Initially even by a little *more*, in order to transfer the surplus to those who after all cannot do anything else. I hope the goods keep. [Made] of this nature of course, they remain [the same] if they entered into foreign trade. [264] — If something should be lost in all this, the trade profits must shoulder the risk. This was the remaining matter [we] owed above.

[Now we can treat] the standard for the value of money. — Whenever one of the trading states manages the money, then [this applies]: whatever the goods that I receive in the exchange are worth in money, the goods of my country are also worth, and since these goods have a determinate relation to the bushel of grain, and this bushel a determinate relation to all other goods, [that means] the bushel of grain is worth this much money. This price is the completely correct one. I can permit all my citizens who have money to conduct foreign trade themselves if I sell for the price [set by] the foreign country. What can be bought abroad at an advantage, I sell at just the same rate. What cannot be bought [abroad] at an advantage, they will not seek there, but rather will [buy], I think, domestically, (186) where it is cheaper. Thereby metal money is condemned to lying around uselessly, and becoming something for the state to exchange, at just the right price, and is eventually added to the state's domestic currency. — It now becomes a good and we have gained an excellent good either for the private man, who can pay for it and who is calculating for the perpetuation of his family or also for the eternal state, which makes this calculation with more reliability.[164]

*Labor* is only relative property, and everyone has a claim to this matter. The form it takes is his. *Freedom* from work, and the representative of that freedom is money: *absolute* property. *Freedom* [is] the *freedom* to use, like in the *book*.

[Fichte reads here from FNR, pp. 206–9, Section 19-F] (187–90)

How to indicate property. Through use. Through the household. (Nothing else). No inspection, accounting, or the like. "More freedom from the *state*, and reciprocity." — Of course, "brought about" by ability, here simply the standard. What is *rightfully* in the house. But this is assumed. That is what is common. Only now have we returned to the ground of the ordinary doctrine of right.[165]

[Fichte reads here from FNR, pp. 210–217, Sections 19-G, H, I] (191–200)

Every[166] personal attack is a violation of right and is punishable. (How [punishment occurs] does not belong [265] here just yet). *Self-defense*.[167] 1) Making myself the judge, which I have given up by entering into the state, self-defense is therefore completely forbidden. The will of right lies with the state. — 2) Only where the state *cannot* [act], there is no state, and we enter into the sphere of the state of nature. Where the state cannot [act], it thus hands over the right to self-defense. (201)

1) Designated property. Here there is no [right to self-defense].

[Fichte reads here from FNR, p. 217, Section 19-I, "The right of self-defense . . . who the transgressor was."]

2) *Undesignated property*. Here there is *indeed* [a right to self-defense].

[Fichte reads here from FNR, p. 217, Section 19-I, "By contrast, everyone has the right . . . *irreplaceable property*."]

Also against the objections that the possible damage would not stand in relation to the value of what is defended. — I must be answerable for this [self-defense] before my conscience. What the state would have to do [in this case is to] fight to the death (like it does in (202) war), and this never changes. It is its obligation. This is why the state exists: right, mere right, is its morality. Since I am taking sides now, how can it reprimand me? With it I am secure. Of course, right is not my morality: that I will have to arrange for myself. (I am not saying that it is better to beat the other to death so as not to lose a penny.) That is, [the right] to begin the fight. That is the crux of the issue. Meanwhile, moral assessment is difficult.[168]

Crying for help and witnessing [crimes].

To what extent is there an obligation of right to come help? We must prove this more precisely. The duty to protect is the original duty of *the individual*. The duty is only transferred to the state where it can [protect]. Just as each person is once again placed in their natural right to self-defense, so everyone is again placed under the natural duty of the defense [of others].

[Fichte reads here from FNR, pp. 218–20, Section 19-I, "This also implies . . . sole protector and judge"] (203–5)

So once again, the principle: the state should be able to [help], thus the individual may, if need be, *separate the conflicting parties*, but must not judge or punish [them].

And now this material, often badly ordered (due to a certain malleability of legislation and admixture of the moral point of view, and the influence of religion) should be clear as far as legislation is concerned. — Why undertake a lengthy proof here? To take up the status causae.[169] The very necessity of an investigation provides the factual proof to the state that its supervision and protective power were not at hand. Why make self-defense more difficult by prohibiting weapons and their use where one clearly cannot protect others? Pity for criminals is *often* greater than for rightful individuals due to the jurists' excessive sense of equality.[170]

Right of necessity and [the discussion from FNR] mentioned above.[171]

[Fichte reads here from FNR, pp. 220–22, Section 19-I, "There is yet another kind of self-defense . . . made more secure"] (206–8)

Nature or God must decide and they decide in light of the fact that I am the stronger, the more determined. The abandonment of deliberation, the entry of the powerful urge for self-preservation is the law of nature here.

Which investigation is to be recommended here? How do I know? God may talk, but here he speaks through nature.[172] [266]

[On Acquisition and Dereliction]
Acquisition:
[Fichte reads here from FNR, pp. 222–26, Section 19-K] (209–14)
[The first case. —] 1) Wealth increases in terms of value, or 2) it changes its nature, from relative to absolute, and vice versa.[173]

The second case. — Supervision of the state. Conditions: 1) that the earner of relative property needs it. 2) that the buyer is able to live. [Thus there might be] *privilege* [in conflict] against *privilege*. In this case, it would only involve a declaration to the state.

The first case: *gifting* and inheritance (a third does not exist). Gifting involves [swapping] relative for absolute property (surrendering a right): from hand to hand, the state has nothing to do with it.[174] — (215)

[Inheritance]
Inheritance.[175] — Here too our discussion can only be about absolute property: that is, money and the value of labor products in money, machines, and similar inventory. No privileges are to be bequeathed. They *are to be* awarded by the state after death.

*Absolute* property would become res nullius[176] in the event of death. It would go not to the prius occupanti,[177] but rather to everyone in parts, and would therefore fall to the state [to distribute]. Every other tax is canceled. — This would be the rule. But certain obligations and presumed intentions can reside in the absolute property of the deceased. The deceased leaves behind some without care and provision, children who have not yet left the family, a widow. — In short, a family remains, even if its head has been lost.

Tell me, if this wealth had not been left [to the family], what would the state have to do? Maintain them. Now it can absorb the wealth and maintain them. If it were to allow both, they amount to the same. — Inheritance ab intestato.[178] The basic principle: *the family is the owner*. As long as this family does not die off, the wealth is not without a master. That is thoroughly fair and appropriate. Who could know how contributions were made to this family's wealth through work, caretaking, and sacrifice? Who should involve themselves with these matters, concerning absolute property? The husband [for] the wife, the wife for the husband, and both for the children. [267]

From this follows, however, a right of supervision, of supreme guardianship.[179] The state has this right in any case. So it is no different with the mother. For is she any less (216) the head of the family? Only she must be secured with more protection against brutal acts, if this is required.

This right protects the family and its total property. Thus, the right does not encompass distant relatives, strictly speaking not even the already established adult children. (But there is a right to preserve the old family relations).

Inheritance through a will is different. It is a gift [made] in the event of death. How can the will of the dead bind the living? Answer. The living *wish* it for their own sake. (as a matter of fact, they required the use of their wealth in their lifetime, which is a kind of usury with absolute property rights). They wish for the universal belief in the validity of wills, therefore [for] a law. — They have no absolute right to cite it, because all right extinguishes with death. (not in the way that they can cite *other* laws. Take note: the matter is *unique*). But the state also has no reason to deny it. The universal wish makes the law here. A rightful relation can exist without this setup. The only thing absolutely necessary is only what lies in the rightful relationship. [Anything else is] arbitrary.

Limitation on the bequest. Those left behind must be able to live as appropriate to their station, and the children must be raised and educated. — The intestate inheritance (which is indeed the possibility of life) goes beyond the will and limits it. — The Romans distributed [property among the family]; that is not the right principle. — One can bequeath just beyond a certain valuation of assets according to one's status, but nothing besides that.

[The Second Part of the Doctrine of Right: Civil Contract] (217)
[The first section] Criminal Law

In the depths, there is clarity. And we have already laid the foundation for this clarity. Here too there are peculiar confusions, conflicts, misunderstandings. These questions are especially raised because they hover over the surface, without question and answer emerging from a systematic overview of the whole. At that point, the mistakes disappear by themselves.

1) The individual only has rights in the state by recognizing the rights of everyone else.

2) The recognition must be an active one (not just through words) and for all time, independent of the changeability of his will.

3) This unchangeability of the individual's will is only achieved when it can display the impossibility [of changing its will], as though it follows a natural law that his will might ever be other than the required rightful one.

The task is to find and actually realize such a principle that abolishes all wills contrary to right, and only by establishing such a power does everyone provide everyone else the guarantee that alone grants them rights.

4) Such a power would be a power that coerces the wills that are, in themselves, free.

If they want to have rights, everyone should have a certain determinate will for this [power] and for this content [of rights].

This will cannot be expected of their freedom, because this will is the condition under which one can grant them rights. Hence, they have to prove this will is in place before one gives them rights. To prove (218) means to show the impossibility that they will ever have another [will]. They therefore must place themselves under a principle of such an impossibility, i.e., under a principle from which the [rightful] will follows necessarily, a principle which enforces the [rightful] will.

NB. The subjection to this coercive law — [and] previously the establishment of it — is the condition of rights and of a citizenry. — What we have proved before in general, [we have] now demonstrated in particular, as applying to coercive power. The state is such a [power].

Just as a body falls according to the law of nature, so too shall the rightful will occur according to this law, [such that] the will contrary to right [shall] therefore be surely impossible.[180]

At least, this is the task. [269]

Now how can *the will, as such, be coerced*? How is a coercive institution possible?

1) We are not talking here about the internal will, about the wishes of the human being, at all, but rather about the will which erupts into action. Neither a positive nor negative violation of right occurs through internal wishes, but only through a will erupting into action. (219) Thus, only in this light are we speaking here of the will as a principle of action or inaction. Completely excluding that of inaction.

2) The will of the human being generally aims for *well-being*, freedom of the person, the noble one as much as the ignoble — in this they are the same. The ignoble merely wants to have it [its freedom] and feel it and enjoy it, [whereas] the noble one wants to use it. This will cannot and should not be coerced, changed, or modified. All its *active* willing and efficacy have the intention of bringing about the means of this freedom. If such a nature — in which this purpose could be achieved only through the use of the rightful means and through rightful action, but the opposite through actions contrary to right — could be constructed around the human being through art, then the will would be coerced through itself.

*Moral world.*

Our task[181] is thus: to coerce a certain will, i.e. to bring it about as the result of law that commands with natural necessity. ([That is,] to make it into a product of nature).

1) A certain will: thus not internal willing and wishing that may remain in the heart, but rather the external will, which erupts into action. One does not will an unjust action, and if that does not happen, then one is content, even when one hates coercion from the bottom of one's heart. Wish what you will, lust after injustice; but we want to prevent your decision [to perform] injustice. Willing in this respect = deciding.

(We must, it is demanded, be able to love the law. It should be worthy of love, worthy of desire. Then it would never come to be a law. — Love of the law arises solely from insight and moral refinement. (220) But for these [individuals] the law is destroyed, as we will see further below. The usual path of human beings, however, is that they only come to morality through legality, that the wildness has to be tamed, licentiousness[182] has to be broken. Thus, their will first has to be tamed by the law. This is the preparation. But the law, where it is effective, is necessarily hated, because the desire that it [270] assumes is contrary to it. The law can only arouse fear, not invite love. They would like to sin, but do not want the punishment.

Wherever the law — its content — is loved, there is no more law, according to form. [That] we must be able to love the law therefore means there should be no law at all, which, properly understood, is also true and appropriate.

2) All human beings necessarily will an end by their nature: their freedom in the sense described above, that is, the capacity to set their ends for themselves with freedom (arbitrary will): for the noble person makes use of it, [while] the ignoble one enjoys it and takes pleasure in their gratifying sensation; that is why it is called *well-being*.[183] This is the substantive end of everyone. A. If only nature were arranged such that this end could only be achieved through the individual deciding [to do] that which is rightful in every instance, while every decision [to do] what is contrary to right would lead by itself to the opposite result of the deprivation of freedom and well-being, then the accidental will, under the command of such a nature, would be forced by itself and its permanent property to decide only what is rightful. Since it cannot help but will the well-being of the person, then it must will what is right as it otherwise cannot attain well-being. The task is solved: the rightful will is coerced.

Some desired and regretted the absence of such an organization of the world[184] in general under the government of a just God, in which virtue necessarily has good consequences for happiness, (221) vice has the opposite; the former yields rewards, the latter punishment. I hope that the current presentation has already shown why such a demand is quite mistaken. For then morality would have to be enforced and there would be no love for it, but only a love for the reward, no hate for vice, but only for punishment. (And those who desire such an organization of the world also defiantly assume this and they despair at the possibility of morality without such an organization. And they themselves do not even will morality for its own sake, but only for its good consequences.) All notions that set out to feign such an organization of the world if not in the present one, then in the future world, and to enforce morality through a visible reward for it, thus set out to fully eradicate it at its roots from the minds of human beings.

Thus in regard to the entire organization of the world. — The civil order of the state has however nothing to do with inner morality, with the love of the good for its own sake, but only with the legality[185] of external actions. Hence it [271] can arrange an institution, in which only rightful actions produce their ends, the ones contrary to right securely lead to the opposite, and the decision is coerced. The institution can put up with the citizens despising this order, in that they would all rather steal than labor for the end they actually have, if that could somehow be accomplished.

3) Grasp the disposition well, that the establishment of such an order of things assumes. The rightful will is tied to the desired consequence, and the

consequence that is hated is bound to the will contrary to right, since it is assumed that (222) everyone will do what is right only for the sake of the good consequence, [and will] forego what is contrary to right only because of the bad consequence, but not do it for love of right and hatred of injustice for their own sake without any consequences. — Whom does this institution have an effect on? Whom does it *coerce*? Of course, only that person who really relates to things in this way. But, whoever wills what is right for its own sake without any regard for the consequences, how could he be forced by a law that only speaks of consequences? Even before the introduction of the law, he already wills what the law wills not because the law wills it but because he does. As far as the introduction of the law goes, and its coercive force, that can only be relevant for the will tempted to violations of this law, one that would surely decide to [act on] them [the violations of the law] if the law did not arouse its fear.

Hence it is clear that the law does not exist here for such an individual, as he wills nothing else even without any laws, and does nothing else, other than what the law also wills. — If the law were to command something unjust, he would nevertheless not do it and quietly submit to the consequences. He is above the law and gives the law to the law itself, through the morality of his will, the supreme model[186] for all laws.

Hence it is clear that such an institution absolutely does not intrude on morality. (The hatred of laws that arises everywhere from the weak administration of them, has expressed itself in this statement: "We want to do it freely, not just following the law. Nobody should command us to do it!" Very well. Does the law stand in the way of your free performance if the law does not move you, but only your insight and love? Then you are indeed doing it freely. — "Yes, but one should also be able to recognize [our freedom of action], as it might look as though we are scared of the law." So, are you this vain? This is a bad (223) testament of your freedom and morality. — "So that it does not appear as such, we do it precisely because it is prohibited; if one left it up to our good will, oh how moral and appropriate we would be. The law is for us precisely a way to provoke us into transgression." You might be under an unsullied administration of the laws, if we cannot [272] rid you of your desire to defy the law. Morality can and also should never show itself in external legality, because morality resides above all civil law and cannot be commanded. This morality shows itself in other expressions. And only just when one has passed through the sphere of civil right. It is therefore annoying to hear those people speaking of morality and freedom, from whose mere, natural being external discipline and rightfulness do not arise simply of themselves and who show themselves still to be bonded servants of the meanest crudeness.)

4) Now it goes without saying that the state cannot bring about a different natural order from the one that simply does exist. Thus, the state must itself be the free and reflective force of nature that secures the end of the just will, (this has already happened through the entire constitution as we have also described it until now, and what may be lacking in this regard will be shown) and that links punishment, the opposite of the intended end, to the unjust [will]).

5) This natural order should coerce the will. But the will is coerced through representations: hence the *representation* of this order is the actual element that joins it to the will. — Several things follow from this: 1) The representation must simply be true, otherwise it does not move [the will]. The threatened bad consequences must inevitably occur as a result of the action contrary to right, like a body falling with a push. Whoever sins must know that the punishment (224) will not fail to come. It has to be as certain to him as the sin itself. If it is not this certain to him, he will risk it. Whoever learns about sinning always also must learn about the punishment. Thus, a) the state must securely identify each transgression and its perpetrator. b) [the state must] punish the transgression in the threatened manner without any exception or leniency. Then, the *representation* of the matter is inevitably what should coerce the will. The state must therefore announce the order that it has made, the law that it has given itself, and say what consequence each transgression will have. The announcement of this is its criminal law.

6) For what end is all this? So that the right will is compelled and the unjust will is repressed through the introduction of the order achieved in the state.[187] So is punishment ever the end in matters of right? Absolutely not. The intention is that the threat of punishment annihilates the will contrary to right everywhere.[188] Can it come to punishment? Oh yes. Why? To secure the reality of the representation, and for no other reason. Thus, punishment always enters the organization of the state in a mediated [way]. *Representations* about this should not be punishment. *Making itself rightful*, the justification, this one certainty. This rightful force is its criminal law.

*The criminal law*[189] is foremost: the punishment itself is only for the sake of the law. This is precisely how they spoke of God.

*The right to punish*[190] is the means of the means: punishment only for the sake of the *form of the law,* so that the representation be true and persist. This, the punishment, enters the organization of the state not at all necessarily, but only arbitrarily. [273] (225)

The[191] deduction of punishment and of the right to punish is not at all immediate. — Only criminal law is immediate. This is the condition of rightfulness in general — and we infer from it. Everyone should recognize the impossibility. The punishment is only *for the law's sake*. Therein lies the error, that they would want it to be *immediately*. This is a violation of right,[192] not willing to enforce the legal condition by means of punishment, in order to justify punishment as a fact. From this arises for them an absolute right of punishment.[193] — a) Every action must be able to be regarded as given by freedom as such (correct) — that is, [as] giving the norm and the pattern for the actions of all free beings. Everyone who acts in a specific manner would have to admit this. b) He could not therefore *prove* that it would be contrary to reason if he were similarly treated. — Quite correct. The proof applies, but does not prove anything more than that *it* cannot prove the injustice. It is then not about this. Who has the right to do right to him, if that is his right? — Not *he*, but then how do

I? How do *others*? Between that which is *not prohibited* and that which is *positively permitted* there still is a large gap.[194]

Mandate: that is a heuristic principle, and in this regard also an arbitrary one. Who calls on you to make this into a constitutive principle? Did someone erect such a law just for that? As universally applicable *to* everyone, too. If anyone steals, therefore everyone has to steal? You are not saying this either. — But, then, is it applicable to *him*? Well, he could not *reject it on the grounds of reason*.[195] But who has the positive reason to use it? (226)

Now is it any different *with us*? If the same actually unrightful result is tied to his unrightful will, is he not being treated according to the law that he would have established, if he believed himself to be acting in a universally applicable way? Correct, but not because of that, [but rather] because this is the means for destroying his unjust will. — They converge [on their outcomes]. This convergence, too, has its good reasons.

In case there is consensus here, then [the question about] where the positive right originates has been answered and the missing reason [is found]: through the mediation of criminal law, as by reciprocal guarantee. There is no leap here, just as there is none previously.

1) From theology. Where God's justice is understood as the essential, inseparable property of God. According to these concepts he is a nature that treats everyone equally according to the law that he establishes. Anthropomorphic concepts of God, based on such a ruler who treats everyone according to the law that he establishes. That would attribute to God a type of justice that is itself something so subordinate even among human beings. [274]

2) Punishment is *precaution*. That one does not act [in this way]. Certainly, but where does the right to this come from?

3) Is it for his *improvement*? I hope it is for *civil* improvement (because if it is for moral improvement, for love of right, it does not suffice.) That is why the law was already there. But from where do we get the right to improve him?

4) Is it to make an example for others? Quite so, amongst other things. But where does this right to make an example out of someone for others come from? I give thanks for this representative dignity. (227)

5) As to the content of criminal law: 1) the *antithesis* of the end should be the consequence for the unjust will. Condition: a material success is intended, *profit*. No: precisely this should be lost.

Punishment of equal loss. The smaller the punishment would be, the more secure the opposing incentive.

[Punishment means] whatever you want to take from another, you take from yourself. To expel the will.

2) The same applies to injury done without this material will, due to *carelessness*. Whatever harm you do to the other, you do to *yourself*.[196] Creating for someone the will (the attentiveness) that he should have. As *compensation*: the wretch works off [the injury done] under supervision. [Consider the] difference between dolus and culpa.[197] So, make note of the moral investigation of the incentives that the jurists discuss. (This is very presumptuous, especially when

it is applied in order to make the law for the case.) The law *must fit exactly the temperament* of the person who is tempted. Hence what fits here must be applied. — Thoughtlessness regarding another's goods and coveting them are two different things!

The outcome shows how things stand, and this must be established. [For example,] has someone been ruined? Must he be supervised? (228)

6) The assumption is always that the will wills its fundamental end, happiness, and only errs in choosing the means. Established criminal law is calibrated for such a will as this. [The criminal law's] content is intelligible only to this will.

But now if there is no determined will — which is the first case — and no reflection,[198] the human being acts like a wild incalculable force of nature. Or if the will to violate right, to damage it, is there, positively present and not arising from another desire and as a modification of it, then the law is not effective. Now which law should be applied here?

What does this show? A will that *cannot* be moved *through the coercive law*. [It shows] the impotence of coercion, the absence of civic virtue. Reflection as the formal [quality of the will] and self-love as the material [end], such that the self can be made into the incentive. — All for the self's own sake. The state can well tolerate this, and must even assume it most of the time. Whoever does not have this is also not even a human being. [275]

Thus, in brief, they are incapable of providing the other citizens with security. Their incapacity now shows itself, when we admitted them [as citizens] according to a general average, we erred. — There is only one exception: that of the stubbornly careless, who transgresses only by damaging property. As long as he has [property of his own], he provides security through what he has, as we are only discussing damages and compensation.[199] If he ceases to have [property], then of course he falls under the general rule. — Hence nothing else can follow but their exclusion from the state: their declaration of the loss of *civil right*. The nervus probandi[200] is clear — achieving security, the bond through which all are held together, expires. (229)

7) First of all, this comparison. Strictly speaking, whoever violates right in any part proves that he is not suffused with a rightful will that rules inside of him as a natural law. Thus, he stands to forfeit his rights, since that is the condition [for having rights]. In the first case, for he who actually has the character that offends against right not for right's sake, but rather for the sake of a desire, disregarding the fact that the desire is incidentally contrary to right, a punishment occurs, and an expiation contract[201] regulates it. Once he has suffered his punishment, he is returned his civil rights. In the second case, where there is either no will at all or one that is positively directly contrary to right, such an expiation does not take place, and instead civil rights are lost.[202]

The former is a *civil* criminal law, the latter a capital criminal law.[203] Law counts on [someone having] a will — whoever does not have it or [whoever has] an evil [will] has forfeited their status as a citizen.[204]

8)²⁰⁵ First of all, which cases belong here? 1) Whenever someone who has been punished according to the law of equal loss repeats the same transgression. The criminal law has no effect. At a minimum, there is a lack of will, the criminal is in an affective condition which cannot be moved. — One might say: his punishment must be made more severe! But this would be the course of action only in the case that evading detection is probable. This should not be [done] ahead of time, and I am not discussing such a state. Rather, it must be that the law is calibrated as we have seen, such that what you take from another, you take from yourself, that we can hope for this effect. After all, that is why it was implemented. It can inspire no further trust.²⁰⁶ 2) The case of the formally evil will: violation *for the sake of violation*, partially of property, (This case has a similarity with negligent injury, as was shown in the proof above. How both cases are to be distinguished (230) and determined we will discuss in another suitable place.) partially violation of the person, as in every personal assault. The human person is holy and inviolable; whoever does not [276] honor it, honors no right at all. 3) [The case of a] direct assault on the condition of right as such, through rebellion and high treason. The difference between these two.²⁰⁷

9) Loss of civil rights and expulsion from the state. The punishment of compensation, equal loss, treatment according to the law that has been established can still be connected to it, to the extent that the maintenance of right requires. a) the confiscation of assets follows the expulsion from the state, anyway. He earned the assets in the state, to which he, as he shows now, had no right to belong. From him, [the assets] can be restored. To which modifications this confiscation could be subject, more on that below. b) Physical abuses of others should be punished with the same in public, in front of everyone. Not as the absolute consequence of that law of equal treatment, as of a categorical law, but because in the hands of the law, this should become a tool to eradicate this transgression fully, to tame the greatest rashness and to provide a counterweight to the most evil will, such that at least he does not transgress so far. The human form should (231) become holy and inviolable for the human being. From the human form, all intuitions and all concepts of right emanate. Hence everyone should know that however much this disposition is worth to him in his own person, that is how much it should be worth to him in every other person, because it is not the person, but humanity as such that sanctifies it. That one can atone for physical abuses with a fine or with some time in prison appears to me to express a barbaric contempt for humanity as such. Murder belongs at least among the physical abuses, as the highest level of them, and therefore belongs foremost under this law. Whether it should be punished by death we will only be able to assess further below.

10) Is civil right simply all there is to right, or is there another right beyond that, and, [if so,] in what way? This is a question that cannot easily be answered, and what shall follow the loss of civil right depends on its determination. If it encompasses all of right, that means, banish without mercy, and beat [a criminal] to death like a wild animal if we cannot protect ourselves from him. But if

he retains after losing all civil right a purely human right, then we have to preserve at least this [right] and see what limits it places on our treatment of him.

Of course, there is such a right, since everything human can be a tool of the moral law. This, after all, is what formal freedom is for. If he is now clearly not a tool, he might nevertheless possibly become one. Everyone in whom reason has broken through into clear consciousness recognizes this in everyone else. [277]

Now does this grant a claim of rightful *protection* to him who obviously does not display the apparent condition for this capacity for morality — formal freedom and reflection? Evidently not: the concept of right is a *shared concept, one that is reciprocal among individuals*, based on (232) a fact to which both can appeal, and based on which both must be able to convict one another. The premise of the proof: "I am in the right" is always: I have a free, that is, self-directed, reflective will. The one under consideration [who lacks formal freedom] cannot put forward this premise, hence he can provide no evidence of right before the community or the state. Hence if it depends entirely on right, there is no reason to spare him: it is not contrary to right that the state treat him arbitrarily.

He thus cannot prove [this premise] externally and with objective validity. But the community and the state recognize it in his conscience and know it well. (NB. Thus we posit: the doctrine of right develops the state of reason, valid for all times, in which reason has broken through, not the raw state of reason only possible in earlier times. This examination does not concern us [here].) That condition thus imposes a *duty* on them. Although it is not contrary to right, it is indeed contrary to *duty*. Right, however, can never command something contrary to duty.[208]

Thus, his human right, which he partakes in not through *his right* but through the *duty of everyone else*, is to be preserved. — This means that he can become free and therefore moral. His life is the condition for this, and hence his life is to be preserved. — What is the vocation of his life? To develop reflective *freedom*, civic virtue. Nothing further: and so his life must be limited completely to this condition. He cannot be a *citizen*, but he can be educated into citizenship. (Just like a minor child). He belongs in a house of improvement[209] after the state has carried out the particular punishment that his transgression deserves. That punishment is not for improvement, but to prevent some crime from him and from others. Just (233) as [there is] corporal punishment for physical attacks, so too for murder, corporal punishment, to the house of improvement.

However, capital punishment[210] is never permissible. (I have made an effort in this very contentious matter to be as clear as possible where the investigation has led me to results that contravene ordinary practice.) [278]

The universal consciousness recognizes that one is not permitted under any conditions to kill a human being with foresight and deliberateness for any end whatsoever. Who would think it is permitted to kill the insane,[211] whose recovery is doubted by all experts, or an incurably ill person, to relieve oneself of the efforts to watch over the former and to shorten the pain of the latter, not to mention that no one has hope that those will ever become useful to themselves or to others? We make this exception only for the criminal. Why for him? Because we regard his condition as self-incurred, with freedom, which we cannot see in that of others. Because we expect morality from him. With what truth, more on that later. Because in accordance with the premise that everyone will be treated according to the law that he establishes through his action, we establish an absolute criminal law. Admittedly, right is not against it. Thus, whoever knows nothing higher than right also does not have a positive reason, but only the principal reason, even if that reason is only that he does not know what to do with the criminal, it suffices for him to cast the criminal out, because nothing goes against this. However, whoever has a moral conscience and religion of absolute devotion to the will of God has a duty to the contrary, and the duty is placed upon him to tolerate the criminal in the world until nature, i.e. God, takes him away. — They lack a free will. This is (234) the reason for their expulsion. They are indeed insane, but of a more dangerous kind than those we recognize as such. The latter lose the actual sensible world and the connection of the things in it. The former lose the world of right and the connection of expressions of freedom.[212] This is how one should regard them and treat them.

The correct maxim: one must absolutely treat each person as though he [must be] free and receptive to morality, not forgo this demand for anyone. (In real life one frequently falls short of this [maxim] by ascribing psychological reasons as explanations.) Namely, *so that he may receive morality* (the wise man knows well that he does not [yet] have it). Hence, in life: it cannot be said that I should beat someone to death who lacks freedom in order that he receive freedom. So, right does not go all the way to the death penalty.

The subjective condition of the correct judgment on this matter is: that one perfectly separate morality and legality, and not view the latter as part of the former, but only as its precondition. — Something cannot be [279] right that is thoroughly immoral.[213] In practice it is critical that (235) a people and their government have really elevated themselves above mere legality into the insight into morality. However things may be in practice, in the philosophical schools, the answer to this consists only of reasons.[214]

My interjection. Who should guard the murderer and how? Whoever guards the one who has been declared insane by our doctors. We do not kill for that, and rightly so. Treat him like a dangerous lunatic. (236)

House of improvement: aside from improvement, these houses have the vocation to secure the commonwealth.[215] Thus a secure prison, and no earlier release until one has become convinced of the improvement. What kind of improvement? [Fichte reads here from FNR section 20-IV, pp. 237–38; "Furthermore, this second expiation contract . . . once again about his own security" and pp. 238–39, "The rebel may often be . . . because the state has confidence in them."] (237)

Distinction[216] between a pure violation (not petty theft) out of negligence and out of an evil will. [Fichte reads here from FNR section 20-II, p. 231, "There are two criteria for identifying intentional harm . . . such suspicions about him"] (238)

Constitution: Absolute Grounding of Right in Actuality

No one has rights until he has assured for everyone the safety of their rights, [and so] proven to them a law that commands with mechanistic force, so that they cannot be harmed at all.[217] So far we have only partially applied and subordinated this principle, namely, with regard to the subjection to the law as such, and the subjection [280] to criminal law for safety. — This applies only when the just law is there and administered securely. However, this occurs only through a will that manifests itself in general (in legislation), as well as in each particular case (in the application of the law), and which rests again on two things. 1) that the law actually be applied in all cases, 2) that the correct law, pertaining to this case be applied.

Security is therefore provided only when *such a will*, and necessarily only this will, has been established. *Right*, transformed into a living, infallible will, posits: 1) *knowledge* [of right], 2) positively: infallibly willing what is known — negatively: never not willing [right]. Never willing something different.

(The value of the formula: this is undoubtedly good.)

Now this will is the *supreme rule*,[218] *sovereignty*. No one can have a different will without forfeiting all his rights. This will, which should rule like an all-powerful natural force, must be equipped with a power against which all other power would disappear into nothing.

To erect such a will is clearly *easy and simple*.[219]

2) So now, how should that [will] be brought about? An actual will is only in persons. Thus our task is: to make the will of certain (239) persons into this will and produce [it] as such.

First of all, *certain* persons. The principle of the division of trades already required that one or several persons are concerned with nothing else and are responsible for nothing other than universal right, applying their time and power exclusively for this, having been relieved of all other business.

Government must be *delegated*: thus there is no pure *democracy* here. The will of right must not exist [only] from time to time, but must always live.

3) These persons now have their personal measure of cognition [of right]. But now, who provides the assurance that this cognition would be of absolute right, that they do not err? Even if they did have it, and could have it, they also have their personal will, inclinations, wishes. Who provides the assurance that they will always and without exception subordinate these to the recognized right?

But without this assurance, neither the right of the individual, nor his rightfulness (that he wills the right of all, and is strictly answerable to the whole) is secured. Yet they are nonetheless subject to a will. But it does not depend on that, but rather that this will is right personified, turned into a human being. — Only under this condition is *right grounded*: it amounts to a *constitution* of it. Only under this condition, too, is this representative sovereign. [281] We did not place sovereignty in his personal will, but rather in the will of right that has burst forth in him. Rex eris, si rechte facies.[220]

The personal will of right is to be granted supreme rulership. (I include cognition here.)[221] (240)

4) Two solutions are possible here: to bestow supreme rulership on either the personal will of right, or, if this cannot be attained, that will which most closely approximates it. The best individual should rule. Or, the other way around: to make the personal will that rules into the rightful one, or into that will which most closely approximates it. The ruler should be the best individual.

The investigations so far, also my own earlier ones, have usually approached the task from the second side. We would like to begin there, too.

The means that presents itself first for this would be: his will has to be brought under a coercive law, like the will of every private *person*. The rightful will must be compelled by punishment, which is to be tied to the violation of right by other free intelligences. It is clear that this is not possible. For how does one will to ensure such a second free intelligence, one that then becomes the true highest will? Through a third intelligence, and this through a fourth, and so on infinitely. — To be sure, there will be subordinations, supervision, and responsibility of one before the other in government personnel, but this hierarchical series has to end at some point and we have to come to one will that coerces all the others without itself being able to be coerced, i.e., a will also externally sovereign.

Obviously, then, physical coercion is not to be applied but rather criminal law.

The second way: a moral path through moral motives. 1) negative [motives]: the externally sovereign person or persons must be so positioned that they have no temptation to be unjust. If possible, they must be without personal relationships to the citizens, without relatives, without associates in another sphere — without temptation through self-interest, [achieved] by their having everything and being able to subsist in this way. In addition, their (241) children, relatives [must] be positioned in the same manner. — Such as in hereditary monarchy, which has its advantages over other forms of government here and in the strength of government. 2) positive motives: honor, glory, love of subjects. To [achieve] this, [there should be] publicity in all acts of government. — This is part of the constitution in any case. Because it belongs to the right of each citizen to demand that the rightful will rule and that therefore the publicity that can call for accountability, regardless of any relationships. [282]

This is all good and honorable. But with a heartfelt good opinion that we wish to grant all such hereditary monarchs without exception, who assures us of their insight into what is right? Some say, we want to give them an excellent education. Great, but who educates the educators, and who educates those who elect the educators?

Another[222] rational means of coercion in an artificial constitution, the separation of the legislative, judicial, and executive power (since the French Revolution), is facing criticism, and it belongs among the astonishing events of our time that even thoughtful Germans could utter something like this. If you want to have a state you must have an externally sovereign power that coerces everything and cannot itself be coerced, a first motivating force[223] of political life.

This you likely posit as the executive power (*pouvoir executif*). Now you let a second power, the legislative power, make laws until the end of time. [But] they remain scripta[224] if the executive power does not want to put them into practice, and you cannot coerce it into doing so. Or should the legislative power *coerce it*? In that case, it is no longer merely legislative, but at the same time executive, and what you call the executive power is not a primary power at all, (242) it is without a sovereign will, but is instead subordinated. The legislative power is now sovereign and you have separated nothing. Or assume: the executive power voluntarily accepts the laws of the legislative power, and thus only thereby do they become laws. The executive power is at once the legislative power, and the legislative power is only a law-proposing[225] one, without sovereignty. The sovereign will now *undoubtedly establish* such a council[226] of its own accord. It will even establish the judicial power. This judicial power is subordinated by its nature, as it certainly judges according to a law, and it must remain under supervision and coercion, to see that it judges according to the law. If this is not the case, it is simultaneously the legislative power. So that its judgments do not remain mere scripta, we must also give it the power of execution, directly or indirectly. Now it is the sovereign and we have not divided [the powers].

In sum, the sovereign will must be able to coerce everything without being coerced. It must have, therefore, free discretion within itself about what it wants to enforce. A division of [its powers] is not possible.

This was precisely the sleight of hand[227] of these constitutions, that they wanted to have a sovereignty and also not have it. It should not be in any one individual [283] part, but it should well be in the whole. They just have a different whole than the sum of the parts. According to them, something can be in all of the parts that is not in any one of them, just as according to them life and thought, too, are merely the result of the composition of the whole. One certainly sees from which philosophy such state creations have emerged.

I myself made a proposal in the past for a highly concentrated coercion, to place alongside the positive state power, an absolute veto, an ephorate, (243) which, in the event that it believes the will of right is not ruling, should assume responsibility for revoking all state power through an interdict and for calling the people to judge between itself and the state power.[228] The principles of right that lie at the basis of this are quite correct. The government personnel, however, are answerable to everyone that their will be the will of right and here it would be quite good, then, if this accountability can take place in the world of senses in a court with real proceedings. Furthermore, it is wholly correct that he cannot be their regent whose insight into right is surpassed by that of the ephor or the people. But as far as the practicability, i.e. the enforceability of this coercion is concerned, I must decide against it now upon mature consideration, because 1) who could in turn coerce the ephorate not to start the revolution for any reason even though right has not been violated, and indeed to start it when right has been violated? How many contrary temptations can be conceived? 2) The government, which holds all power in its hands, will doubtlessly make use of this power to oppress the ephorate right from the beginning. Consider the Roman patricians. They beat the people's tribunes to death. Once they can no longer talk, the justifications, the most poisonous accusations will surely be found. 3) Precisely because there is no higher judge proves that the judgment of the people is formally in accordance with right. But how about materially? One can always have more trust in a selection of the wise than in the majority, which came about God knows how.

This was not lost on me back then, either. What I am saying here is acknowledged there, and thereby decided: a people, whose ephorates, as the selection of its best, have so little virtue as to fail to resist those temptations, who are incapable of protecting even them, and who pronounce an incorrect judgment, simply do not deserve a better (244) constitution, and are not capable of a better one. — This is simply the truth of the matter, [284] and what should be universally accepted. The realization of an ephorate, as a part of the constitution, is impracticable, because human beings as a whole are far too bad. By the time they improve as a whole, though, a constitution not in need of an established ephorate will surely have emerged.

Only one consideration escaped all those who found themselves alienated by this idea, [namely,] that by articulating a constitution, it in fact creates itself by itself, without a particular, artificial institution, everywhere there is an educated and self-educating public. Wherever thinking develops, so too does thinking about government and its conduct. A vigilant ephorate: the ephorate should do two things: first of all, warn the regent, and if this does not help, call in the people. The first usually works, only if one does not prohibit the ephorate from talking (and this is quite dangerous), and secretly the government listens and complies. No one dares to remain too far behind the education of the nation, and so government should allow them simply to express themselves in the affairs of state, so that it does not happen to them. If this occurs, then the second follows: the people are called in. As certain proof that such a thing can happen, this has occurred in our age under our own eyes, and the governing personnel were killed over it.[229] But to the extent that we can judge, it also turned out badly for the people, and not by chance, but according to a necessary law. For as long as there are more bad people than good, we can expect with certainty that it is not the counsel of the wise and good but that of the unwise that will win over the majority for itself. The way of calling in the people through the ephorate, that of revolution, is therefore, until a complete reversal occurs within the (245) human race, to be regarded with certainty as inviting one evil instead of another, and commonly an even greater one. — A greater evil [is for instance that] the government's maxims declared by the era will not change, but the regent of a revolutionary nation will firmly establish his power such that it not repeat it.[230] Thus, the only area in which improvement can be expected is progress in education to reason and morality and the quiet effectiveness of the ephorate in this progress.

Thus, viewing the matter from one angle, that the ruler should procure itself the just will, in no way promises security for us. [285]

The second case originally posited remains, that he who has the most just will become the ruler. It is clear that then the government will be the best of all possible governments. Thus, this is the true solution and the former solution must be discarded completely. If only it could be solved by itself, i.e. if the possibility of its realization could be shown.

There is no doubt that in the progress of education men will be produced who are entirely moral and rightful, who will sacrifice everything and [even] life for right, and in whom this morality also breaks through to correct cognition. (The right will enlightens itself.) The first thing is that *they are* [there].

Another thing is how they become *rulers*. 1) Those who are in possession of rule, even if they recognized them, will not surrender their place for them. If they themselves are bad, but also if they are good. For even the best human being, precisely because he is conscious of his honorable intention, but does not grasp the intention of another in such an immediate consciousness, can hardly be moved to place more trust in another than in himself. (246)

2) The masses also will not elect him and appoint him with their power. Because, assuming they would recognize him — but only the good even believe in good people at all, and recognize each other among themselves — but even they do not recognize themselves. And it could occur in a gathering of the best that each, with the most divine purity, nonetheless trusts himself most and therefore — without any self-interest — and from pure love for the good wills himself as ruler. As long as the government is not good, the majority will always be bad, and human affairs are caught here in a circle. Good majorities emerge from good government, and thus, no good government comes from a good majority.[231]

Hence the task of constituting right, which now leads back to the task of making the most just individual of his time and nation into its ruler, cannot be solved through human freedom. It is therefore a task for divine world government. — However, *justice* in the state depends in general on the solution to this problem. This is therefore also a task of divine world government.

At some point, a government will and must come, in which the most just individual among his people is the ruler of them. This government will also find the means to maintain a succession of the best. (This is quite easy.) Until then, governments will be as good as God gives them to us. The only tool in the hands of nations for forcing themselves to progress is progress in understanding and morality. Except, in this historical regard the origin [286] of supreme rulership cannot be inquired into. So we must subject ourselves, not blindly, to be sure, for we should always see clearly and I have tried to convey this insight, but because we see that the resistance interferes with the quiet progress of the times, it only makes evil — i.e. injustice — greater and is therefore immoral. (247) When one argues from strict right, one will always be right that the rulers have no right to rule. For they would only have this right if they could prove that they are right personified,[232] [but] they will always lack much of this proof.[233]

The blind proceed in their blindness and nothing contrary to right is done to them as they do not see what is contrary to right. The wise and virtuous individual, who would be worthy of a better order of things for his person, thereby has the duty laid upon him to labor with all his might to make all others worthy of and receptive to this better order, the only [order] in which he could live together with them. Hence this condition in particular is assigned to him by his duty and one must not will to withdraw from it. If he did live in this better order of things, all would be worthy of it and would be capable [of it], and he would not have this duty, but he most surely would have another one. But the life of the just human being proceeds from his duty for duty's sake and he does not choose his duties. He does not want a different life and therefore every life is right for him.

If we should speak about the police separately.[234] [It] is dealt with there. It does not require a special chapter. (248)

The establishment of right in general, the state as its foundation. Property contract, the contract over state borders.[235] — this is treated adequately.

The individuals are both citizens and families here. That is actually *one thing*, [that] the state must separate in law. In the doctrine of ethics. — Examination, observation, still a higher [perspective] above the state.[236]

The Right of Nations.

¶1   Clear.

¶2   Different states.

¶3   Standing in no relation to right, which they do not know about one another.

¶6   is difficult. — The individual has the right to demand a contract because he is a human being.

Is it equally clear that the other is a *state*? How should it *risk* it? *Non-recognition* yields *war*, this is clear. Thus, I want to posit now *coercive right*. [287]

Who has the right to exist as a *person*?

Can I express this more clearly? *Coercive right* means coercion that the other must *consider right*.

¶9   requires *reflection*. The way is only negative. [Namely,] no one may get too close to any other. (249)

I will probably have to *treat* cosmopolitan right also. It is quite clear. It only stands *negatively* above the laws of the state.

The[237] Right of Nations. *Deduction*.

¶1   [Fichte reads FNR Second appendix, (I) 1, p. 320]

Addition to ¶1 Everyone who lives in a common sphere with others must guarantee them, if he desires [to have] right, the security of their rights, i.e. [he must] enter into a state with them. One enters the common sphere of efficacy through the unity of the concept. The consequence. And so forth.[238]

¶2 [Fichte reads FNR Second appendix, I (2) pp. 320–21] (250)
Addition to ¶2 Several states.[239]
¶3 [Fichte reads FNR Second appendix, I (3) pp. 321]
Addition to ¶3 Clear — separate.[240]
¶4 [Fichte reads FNR Second appendix, I (4), pp. 321–22] (251)

Addition to ¶4 Now the point. *The citizens* come together. They demand with right the unity of the state: *according to the law by which you treat me, I treat you.*

Your state provides guarantees about you to me, my [state provides guarantees] about me to you.

The states together are responsible for the inviolability of the other [states'] citizens by their own.[241]

Corollaries [Fichte reads FNR Second appendix, I (Corollaries), p. 322] (252)

Addition to the Corollaries. 3) a) especially *closed*: it does not lie in the civil contract. The state is as big, because everything else was unknown. b) announced in a law — otherwise the transgressor is *immoral* and *contrary to right*, but not punishable by law. He does not know that someone vouches for the foreigner.

New ¶ — Content: extends only to property right; purely negative, not positive for any kind of performance.

Actually *everyone's own state* is responsible to him for this right. This [state] compensates and supports the other state.

¶5 [Fichte reads FNR Second appendix, I (5) pp. 322–23] (253)

Addition to ¶5 The *guarantee* assumed *as valid*; hence the state recognized as rightful.[242]

¶6 [Fichte reads FNR Second appendix, I (6) p. 323]

Addition to ¶6 *Coercive right* to *recognition*, i.e. to a contract that [is] recognized here.

The person has the right by their nature. The state has no such natural characteristic, but it contains it in itself as a consequence of the civil contract: the rightful, mystical personality. [288]

Of course, the state cannot know whether the other is peaceful enough. From this the right of war follows. (254)

Coercion that the other views as right, i.e. that he himself also wills and must will. Denied recognition turns into war. ([This is] understood [to be] among the preconditions. Russia, France.[243] People take their right for themselves.)[244]

¶7 [Fichte reads FNR Second appendix, I (7), pp. 323–24] (255)
Addition to ¶7 Clear.[245]
¶8 [Fichte reads FNR Second appendix, I (8), pp. 324–25] (256)

Addition to ¶8 Property of the citizens, the *border*, purely *physically*. They do not have *commerce*, and this could not be guaranteed anyway. [It] is in the *civil contract*. Clearly. The contract is purely negative. No one [is to] get too close to the other.[246]

¶9 Eliminate [this section].

¶10   This contract is very simple. The harmed border resident will complain, and the state will demand satisfaction from the offender state. For quick satisfaction, a diplomat. (How wrong the reasoning is there. Then commerce and underselling are implicitly assumed there. [It] is quite false.)

All of this, as far as it goes.

¶11   With limitation. Make note of how very much truncated this is. This also concerns *commerce*.

¶12   War is possible only because recognition was denied, violation of the borders or violation of a direct *trade contract*. Rebuilt relationships later.

¶13   Destruction. No rightful relationship is possible with it *as a state*. A declaration of war denies that the other is a state [at all].

¶14   Only the *armed power*. The others should, after all, become citizens.

*Simple*:[247] prohibit injury to the foreign citizen, punish, compensate, as it accords with the law of *justice*. — This simplicity through the cut-off of reciprocal commerce. This goes very *far*. — The *community* of Europe. — Remark about my printed doctrine of right.[248] [289] (257)

We can include *trade* for this. This is an arbitrary contract, resting on mere agreement, without the higher data[249] of justice. It does not provide a law to prevent taking advantage [in commerce]. Neither are bound to the other's rights. Like citizens, in whose union justice itself should be represented in general. What applies here is whatever the citizen wills to make valid in a solid trade. A relationship put together through a circumstance to be mentioned further below.

How to procure all of this more quickly. Through diplomats. (Emissaries. Distinction between the two classes.)

They represent their self-sufficient, independent state: thus they are not under the coercive power, and have legal immunity.

¶ 10, 11   [Fichte reads FNR Second appendix, I (10–11), pp. 325–26] (258–59)

However, the emissary stands under the *police laws*: for these define the person who can become harmful, harmful in an intentional manner. — For the emissary, not civil law. — Thus, he cannot have this at all, otherwise he would have to submit himself [to the law].[250]

¶ 13   [Fichte reads FNR Second appendix, I (13), p. 327] (260)

Addition to *war*, ¶ 13

Our alliances are such *leagues*[251] and these then provide the opportunity for war. Partially because relationships thereby become more diverse in them, and right certainly becomes more disputed. Partially because of the unjust will, *subjugating [it] preemptively*. Fear of all against all. Belief in general injustice. All of it, because human beings are unjust.[252]

A federation of states,[253] i.e. the establishment of a coercive institution that wills right in the relationship among states, with a rightful will equipped with coercive force, [290] will secure right among them. 1) It will not pronounce an unjust judgment lightly. 2) It will always have the power to execute its judgment.

Now if all states gradually entered into this federation, secure and perpetual peace would emerge. No one will dare to violate the known laws of the federation, [if] his self-preservation is dear to him.

In this manner, the right that also expresses itself in a federation of peoples[254] would ultimately come to apply everywhere. We might cast a glance into the actual world. Whoever is familiar with it will say, 1) [that] it is not at all impossible for the federation to pronounce an unjust verdict. 2) that in the federation, the voices (261) of the powerful prevail and are only concerned for their external interest. [3] that] the powers of the federation in the hands of the powerful members could themselves become a tool for the subjugation of the weaker ones. So strictly speaking, this would be an arming of what is contrary to right, against which we want to praise the current condition without a federation.

The usual alliances (one can well keep the foreign word here[255]) remain in the same federations for a time. They guarantee each other the integrity of their countries and rights. Often one wants to ask: who guarantees them against the guarantor?

Where does this condition of things come from? 1) From the incompleteness of right in the individual states (as remarked already). Travel among one another, commerce and various connections. This diversifies the relationships and makes the question of right more difficult. 2) Where then does this condition come from in turn? From injustice in the relationship among states, as a result of which everyone must be continually armed for war. Hence every profit is allowed, even only apparent profit, with no consideration calculated for the future. These states cut the tree down, only to reach its fruit more quickly. [They invest] no power for long-term operations that promise profit only much later. None for education to rightfulness and morality. This inner injustice again becomes externalized. The disordered power must be occupied with giving those sucked dry a means to enrich themselves again — through theft in other countries. The eyes of the nation should be steered away from contemplating internal wounds toward external glittering undertakings. [There is a] reciprocity of internal and external injustice. So — the external is brought about through the internal, the internal through the external: a circle. Where does one even begin? I say, with the *internal*. Only at first (262) construct the model[256] of a state completely just within itself. This state is to some degree very powerful. To some degree, it will tempt the neighboring states through the sight of its happiness to become as happy as it is.[257]

What[258] is the rightful relationship of states to one another presently? [291]

1) Every state has the right to self-preservation as a state. Indeed, the more honorable and educated the state is, the more valuable this preservation is to it, for it has a determinate, infinite plan for further education that only it knows, and that must proceed without disruption, lest the earlier gains are lost.[259] — Subjugated ones are thrown into an entirely new field and an entirely new plan.

2) This preservation is in no way guaranteed, other than through its own superiority. Thus the state must continually seek to achieve this superiority for the sake of its most valuable end, to always strive to supply itself, in order to

conquer around itself and to enlarge itself. It must not waste any opportunity, when it can act in security.[260] People have asked — not with total mockery — what do rulers gain from conquests? Can they somehow eat, drink, and clothe themselves better now? The matter stands thus: everyone has to expect an attack on his state's self-sufficiency as soon as it becomes possible. If it does not occur today, [it is only] because the other does not feel strong enough for it. It will then be better if *he* possesses this or that power than if his opponent does. Hence he should waste no time in acquiring it. Assuming his state loses one day, he would always blame himself (263) that this would not have occurred if he had not passed up the opportunity to increase the state's power. (This is what happens to many states, as experience shows.) A state must guard itself from this reproach while there is still time.

So it follows from the attack we assume to be certain. Is right on the state's side in this assumption? How could it not be, when it only considers that every state it faces must think and calculate in the same way as it does. I must obviously seek to incorporate its powers, if possible, even if it is only to arm itself with these others against the attack of a third [party].

Hence it follows that all are necessitated by right and by duty for self-preservation to view one another with suspicion constantly, always be armed, let no opportunity for strengthening themselves pass. For each gain that is passed up could someday be the reason for their downfall.

Thus, everyone views everyone else continually as without right. No right binds them, but only weakness. It alone guarantees peace. How? For the sake of universal mistrust, but where does this come from? Because no one is capable of guaranteeing to the other. (My theory of right is clear. Whoever does not provide a guarantee truly has no right. Only [292] the guarantee brings about the condition of right. [This ultimately means] incessant war of all against all, and this for the sake of right. In this condition of things because they have no secure right.)

Whether the rulers of all states have understood this situation clearly remains to be seen. But whoever thinks it through logically regards it this way. Of course, it has not been stated. Because if no one risks it and everybody believes, we do not risk it either, so this is to our advantage. Only (264) the philosopher is permitted to say it: the statesman, however, always has to deny it as a matter of his office.

From all this [arises] the phenomena of modern European history especially. [The] balance of power thereby replaces the guarantee. [As such, there is] no advantage in attacking. Now this is good to say to the other: see, I cannot direct anything against you. If the other believes it, he starts to feel safe and we assume their guarantee for ourselves. Why, then, have they not attacked one another yet? In the hope of victory. Hence, they personally must not believe very strongly in the balance of power.

That is where pointless[261] wars [begin]. But still some [states] are conquering provinces again. [Claiming,] this is mine from now on, and not the other's. Then we rest again and recover from the damage that this victory obviously has done to us until we find the right opportunity to start again. Thus, a *ceasefire* comes about, out of exhaustion from the ongoing warlike way of thinking. — For if you really make peace,[262] why do you keep the conquered provinces? Only states whose rulers have observed this most actively, in every other time period, and who did not miss any opportunity, have raised themselves. Those that passed up opportunities have sunk. One can offer to prove to each specifically where he failed, i.e. he did not take an opportunity where he could have taken the opportunity without danger. Because in this realm, there is no other mistake.

Where does all this come from? Because [there is] no guarantee, i.e. no rightful will equipped with force. For this would be the federation of peoples. This can be said. But how to get there? This remains an insoluble task for the divine (265) world government. — Until then: every state guards itself and protects itself until the last drop of blood because it does not know what could be tied to its survival. The state, I say. But the citizen obey the commands of his state, because for him these are the voice of the world government. If the rulers have made a mistake, they may bear responsibility for it. [293]

[Cosmopolitan Right]
*Cosmopolitan right*; question of right.
The foreigner is subjected to the remaining laws of the state, as far as they apply to him. He is no *active* member.
I have answered the genetic question — how to portray right in the world, the art of this portrayal, and set down both it and where its limits are, as well.[263] I conclude today therefore and hope that I have contributed somehow to the purely scientifically educated human being's ability to gain clear insight into these relations, too. Hence I conclude.[264]

# Notes

1. Pagination references are to GA II/13.197–293 in brackets, and J. G. Fichte, *Die späten wissenschaftlichen Vorlesungen III*, ed. Von Manz et al. (Frommann-Holzboog, 2012), 71–266, in parentheses. Supplemental citations in footnotes are from the student notes, cited by student notetaker's last name, from GA IV/6.7–70.
2. Beginning of the first lecture, 20 April 1812.
3. (HALLE) Chapter 1: What Type of Concept is the Concept of Right (7)
4. (HALLE) Above all it is important to capture the doctrine of right from the point of view of the *Wissenschaftslehre*, and to determine its place in the domain of knowledge according to general scientific concepts (7).
5. Zusammenleben
6. (HALLE) In a way a law of nature occurs here, for in knowledge, for example, no interruption of freedom is possible because no one can think something for another. It is made impossible by the natural existence of individuals.

Likewise the movements of the body, insofar as they are arbitrary are completely independent from the will and decision of another. This therefore would be following nature without the law of right (8).
7. (HALLE) Through nature perpetual war is given. Thus it is not a law of nature. Is it a law for freedom? Just as little. This is directed at freedom in immediate consciousness. This, however, is an individual: I should! All laws of freedom are laws for individuals. The law of right is for all (8).
8. Beginning of the second lecture, 21 April 1812.
9. Gesezmässigkeit
10. (HALLE) Here nature will become freedom itself and freedom will become nature. The laws are laws of nature and laws of freedom. These are united through the mediating term and this is quite certainly the law of right (9).
11. "Do not wrong anyone, and render to each his own." These imperatives stem from Ulpian's *Digests*, 1.1.10.1, but were formulated as imperatives by Kant in his *Metaphysics of Morals* (Ak 6:236–237). Kant's discussion also contains a first imperative of right, "to be an honorable human being [*honeste vivere*]."
12. "Do not do unto others what you would not want done unto you." The golden rule, expressed in its negative form.
13. Cf. Immanuel Kant, *Groundwork of the Metaphysics of Morals*, which contains many formulations of the categorical imperative cited here, including: "Act only in accordance with that maxim through which you can at the same time will that it become a universal law" (4:421). Also in the *Groundwork*, Kant rejects the "golden rule" as a proper moral principle: "Let it not be thought that the trite quod tibi non vis fieri etc. can serve as a norm of principle here" (4:430n).
14. Fichte's *Foundations of Natural Right* was published in two parts in May 1796 and September 1797. The first part of Kant's *Metaphysics of Morals* on matters of right was published in 1797.
15. Kant's *Perpetual Peace*, published 1795.
16. (HALLE) Only later his *Doctrine of Right* was published, which like much else by Kant (e.g. the *Anthropology*) was copied from old lecture notes and hence does not contain any of these refined concepts. But the introduction to it is superb. (9)
17. (FICHTE'S NOTE): No chapter from the doctrine of ethics. — It's true that you ought to will right; in your position you should not violate it, and should be just. — But what does this mean? In part, it means not to assault another's body and life. But in the case of things in another's sphere of efficacy? [Wirkungssphäre] Only to tolerate, to yield, to give in, as some have assumed. This is how injustice occurs. Thus, 1) one-sidedness and interferences, 2) an important and meaningful form of knowledge is completely overlooked, thus confusing judgments about objects lying so close to human beings.
18. "This law is not written, but born." Fichte is citing here Cicero's *Orator*, line 162, in which Cicero is describing natural law.
19. An inborn law
20. (HALLE) This lasts until they have reached a certain measure of formal

education; then the complications of their relationships demands artificial institutions to administer right (10).

21. "The war of all against all." Fichte cites here Hobbes's famous description of the state of nature from his *Leviathan* (1651), part 1, chapter 13.

22. The South Sea Islanders were considered by several thinkers at the time to represent human beings in a natural condition. Georg Forster, for example, describes the South Sea Islanders as in a condition of "profound barbarism," knowing only the "law of the strongest," such that they are "more inclined than any other people on earth to kill their fellow human beings at the first opportunity" (*Travels around the World during the Years 1772–1775*, p. 131). Kant describes them as a people devoted to letting their "talents rust" and "concerned with devoting [their] life merely to idleness, amusement, procreation — in a word, to enjoyment" (*Groundwork of the Metaphysics of Morals*, Ak 4:423).

23. Staatsrecht

24. Beginning of the third lecture, 23 April 1812.

25. (HALLE) First of all, the concept of right rests on the fact that several free beings coexist in a communal sphere, which transmits the efficacious action from one to another. Only if this precondition is met does the concept of right apply. *Understanding* and *will* have entirely different spheres, and no infringement of freedom is *possible* and hence no law of right either. But the question is: where does this coexistence come from? (12)

26. Selbstanschauung

27. Selbstbegriff

28. (HALLE) Neither in the whole nor in the individual can the human race raise itself to morality right at the start. From the condition of anarchy, where war of all against all is the motto, one must first pass through the condition of right. It is a condition of the factual possibility of the moral condition (13).

29. Beginning of Lecture 4, 24 April 1812.

30. substantialiter

31. (HALLE) Of course, in a certain manner everyone has his particular sphere and is in this sense separate from all others, i.e. *understanding* — into which no stranger can think — and the *will* — by means of which he solely determines the movements of his *own* body. Here we cannot speak of a disturbance at all. It is clear: first of all the limits of individuals are determined by the nature of being. Everyone has his body for himself. This is a willing and obedient organ of his own (14).

32. Naturverfügung

33. (HALLE) What is essential is a boundary for free action. The concept has to be put this generally, for if one were to limit it further, e.g. to only spatial relationships, this would be one-sided. By misunderstanding property, the doctrine of right has suffered the most acute damage. Here an artificial agreement through contract occurs. This is not the case with the body. The body of each is a natural property. This is all conceived of in the mere concept of right, i.e. in the thought of the coexistence of several beings without disturbance (15).

34. Das Willenbewegende

The Doctrine of Right (1812) | 207

35. Beginning of Lecture 5, 27 April 1812.
36. (CAUER) But who can ask this? Only a moral being, because the moral law is always addressed to each individual (16n).
37. (HALLE) 1) The constitution of right completes a closed organic community of individuals who know one another and in which I as an individual have the right and bind through my right those whose right I recognize. Hence I must know them directly or indirectly because of the reciprocal relationship (16).
38. Allheit
39. Beginning of Lecture 6, 28 April 1812
40. (HALLE) When one wants to secure personal freedom as a right, one must respect the personal freedom of others. Only through this recognition of the rights of others does one receive right in general (17–18).
41. For I), see page 137.
42. (HALLE) Desires and proclivities do not lie in the realm of right (18).
43. Ex professo
44. Macht
45. Nichtwollen des Unrechts
46. (HALLE) The community alone would have to be able to establish such a power and it has to want to establish one insofar as it wills right (19).
47. Beginning of Lecture 7, 29 April 1812.
48. Obergewalt
49. [FICHTE'S NOTE] If everyone is to be bound only through *right*, then only everyone can constitute this power. However, some are bound through coercion, fear, and so on, as was mentioned earlier.
50. (HALLE) But the condition is that such a power be established by those whose intention is no other than to achieve their own right. This would be against the form but qualitatively rightful, since it would have to occur with force against those who have not yet understood right (19).
51. Rechtssubjekt
52. Leistungvertrag
53. Staatsbürgervertrag
54. There are some unreadable words in Fichte's manuscript in this sentence, so we insert some terms here from the Halle student notes (p. 20) to make sense of it.
55. (FICHTE'S NOTE) Here everyone is a legal subject through the absolute freedom granted to him, through him being a free [being].
56. (HALLE) In personal freedom certainly, for here nature has divided [us] (21).
57. (HALLE) Through which power? There are two powers, moral and physical. The latter would have to be established (21).
58. Beginning of Lecture 8, 30 April 1812.
59. Beisammenstehen
60. (HALLE) The state has to see that no contracts but rightful ones are entered into (23).
61. (HALLE) By themselves, these principles lie at the transition from right

to morality in the realm of education to morality. For here it is necessary that one becomes accustomed to view one's will as holy and eternal — here what one calls *honor* enters the state; hence the declaration of will is called a *word of honor* (23).

62. "I do that you may do," a civil contract of services, an agreement to perform certain positive actions toward one another. "I give that you may give," a civic contract of goods, "I do that you may give," and "I give that you may do," civil contracts that mix service and goods exchange.

63. "I give"

64. (HALLE) Property consists in the exclusive right to an action. Afterwards they [the other philosophers] found that the object does not have a sole value but also [has a value as] work and so they divided property into property of objects and of powers. Wrong. [There is only] property in powers: the objects follow automatically. The objects can be considered insofar as they are objects of acting, for this is clearly only possible in objects (24).

65. "I don't do that, you don't do that."

66. "To a willing person, it is not wrong," a common law principle that holds that a person who willingly risks danger cannot sue for any resulting damages.

67. Beginning of Lecture 9, 1 May 1812.

68. (HALLE) [24] Above all, two investigations belong to the doctrine of right. 1) *What* the right of everyone is, 2) *How* this should come about.

The first is the matter, the second is the form. The matter expresses itself in property, the form in the civil condition [Staatsverein]. Both have to be preceded by an examination of the personal right of everyone, as property right is developed from this.

On personal right.

The ground lies in right itself. Personal right is the *original right* — here no contract occurs. The ground of original right is the *concept of freedom* alone. The freedom of many should coexist. The concept is formal, a character without any quantity: everyone should be free. What belongs to this concept of freedom? [25] Evidently, that everyone is a principle in the sensible world, a cause, not something caused, a second or subordinate member in a chain of occurrences. That is, 1) the whole effect calculated according to a basic concept has to be ground about by a free cause alone.

2) Success in the world of senses has to correspond to the freely devised concept. [CAUER: that success emerges from it exactly as it is conceived.] In *devising* the concepts no one can disturb the other, for understanding and will are completely separated from one another. This is forbidden by nature. Hence this is only noted here for the sake of completeness. In the relationship of right, the free being initially exists as an articulated body. In the realm of right, the body of the person is equal to freedom itself and thus the closer determination of *original right* follows:

I) The body viewed as a person must be the final cause of its determination to an effect. What everyone is capable of is determined by nature. What each is capable of he also has to be able to execute unhindered. Hence he may 1. not be used as a means for another's ends, and 2. no one else must impede him in his efficacy.

II) The efficacy that this makes possible in the sensible world must result from the purposive determination of the body. This is given by the inviolability of objects of efficacy.

Through the first determination, the inviolability of the body became a right; through the second, the inviolability of the objects.

III) But a concept of purpose presupposes cognition of the object which is being effected, and a certain concept of purpose presupposes a certain knowledge. To have this is up to each by himself. But if the object that someone has subjected to his concept of end is *changed*, this amounts to a disturbance of his freedom. Thus, objects have to remain in the condition in which someone has subjected them to his concept of a purpose, because it is with this shape that he calculates [how he achieves his ends].

IV) In this concept of an end, a person comprehends a future, which posits a duration for itself. The appearance comes to be only after some time has passed, for only in time can what was intended come about. Thus, with persons, every use of freedom implies a desire for a future, that is, self-preservation. [26] Hence this self-preservation belongs to personal right. The property contract could end up in a way that someone could not persist under it. By contrast, this principle is peculiar, in that it already lies in the first principle.

Taking all this together, we get the following as personal right. It consists of the continued existence of the reciprocal effect between the body of each and the sensible world of everyone. It ought to continue into the future and it should be determined solely through his concept.

This is merely a formal analysis of the concept of freedom. If one extends this, then the impact of each on the *entire* sensible world follows from it — without any determination of quantity. [CAUER: From this what follows is a dominion of each over the entire world] Now several enter and everyone demands it. Hence everyone's freedom must receive a quantity.

A distribution of objects of effects must occur, [since] everyone has to receive his own world. The original right that was expressed remains, the concept of quantity is merely applied to it.

Now the question is: what is everyone allowed to do in his world? With this we enter into the right of property.

69. 1) and 2) refer to the numeration in ¶11 of the FNR, 103.
70. Beginning of Lecture 10, 4 May 1812.
71. Erfassung
72. Wechselbegriff
73. erste prius
74. Wechselwirkung
75. (HALLE) So this contract issues the law and the norm according to which the objective sphere of the effect of each is to be structured and maintained. About the objects themselves it cannot decide on something that is perpetually valid. This constitutes the object of civil legislation as such (27).

76. (HALLE) Everyone must be able to live from his work or else the contract would end. Hence the conditions are:
The kind of work must be such that one can live from it in this association. Enough room and sphere must be accorded to each for the work.
Others must maintain him if he does work but nonetheless cannot live. In a well-established state no one is poor and in it charity and such are a sacrilege. Everyone must be able to subsist. Because he demands it as a matter of right, one must know that he may work in his sphere. (27).
77. W.d.E.W. (Was das Erste Wäre).
78. Beginning of Lecture 11, 5 May 1812.
79. Rechtsbundes
80. Principiat
81. (HALLE) It is part of freedom that the individual come up with his concept of end himself with absolute inner freedom, that it not be imposed on him through external necessity. This is apparently the case here. His end is accordingly the effect of natural necessity and of the artificial institution of the state. Or, I have said the rightful condition is the factual condition of the moral. The moral end lies in the higher world. True freedom is the capacity for supersensuous ends that are not forced [on one] through necessity. A human being who must work to live and who pays taxes does not have freedom. Or, I said above, the establishment of a government consists in making the will contrary to Right impossible. So one's own will is the second effect of the will of the state. We are not speaking at all about a free design of ends from a higher world (28–29).
82. (HALLE) If someone doesn't have this [freedom], he did not enter the contract. Otherwise, the reflective will would stand under an iron mechanism. Without such an institution the state is not a relationship of right but a coercive institution (29).
83. Zwangsanstalt
84. Beginning of Lecture 12, 6 May 1812.
85. (HALLE) No supervision occurs over the use of this freedom; for the form of freedom would thereby annihilate itself, for its true nature consists in developing on its own and by itself. However, direction and schooling can be given for this self-development. To care for this is the duty of the state, since the entire relationship of right is only to be viewed as an education to morality (29).
86. Moses
87. Exodus 20:10
88. Exodus 23:10–11
89. anschaulich machen
90. (HALLE) The first product of the higher freedom (of the state) is the creation of this freedom itself, that I no longer do it for the state's sake but for that of morality. Here freedom is everywhere its own reason and posits itself. The inner spirit of obedience lies with the individual (30).
91. Werdens
92. Dressur
93. aufzuheben

94. Beginning of Lecture 13, 8 May 1812.
95. (HALLE) The highest end would of course be for the human being to be completely free (32).
96. Beginning of Lecture 14, 11 May 1812
97. See FNR: "All organization takes place . . . Accordingly, we must discuss" (189).
98. Or "real estate:" Grundeigentum
99. (HALLE) With regard to property in the land, the contrary system claims a right not to work on the soil but to exclude everyone else from it. Thus, only a negative right. But where does this right come from? Only from contracts with others and in particular with those who claim the same right to their use of the soil. But these individuals don't even work their soil themselves, but *transfer* it to others on the *condition* that they will work for them. He pays others for the work [on the soil]. He does not regard these others as equal to him in right at all. In this contract, a natural inequality of human beings is posited. A class is posited that is never to have claim to property in land. So no equal rights for everyone. Rather only those who obligate and those who are obligated (34).
100. (HALLE) Thereby two classes of human beings are posited — *those* who *exclude* all others from their ostensible property, and *those* who *are admitted* conditionally. The former cannot say anything to justify [their ability to exclude] other than that they got there first. –but by seeing the field first they did not come to possess it! The entire demand here can only be grounded in power and force, which is the extent to which they remain in possession. Here too a contract would have the ground the so-called property in land, specifically a contract *among land owners* — they mutually respect their so-called property and *all stand together* if one should be harmed. Precisely in this earlier contract their power lies. Power gives no right. Right of the stronger is merely an ironic ridicule of right. By having the right to exclude all others, owners of land become protectors of the soil against all foreign force for their own interest, but not for the sake of the rights of man (34).
101. (HALLE) It was fortunate that the conquerors were Germanic tribes, standing under a leader. This is how monarchies came about (35).
102. (HALLE) In Old Europe the same came about through the colonies, but here republics emerged because they [the Germanic tribes] did not have attachment to their leader (35).
103. FNR 190–91: "Every agriculturalist . . ."
104. Beginning of Lecture 15, 12 May 1812.
105. (HALLE) [35] By having received the field to use for a particular end, the farmer is not at all justified in preventing another's use of the same field which is not harmful to his end. [For example,] one can dig for metals under his field. Every farmer should be able to live off of his labor. He should also be able to afford to pay taxes from the products of his fields in the condition in which they stand now. What remains after he pays his taxes is his absolute property. It is his absolute freedom which the state must protect.
First, what about the fruits that grow wild in the soil, which the owner does not

work on? They belong to the owner, whose end certainly is [36] not to work the soil, and based on this end the wild fruits thus grow.

Secondly, what about the land that is not distributed? Here we have to distinguish between the substance, the land itself, which belongs to the state, which is the state's property in the land. In terms of its accidents, that which grows on it must be used, for otherwise it spoils. Either this belongs to the state, or it is too insignificant and fall to whoever appropriates it: res nullius cedit primo occupanti [Unowned things go to the first occupant]. The first is called a rule. But wherever there is uncultivated wild growth, this must make way for culture. Thus the rule should not remain, but should fall away and be replaced by the lawful tax on the lawful owner.

106. (HALLE) [Mining] stands in the middle between raw materials and organized nature. But nature does not let itself be led here. Metals cannot be built but [must] be looked for, and where to find them of course follows a rule. They are searched for. He will be driven best [to find them] by an eternally persisting society which can sustain the loss through [the promise of] eventual gain. The state is such a society. Individual workers would thus enter into the class of wage laborers. The state also must find itself in sole possession of precious metals. The same with all similar things that are not created but have to be looked for, e.g. gems, etc. All these things are under the state's sovereign ownership. The main condition is that a law has to exist about all these things. The state has to make pronouncements on them. Otherwise it is res nullius. [Unowned thing] (36).

107. (HALLE) [36] Animals have a value for human beings. So there must be a law. The substance of the animal has a value, as does its accidents: the power. Above all, one must have dominion over animals and preserve them according to a rule. Therefore, the animal must be lent out for exclusive use. So who does the animal belong to?

It moves freely. The property would have to be designated differently. First, which animals can be exclusive property and which cannot. Tame animals are never without a master. Which owner does each animal belong to? On this, the law has nothing definite to say. With the horses of the army the state has a symbol. Now the animal speaks for itself by running into its master's stable.

With other animals the place is decisive, such as [in the case of] fishing ponds. [But it is] different with wild animals, and hence the basic law of the state: that this one has a master is excluded in this case. They also have a value, but are a common good. [37] They fall under the analogy of fruits growing wild. Either they are included in an element, which is not subjected to the human being, as [for example] with water. Or they live in an element shared with human beings. They are either not harmful such as birds, [or harmful]. Wild fishery has to be conducted exclusively by individuals. For the sake of order, there are [designated] realms [for fishing] here. (Small birds are insignificant.)

Of a completely different type are harmful animals, actual game, especially larger game. These fall under the protective function of the state: the state should not let them suffer. This is the actual end of *hunting*. — Hence hunters are called to hunting as a civic matter. This game can well be used when it is dead. It can therefore be anticipated that the state doesn't need to expend power on it: hunters [permitted to hunt in a certain area], who have their property. But the contract with them is different from the one with fishermen. Fish don't cause damage, but the hunter must shoot under [the threat] of penalty. Thus this is an obligating contract.

108. Beginning of Lecture 16, 13 May 1812.

109. (HALLE) Until now we have only dealt with how to gain the *products* of nature, and we can call all those who make this their business *producers*. But the products as nature provides them are not useful and usable for the human being. They have to be treated further and those who are occupied with this can be called artisans in the broadest sense. Thus, a second estate. Nature does not do anything further. Its striving must be killed off. Next, art — the understanding — provides the concept of unity, according to which the parts are to be put together. The material is nothing other than the dead carrier of the understanding's concept (37).

110. Grundstand

111. Verarbeiter

112. Feldbauer

113. Landbauer

114. (CAUER): The state of production must determine the number of artisans in the state, because they all must be able to live. — If the set number is overshot, this is thoroughly contrary to right — whether it is politic and prudent is not to be decided here. The artisans are made necessary through a surplus of products, since the left-overs should be enjoyed, but not for free — they should be earned. As a matter of fact, this is how artisans emerged (38n).

115. Labor

116. Day laborer

117. Work

118. Craftsman

119. (HALLE) The state must have permitted everyone to be an artisan. The state must be able to calculate how many hands it can free from farming and how many can live off of it. (38)

120. (HALLE) Secondly, this contract contains the guarantee of the preservation of the artisan. (38)

121. vogelfrei

122. Beginning of Lecture 17, 14 May 1812.

123. (HALLE): The existence of the estate is conditioned by the law of saving time and power. But where no time and power is saved, it does not occur (39)

124. Provision

125. Beginning of Lecture 18, 15 May 1812.

126. Pentecost Sunday was on 17 May 1812.

127. Cf. Kant, *Critique of the Power of Judgment*, 5:432, 5:434n. (HALLE): Several have established this measure, even Kant (40).

128. (HALLE) Besides the fact that under these conditions the continuation of the human race would be impossible and no state could be thought of, human

life in this fashion would have no value because it would lack self-sufficient free being, and would instead dissolve in its subsistence. It would only form a *circle* (40).

129. Lebenkönnen
130. Cf. Kant, *Critique of the Power of Judgment*, 5:434n.
131. Beginning of Lecture 19, 25 May 1812.
132. (HALLE) The factors to determine the value of all things according to the basic measure therefore are: 1. The production of all agriculture, 2. The sum of necessary taxes, 3. The number of farmers (42).
133. Beginning of Lecture 20, 26 May 1812.
134. Mässgen, an antiquated measure of volume.
135. Fabrikant
136. Lösung
137. Beginning of Lecture 21, 27 May 1812.
138. A reference to the issuing of paper money or *Assignats* by the Constituent Assembly early in the French Revolution to pay off debts. From 1789 to 1796, there was tremendous inflation on the Assignat, which forced the Revolutionary government to set fixed exchange rates and maximum prices for commodities.
139. (HALLE) Whoever hands over a sign that does not represent [goods] is a money forger, be he an individual or the state itself (43).
140. (HALLE) It is clear that I have assumed: all food will be eaten between one harvest and the next. That cannot seriously be my opinion; for in this way the acquisition and expansion of national wealth would be impossible. For this capital is needed. *So about capital* (43).
141. (HALLE) The question is whether the state could secure property under the condition of metal money (44).
142. Realisationscomtoir
143. Halbheit
144. (HALLE) It drives itself around in a circle — it is not quite a good and not quite money (45).
145. Groschen
146. Beginning of Lecture 22, 28 May 1812.
147. (HALLE) In recent times we have talked a great deal about the freedom of trade and business. Thus we demand it so that most individuals rely on it and so that many goods come to market. Through supporting the freedom of business it becomes *cheaper* — for the possessor of money — by making money more expensive (45).
148. Unclear reference. Perhaps Fichte is referring back to Lecture 18 from 15 May where he critiques the idea that trade is simply about preservation of life (see 163).
149. Herr Amtmann: an administrative position in Germany that collected taxes and maintained law and order in a particular town.
150. [FICHTE'S NOTE] Paradox. The product of labor becomes cheaper, labor more expensive. When national wealth increases, the manufacturer gives more goods for his portion; the goods have become more expensive. However,

he does not need as much time to deliver this larger quantity as he previously needed to deliver smaller (173) quantities, [since] his *time* devoted to work is more expensive. Previously he finished 1 portion in 3 hours, worth 4 hours of life. Now he must deliver 2 portions for 4 hours of life. His goods are therefore cheaper. But he needs only 2 hours. His work is more expensive: now he maintains 2 hours of life for 1 hour of work; previously he had to provide ¾ of an hour work for 1 hour of life.

With the farmer [it is] the opposite ratio: his goods are worth more in other goods. [They are worth] less in labor time of the artisan. For the livelihood of 4 hours, he only works 2 hours now, whereas he had to work 3 hours previously. But the ratio remains correct if the farmer also needs only 2 hours to earn this living, when previously he needed 3. Both gain, and nature bears the cost.

To secure the value of the products of labor. How to do [this]. [An established] *standard*. Amidst fluctuating value, the standard persists.

151. GrundKapital
152. Fichte's manuscript continues, "and for the . . ." The end of the clause is unreadable.
153. Absolute Schöpferkraft
154. [FICHTE'S FOOTNOTE] "It will be brought up here, but just do not conclude it." Who says that? I am not thinking of any conclusion. — The transport will have to be paid for right away, and the thought; and therefore that has to be available somewhere until the harvest, and with enough left over. Because no one wants to go hungry himself. Thus also in the world [more generally]. Consider the world as a state, as this is the case under the concept of world money.
155. Beginning of Lecture 23, 29 May 1812.
156. GeldKapital
157. Landgeld
158. (HALLE): The interest of each is not the subject here, but the limit of the tax exemption could be shortened (49).
159. Aufforderungen
160. Beginning of Lecture 24, 2 June 1812.
161. (HALLE) What one does not need is simply too expensive, even if it is free. Each good has to be posited by human need and not the other way around (49).
162. Kunstfertigkeit
163. (HALLE) From this condition both states gain leisure, gain national wealth. This is how nations divide their wealth. In this way the trade between different states is a gain for humanity in general (50).
164. (HALLE) Now we can indicate a measure for the value of metal money: assuming that one of these trading states uses metal money, the situation is as follows: whatever the goods would cost abroad, the goods that I give him in exchange are worth accordingly less. For example, foreign silk would cost 100,000 Reichstaler — now the goods I would give for it are worth this much to me. Thereby a measure is determined and the carrying off of money from the nation

is pre-empted. Money is posited at the value that it has abroad.

In this manner, the state has a means to regulate the exchange of gold and silver in national money and to collect gold and silver for itself. Why does the state need it? It becomes goods and we have gained felicitous goods (51).

165. (HALLE) Here a property of a rather different nature has quietly emerged. The property which consists in the product of labor is not so unconditional, for the product is to be exchanged and the state retains a claim to it. The state lays claim to what is material; because it is grain you should sell it; only the form is property. The value is property. If it became money, it would no longer be of any concern to the state. And so we get a third type of property. Freedom, leisure, and the representation of freedom and of leisure — money. This would be absolute property. The remaining would only be relative property. Above we asked how property should be indicated. With relative property, an indication of money cannot work. It could only be immediate possession. But one cannot carry it on oneself. There must be another representative. This is everyone's house, or one's suitcase and such things. These are signs of absolute property. What I have in my dwelling is my property and I do not provide proof of it. The nature of absolute property is also that it went through the whole process in the state, and all civic duties were discharged. What I have in my house, the state does not need to know.

Here this remark: Only now I join with the perspective of the ordinary doctrine of right. They have understood material objects, they have also counted a great deal as material property (51).

166. Beginning of Lecture 25, 3 June 1812.

167. (HALLE) The material that was analyzed provides the ground of civil legislation. My property reaches this far, and yours this far. Personal right of course belongs here, for it is the foundation of the whole. Personal freedom does not have to be specially guaranteed, because it is not accidental but substantial. Hence a violation of the personality is a crime. How a personal attack should be punished belongs to criminal law. Here belongs the doctrine of self-defense" (52).

168. (HALLE) The state is no moral person. Rightfulness is its morality. The state has to protect my property to the death. Hence when the state is not present I may represent its office. But if I have a conscience about this, I can let it be. I can gift, but not the state. The condition is always that the state cannot defend me. Then I have to call for help myself. This should be committed to memory. Of course, the right to self-defense occurs all the more when the attack happens directly to the person. As when I murder someone and say he attempted to rob me. I have to put myself in a position to collect witnesses. Everyone would have to report the self-defense himself and it would be possible to prove that he did not call for help (52).

169. Nature of the cause

170. (HALLE) Self-defense is the worst case, hence [the need] to call for help. Those who have been called to help cannot do anything but separate those who are fighting. For now the guilty party and the damaged party are back in the

hands of the authorities. It appears that most laws limit the right to defense too much. We demand proof that is not possible. We are not in a position to observe. Also the state must not make defense harder by prohibiting weapons. Such dispositions are based more in pity for the criminals than in considerations of the rights of humanity (53).

171. (HALLE) When two free beings come into the situation — through mere natural causality — that one of them cannot survive — one of them has to perish (53).

172. (HALLE) In the familiar [doctrine of] natural right, [there is a common example] that there are two persons on a plank of wood [in the ocean] which can only carry one of them. I do not know how they got on there. Jakob hence assumes [that they are] on a barge. [Ludwig Heinrich Jakob, 1759–1827, Professor of Philosophy in Halle.] We have pronounced a formula of a case that we do not even know. Some have said: they should assess who can yet do more good. The matter is not a matter of right at all. Both cannot stand next to each other at all. Nature reigns. So nature may decide or, if you will, God, through which nature is an expression of his will. What happens is not to be regarded as the result of the free will. If two citizens run into such a situation, one of them has to report the occurrence. And the state retains the right to investigate, but the citizen does not have [the burden] to prove (53).

173. (HALLE) I only speak of property acquisition within the state, not acquisition in which the state comes to be, nor the expansion of the borders of the state. This belongs in the section about the original property contract. Also not about exchange. Rather, I am only talking about the case in which one's property really is diminished and that of the other really is increased, or where the property changes its nature (53).

174. (HALLE) Wealth can increase or decrease through gifts but not through exchange. It is transformed only by swapping relative for absolute property.
1) Civil privileges stand under the immediate influence of the state — hence it must know about such an exchange. 2) Such privileges must be used. Hence the state can examine whether he who is to receive such a privilege is capable of using it. 3) Through the money he receives, the seller of such a privilege removes himself from the supervision of the state, but everyone in the state has to be able to live. Hence the state will retain the supervision [to ensure] that the seller henceforth remains able to live through the contract — either through the seller retaining a part of the privilege or by placing the money under the supervision of the state — and will have to adhere to fulfilling the contract.
Privileges with regard to money. Why not with regard to privileges? This would be a declaration to the state [of the intention] to exchange the mutual obligations in the state. The state would have to verify whether they may exchange.
Or *gifting*. Here too there are two cases. Either: 1) the given property is a civil privilege, so naturally the state has the right to verify.
It is a demand of the state to substitute this position with this person; the state would [otherwise] do this on its own. The requirement for the state to perform [is that] it leave it to it. The case will hardly occur in our state.

2) The gifting of absolute property. Here there are also two cases: either during one's lifetime or through a will or the doctrine of inheritance (54).
175. Beginning of Lecture 26, 4 June 1812.
176. Literally "nobody's thing," an object with no owner, according to Roman law.
177. First occupant
178. By intestacy
179. Obervormundschaft
180. (FICHTE'S NOTE) First principle: the establishment of a coercive institution and the coercive institution itself is rightful, for it is the condition under which alone the individual has rights and through this alone that a rightful condition, in which rights are secured, is possible. It belongs to securing [them]. Hence the *punishing power* [is necessary], concerning the origin of which [there are] doubts.
181. Beginning of Lecture 27, 5 June 1812.
182. Zügellosigkeit
183. Wohlseyn
184. Welteinrichtung
185. Rechtlichkeit
186. Vorbild
187. (HALLE) The criminal law as such is that which has an effect [das Wirkende]. (57)
188. (HALLE) The punishment should actually never occur. Punishment is always an evil. It shows that the legislation is not reaching its end. The state thereby steps out of its natural course — the commonwealth is thereby damaged (57)
189. Strafgesetz
190. Strafrecht
191. Beginning of Lecture 28, 8 June 1812.
192. Unrechtlichkeit
193. Cf. FNR pp. 245–47.
194. (HALLE) The right of punishment cannot be *immediately* deduced from reason, only mediated by criminal law. Some nonetheless attempted to do this — they spoke of an *absolute* criminal right; namely, they believed that one is permitted to treat everyone in line with his own behavior, so long as one assumed the principle: every maxim of free action has to be capable of becoming a universal law. Of course, he who acts according to this [maxim] will not offer anything against it. But the principle only proves that it is not contrary to right, *positive* rightfulness is not proven. This is merely a *heuristic* principle that cannot be assumed as a universal basic principle. This is a rather decisive proof of the impossibility of proving that an action is contrary to right (58).
195. Vernunftgründe
196. (HALLE) But someone can cause damage purely because of inattentiveness. Here there is not a greedy will but no will at all. Here no positively illegal law is to be suppressed, but a coercive law must produce the will that is lacking.

The precondition is that he pay attention to himself. Here a missing will is to be filled in based on the will that is assumed in the careless person, [so] that he will not damage himself. You should care for the security of the other as much as for your own. What you do to others through your carelessness, you do to yourself. Here damages and compensation are enough. Whoever has nothing has to work it off.
Here the law should look to the determining grounds [of action]. Hence the judge should examine the state of the will (jurists distinguish culpa [fault from carelessness] and dolus [fault from malice]). Some have conceived this as though one has to seek the *moral determining grounds* of the action. Incredible error. (58)
197. Roman legal terms meaning "fraud" or "intentional fault" and "negligence."
198. Besonnenheit
199. Schadenersatz
200. The crux of the argument
201. Abbüssungsvertrag
202. (HALLE) What kind of will do these [cases] display? Apparently one that cannot be moved through principle forcing the will. But the capacity to be coerced is actual civil virtue. The state counts on self-love from all — the love for the neighbor only follows from this. Whoever lacks this self-love in the described manner, is unable to be a member of the state, because he cannot provide security. Civil right is lost here. An exception could possibly be made for the stubbornly careless who only damages property — here one can recover through [his] wealth until he too does not have anything left. (59)
203. Hochnothpeinliches Gesetz
204. Thus, a dual criminal law and criminal court. The first one could call civil criminal law; the punished [party] remains a citizen. The second [one could call] the actual criminal law, the [criminal] right very strictly speaking (59).
205. Beginning of Lecture 29, 9 June 1812.
206. (HALLE) How is such a will recognized? 1) [In the case] when the punished [party] repeats the same violation. To double the punishment would be good in a state where one expects that the punishment is not executed, where the criminal is captured once after several crimes. This is not what the state of reason expects. If the previously applied punishment does not show the effect, one must judge the criminal to have no will left at all and hence he falls with the latter into a category [of people] who desire injustice for injustice's sake (59).
207. (HALLE) *High treason* is when someone to whom the force of the state was partially transferred uses it against the state itself. Only the private person can rebel. The agent of the state commits high treason (60).
208. (HALLE) But it is different internally and subjectively, when the community and those who govern have achieved morality. Here there is a higher right; the moral characteristic imposes a duty on each human being. Even if it is not against right, it is still against duty. He can yet become free and moral. So his life is to be spared. His life has the sole vocation to be formed to the condition of

morality (61).
209. Beßerungshaus
210. Lebensstrafe
211. Rasenden
212. Freiheitsäußerungen
213. (FICHTE'S NOTE) The absolute assumption of freedom and the casting off of human beings without is a strictly rightful orientation in thinking, deserving of all honor. Whoever has not elevated himself to this orientation, but explains all appearances in humanity as psychological phenomena according to a natural law, is (235) deeply contemptible. In him not even the completely common legality has emerged. Both, however, are one-sided. Whoever does not misconceive the realm of psychological necessity at all, and views this assumption as the means of education for freedom, ordered by reason, and limits it to the sphere in which it can be such a means, unites everything in the higher viewpoint of morality. The moral person has no viewpoint at all, other than that of a moral education and perfection of himself and others. For him, this is the purpose of life.
214. (HALLE) One has to separate morality and legality perfectly, and merely regard the latter as a means for the former. There never is a right to immorality. Whoever makes psychological excuses for it deeply humiliates himself. Both standpoints must be united in the standpoint of morality. The moral person must treat everyone as free, and he may not do so as a gift (61).
215. Gemeinen Wesen
216. Beginning of Lecture 30, 10 June 1812.
217. (HALLE) We have posited the principle: no one has right until he has assured all their rights from his side, until he has proven to him the impossibility that he is capable of violating right. This can only occur through a will that actively wills right (61).
218. Oberherrschaft
219. (HALLE) The law and government have to be just and act justly in all cases. This solely through a will that is the will of right itself. This will must reign both in general in legislation and in particular in its application. First of all, the law has to be applied in all cases and second of all the right [law].
Every will carries cognition with itself. Hence an absolute cognition of right that can be felt and secondly the strong desire for that which has been recognized as right. The citizen must be able to say: a principle rules over us transformed into a will that governs. Now this will is sovereignty — no one in the state may have a different will. This will that should reign should be equipped with a power that no other in the state can resist. The constitution of right is therefore one in which such a will be established (62).
220. "If you do right, you will be king," Horace, *Epistles* 1.1.59–60.
221. (HALLE) We want to be subject to the will of right, then we are free. Everyone has and retains the right here to demand accountability from administrators.
This will is sovereign because no one can adopt another will without losing

right. This goes without saying when he is the will of right. "If you do right, you will be king" [rex eris si recte facies] (63)
222. Beginning of Lecture 31, 11 June 1812.
223. Triebfeder
224. Words on the page
225. gesetzvorschlagende
226. Kollegium
227. Kunststück
228. On the ephorate, see FNR pp. 141–64.
229. A reference to the French Revolution.
230. A reference to Napoleon, crowned emperor after the French Revolution.
231. (HALLE) But the masses do not will that the best rule because most selfishly wish for a *weak* government (65).
232. Menschgewordne Recht
233. (HALLE) So the task cannot be solved through human freedom, but is a task for the divine world government. Progress in reason and morality is the only possible means to make the present rulers bearable. Only in this way one can say that the origin of the supreme power is inexplorable, [but] we should subject ourselves but not blindly. Otherwise one disturbs the quiet progress of time (65).
234. The section on the police, which does not appear in the student notes, was likely omitted in the lectures.
235. StaatsGrenzenvertrag
236. (HALLE) We also add in family right.
The elements of the state are commonly not individual physical persons, but *families*. The family does not invoke right against itself as little as the individual does. Only when family members go to court with one another, the family is therefore dissolved, [and] we can talk of family fight. So it does not belong in the theory of right. By the way, I touch on it in the doctrine of ethics and here refrain from the investigation altogether.
The family stands partially in a natural, partially in a moral relationship. When right applies in the family, it takes one step down. But also [a step] up in case states themselves appear against one another and become person[s]. This is *international right* and cosmopolitan right (66).
237. Beginning of Lecture 32, 15 June 1812.
238. (HALLE) 1) Every individual who finds another like him in his sphere of effect has the right to force him to citizenship for his right's sake. If he already is a citizen of a state, the guarantee is that he subject himself to his state. It follows from this: whoever is in no state at all can be forced to subject himself to the state or to leave its proximity. If one applies this principle generally it follows that all human beings will eventually melt into one state assuming there was [only] one state (66).
239. (HALLE) But if we imagine 2) that it was not the case [that there was only one state], but that different states had emerged in different places without knowing one another, no one would be able to coerce the other to enter into his

state; because he could provide him security in another manner. That this really happened this way is made likely by the natural boundaries of the earth (66).
240. (HALLE) Because 3) the relationship of right only speaks of human beings who stand in a reciprocal relationship with one another. Certainly not about those who do not know each other at all (66).
241. (HALLE) But now it is posited 4) that two citizens from different states encounter one another. Each one will demand security from the other. Each will propose: subject yourself to the same law as me. But both will say: that is not possible. The reciprocal right, enter into my state, cancels itself, but the absolute right to demand the guarantee of each other does not cancel itself. The states of these two citizens would have to unify to provide the guarantee in the name of the citizens. Only thus do states take up the position of trading with one another. Thus [67] 1) all relationships among states are based on the relationships among citizens. States are concepts, artificial products, and have no relationships at all. So only border states can come into a relationship of right with one another. 2) This relationship among states is very easy. They guarantee one another the security of [their respective] citizens. Both promise each other security of the citizens. Formula of the contract: I make myself responsible for all damages that my citizens do to yours if you do the same. 3) Such a contract must be actually entered into in time; it is not contained in the civil contract (66–67).
242. (HALLE) 5) What is the material content of this contract? In the civil contract a negative contract: not to attack the rights of others, and a positive one: to protect the rights of the others through the government. In the contract among states only the negative contract occurs. So the subject of the contract among states only extends to property rights, specifically in the objective and material sense that no one take an object from the other. Commerce and exchange cannot occur among the different states — naturally the personality has to remain untouched here as well (67).
243. Russia introduced a new tariff on trade with France in 1812, which France took to be a cause for war.
244. (HALLE) 6) In this contract, something else is present as well: the reciprocal recognition of the two states as states.
A state which is refused this recognition has to coerce it. It must subjugate the other state. For in the refusal of recognition lies the refusal of all right (67).
245. (HALLE) 7) It follows naturally from this that a state may subjugate or force into a rightful constitution a neighboring people who lacks an authority, or drive it out of the vicinity (67).
246. (HALLE) 8) Neighboring states reciprocally guarantee the property right of their citizens. But nothing should be guaranteed as a matter of right where right is unclear. So the borders of the state must be precisely divided; one has to know which of the two attacked the other. Borders result from the nature of the matter. Not just with national borders but also special rights such as fishery, hunting, etc.
This contract is easy. Through possible trade among states, however, it can become more complicated (67).

247. Beginning of Lecture 33, 16 June 1812.
248. (HALLE) Through mere *trade* among states, the relationship can become more diverse. On the whole, the relationship is easy — merely negative. You deliver this and that good to me for this price at this and that time. Original and higher courts of right do not take place here. If you do not want [to trade under these conditions], then do not. Amongst the citizens themselves, things are different (68)
249. data
250. (HALLE) Later, there would still be a relationship constructed among the states. It will be quite good if a state has emissaries in the other, who conduct the business of the one in the other state. Such [an emissary] represents the self-reliant and independent state, which has sent him. Thus, he cannot be subject to the laws of the other state. Otherwise, he could not act according to the will of his state. But he is subject to the police laws of the foreign state. Only he is not subject to the civil laws. He also is not a citizen. Who can and should be punished? In general, if he does not carry out what he is meant to, oversteps his business, the foreign state does not become his judge. He did not come as citizen, but also not as [an] emissary. He is sent back and the offended state has the right to ask for punishment. If one state does not keep to his contract with the other, war follows (68).
251. Bündnisse
252. (HALLE) Formally the right to war is clear: where there is no relationship of right through contract, violence must reign. But the right of war is, like all coercive right, infinite. The state on which one declares war has no right at all. Even if it asks for peace, why should one trust? The natural purpose of war cannot be any other but the destruction of the other state, i.e. to subject its citizens to the foreign law.
Technically it is the armed state that conducts war, not the unarmed citizen. He is not our enemy; he shall become our citizen. One must maintain him, otherwise one hurts oneself. The disarmed soldier too is no longer our enemy. Our ordinary wars are no wars at all, which is not understood well at all. Also they are not waged for the sake of right. [Consider, for example,] how [to understand the purpose of] hand-to-hand combat itself? The purpose is not to beat to death. It is a goal of the armed to drive one another away. It probably will come to combat, and one kills so as not to be killed. Here the relationship of the right of necessity [applies]. But the just cause should win. (68)
253. Staatenbund
254. Völkerbündnis
255. Fichte uses the word *Alliancen*, which comes from twelfth-century French.
256. Muster
257. (HALLE) The just cause should be equipped with the largest power. If one could bring about [69] a state of states [Staatenstaat], a government of states, right among states would be ensured. We would call such an alliance [Vereinigung] a federation of states [Staatenbund]; through the help of this one the most rights would be assigned to the biggest power. The formula: we all

promise to eradicate with joint force the state which does not recognize the dependence of one of us or which does not keep the contract that was entered into. The union of states becomes judge within its sphere, either between two states that belong to the union or between one from the union and an alien [one].
If all peoples were to enter into such a union, perpetual peace through justice would occur (68–69).
258. Beginning of Lecture 34, 17 June 1812.
259. (HALLE) Each state has the right to self-preservation. The more honorable and educated it is, the holier this right is (69).
260. (FICHTE'S NOTE) Principle. As much power as possible to attain it, with an assault [they] surely expect.
261. ungründlichen
262. (FICHTE'S NOTE) Trust.
263. (HALLE) Cosmopolitan right.
Should no one come over the border of the state? Oh yes! He retains cosmopolitan right: all positive rights are based in a contract. The foreign visitor did not enter into a contract, but has the original human right. — Everyone has the capacity for right, even he who is not part of a contract. He has this right to offer himself for a contract. From this follows the right to enter the foreign state. The original question was the genetic one: how right is to be portrayed in the world. Or an art to portray it. This we have done (70).
264. After his conclusion, Fichte announces his lectures on the *Theory of Ethics*, which would begin on 29 June 1812. See theory of Ethics, trans. Benjamin Crowe (State University of New York Press, 2016).

# Glossary

| | |
|---|---|
| Abbild | likeness |
| Abdruck | copy |
| Anerkannt | recognized |
| Anforderung | demand |
| Angesicht | view |
| Anregen | to excite, to stir |
| Anschauung | intuition |
| Ansicht | viewpoint, perspective |
| Auffassen | perceive |
| Aufgehen | to blossom, unfold, unfurl |
| Ausbilden | to cultivate |
| Bedingt | conditioned |
| Belehren | instruct |
| Besinnung | deliberation |
| Besonnen | deliberate |
| Besonnenheit | reflection |
| Bestimmung | vocation, determination, calling, occupation |
| Bild | image |
| Bilden | to compose, form, educate |
| Bildlich | metaphorical |
| Bildnis | portrait |
| Bildung | cultivation, education |
| Darstellen | to represent |
| Dasein | existence |
| Eingreifen | intervene |
| Einsicht | insight, understanding |
| Eintreten | to emerge |
| Ensprechen | correspond to |
| Erfassen | to realize |
| Erkenntnis | cognition |
| Erleuchtung | illumination |
| Erschaffen | creating |
| Erziehung | education, upbringing |
| Ewig | eternal |
| Forderung | requirement |
| Gegensatz | antithesis |
| Gegenstand | object |
| Geistig | spiritual |
| Gesetzmäßigkeit | lawfulness |
| Gesetzmäßig | lawful |
| Gesicht | idea |
| Gestalt | form |

| | |
|---|---|
| Gestaltet | formed |
| Gestaltung | formation |
| Grundsatz | principle |
| Handeln | action |
| Hervorbringen | generate, bring about |
| Kollegium | assembly |
| KulturStaat | cultured state |
| Lehre | doctrine |
| Machen | produce |
| Menschengeschlecht | humankind, human race |
| Menschheit | humanity |
| Musterbild | model image, design |
| Nachbild | after-image |
| Ohngefähr | chance |
| Räte | councils |
| Rechtlichkeit | rightfulness, rightful status |
| Rechtlich | rightful |
| Rechtsgültigkeit | rightful legality |
| Rechtssubjekt | legal subject, subject of right |
| Rechtswidrig | contrary to right, unjust |
| Schriftstellerei | writing |
| Staatsbeamten | government officials |
| Staatsgewalt | government, state power |
| Staatsverwaltende Behörde | governmental administrating agency |
| Staatsverwalter | government administrators |
| Staatsverwaltung | public administration; government administration |
| Stamm | descent, tribe, population, state |
| Stand | estate |
| Stoff | substance |
| Übersinnlich | supersensory, supersensible |
| Unendlich | infinite |
| Unmittelbar | immediate, unmediated |
| Unrecht | contrary to right, unrightful |
| Unverstand | ignorance |
| Urbild | original image |
| Urrecht | original right |
| Verfahren | way of proceeding |
| Verkehrtheit | folly, foolishness |
| Verstand | intellect, understanding |
| Verständnis | comprehension |
| Verwaltungsbehörde | government agency |
| Voraussetzung | assumption |
| Vorbild | model |

| | |
|---|---|
| Vorhanden | present |
| Vorwelt | prehistory |
| Wahrnehmungen | perceptions |
| Wesen | essence |
| Wilde | savages |
| Willkür | arbitrary will |
| Wirken | functioning, effecting |
| Wirksamkeit | efficacy |
| Wirkung | effect |
| Wirkungssphäre | sphere of efficacy |
| Zweck | end, goal |

# Index

*abbild* (likeness), 225
*abdruck* (copy), 225
absolute property, 183
absolute right, 148–149
action. *See handeln*
*Addresses to the German Nation* (AGN) (Fichte, J. G.)
  educational theory in, 53n45
  for English language readers, 1
  fragmentary structure of, 4–5
  geopolitical themes in, 3
  humanity in, 3
  philosophy in, 3–4
  texts prior to, 2–5
after-image. *See nachbild*
AGN. *See Addresses to the German Nation*
agriculture
  property contracts for, 179, 211n105, 212n107
  in *The Republic of the Germans at the Beginning of the 22nd Century Under the Fifth Magistrate*, 63
*anerkannt* (recognized), 225
*anerkennung* (recognition), 10
*anforderung* (demand), 225
*angesicht* (view), 225
*anregen* (to excite/stir), 225
*anschauung* (intuition), 40, 225
*ansicht* (viewpoint, perspective), 225
antithesis. *See gegensatz*
"Application of Eloquence" (Fichte, J. G.), 1–2
  eloquence in, 15–16
  legality in, 16
  morals in, 16
  preachers in, 16
  science in, 16
  stages of humanity in, 3
apprentices and apprenticeship, in *Lectures on the Vocation of the Scholar*, 112, 114, 122
arbitrary will. *See willkür*
art, in "Application of Eloquence," 16
artists, in *Lectures on the Vocation of the Scholar*, 114–115
assembly. *See kollegium*
assumption. *See voraussetzung*
*auffassen* (perceive), 225
*aufgehen* (blossom, unfold, unfurl), 225
*ausbilden* (to cultivate), 225
Austrian Empire, Bonaparte military success against, 2
authoritarianism, Fichte, J. G., and, 5, 9
authority, in *Patriotic Dialogues*, 24

*The Basis of Right* (Fichte, J. G.), 10
*bedingt* (conditioned), 225
*belehren* (instruct), 225
Berlin, Germany, French occupation of, 5
*besinnung* (deliberation), 225
*besonnen* (deliberate), 225
*besonnenheit* (reflection), 219n198, 225
*bestimmung* (vocation, determination, calling, occupation), 225
Beyne, Carl Friedrich von, 2
*bild* (image), 225
*bilden* (to compose, form, educate), 225
*bildlich* (metaphorical), 225

*bildnis* (portrait), 225
*bildung* (cultivation, education), 127n47, 225
blossom. *See aufgehen*
Bonaparte, Napoleon, 2
*Book for Mothers* (Pestalozzi), 47–49
bring about. *See hervorbringen*
burial practices, public burial ceremonies, 80–84

calling. *See bestimmung*
capital, in property contracts, 171, 177–179, 214n140
Catholics, Catholicism and, in *The Republic of the Germans at the Beginning of the 22nd Century Under the Fifth Magistrate,* 67, 76–78
censorship, in *The Republic of the Germans at the Beginning of the 22nd Century Under the Fifth Magistrate,* 59–60, 64–65
chance. *See ohngefähr*
*Characteristics of the Present Age* (Fichte, J. G.), 3, 8
chauvinism. *See* cultural chauvinism
Chivalry Studies, 71
Christianismus, 88n73
Christianity
  Protestant, 4
  in *The Republic of the Germans at the Beginning of the 22nd Century Under the Fifth Magistrate,* 67–68, 76–80
  universal Christian Church, 77
citizens, citizenship and
  as farmers, 57–58, 60
  property rights and, 222n246
  in *The Republic of the Germans at the Beginning of the 22nd Century Under the Fifth Magistrate,* 57–58, 60
  requirements of, 62
  as soldiers, 57–58, 60
civic life, in *Patriotic Dialogues,* 22

civil contract, 9
  coercive law and, 190, 195–196, 201, 218n180
  concept of right and, 141
  cosmopolitan right and, 204
  criminal law and, 188–191
  in *Doctrine of Right,* 184–204
  ephorates and, 197
  executive power and, 196
  in German Constitution, 194–199
  loss of civil rights and, 190–192
  morality and, 185–187, 193, 195
  punishment and, 188–189, 192–193
  Right of Nations and, 199–204
  of services, 207n61
  sovereignty and, 196
  well-being and, 186
civil rights
  civil contract and, 190–192
  Fichte, J. G., on, 10–11
  loss of, 190–192
classroom teacher. *See lehre; lehrer*
*Closed Commercial State* (Fichte, J. G.), 8, 10
coercive law, 190, 195–196, 201, 218n180
cognition. *See erkenntnis*
commercial estates, property contracts for, 162–163
communal sphere of effects, 132–133
comprehension. *See verständnis*
concept of right, 206n33
  allness as element of, 137
  as artificial institution, 142–143
  civil contracts, 141
  communal sphere and, 206n25
  conditions of, 132–133
  constitution of right, 136
  in *Doctrine of Right,* 132–143
  freedom in, 134, 142
  moral law in, 142
  morals in, 136, 206n28
  necessity of thinking in, 134
  power in, 139

principles in, 141
property contracts and, 137–138, 148–149
property in, 137
realization of, 135–137
as shared concept, 192
subject of right, 140–141
*Wissenschaftslehre* and, 141
conditional law, 130
conditioned. *See bedingt*
constitution of right, 136, 207n37
constitutional rights, Fichte, J. G., on, 10–11
contracts. *See also* civil contract; property contract
in *Doctrine of Right* (1812), 143–147
essence of, 143–144
negative contract of omission, 144–145
*Contractual Basis of Government* (Fichte, J. G.), 9
contrary to right. *See rechtswidrig; unrecht*
*Contribution to the Correction of the Public's Judgment on the French Revolution* (Fichte, J. G.), 2
copy. *See abdruck*
correspond to. *See einsprechen*
cosmopolitan nationalism, in *Patriotism and Its Opposite*, 3
cosmopolitan right, 204
cosmopolitanism, in *Patriotic Dialogues*, 22–23
councils. *See räte*
cowardice, in *The Republic of the Germans at the Beginning of the 22nd Century Under the Fifth Magistrate*, 64–65
creating. *See erschaffen*
criminal law
civil contract and, 188–191
dual, 219n204
*Critique of Pure Reason* (Kant), 31
cultivation. *See bildung*

cultural chauvinism, 1
culture. *See kultur*
cultured state. *See kulturstaat*

*darstellen* (to represent), 225
*dasein* (existence), 225
Delbrück, Friedrich, 50
deliberate. *See besonnen*
deliberation. *See besinnung*
demand. *See anforderung*
descent. *See staam*
design. *See musterbild*
determination. *See bestimmung*
*Distinction Between Morality and Right* (Fichte, J. G.), 9
doctrine. *See lehre*
doctrine of nature, 131
*Doctrine of Right* (1812) (Fichte, J. G.), 205n16. *See also* property contract
civil contract in, 184–204
communal sphere of effects in, 132–133
concept of right in, 132–143
conditional law in, 130
contract in, 143–147
doctrine of nature as distinct from, 131
freedom in, 130–131, 133
natural law in, 129–130
natural right in, 131–132, 217n172
practical law in, 130
preamble, 129–132
as pure science, 129
right of reason in, 131
scope of law in, 130
universal rule in, 133
*Wissenschaftslehre* and, 129, 204n4
*Doctrine of Right* (Kant), 7
translations of, 8–9
dual criminal law, 219n204

Eclectics, 41
*Economic Right* (Fichte, J. G.), 10

educate. *See bilden*
education. *See also bildung; erziehung; specific topics*
  implementability of, 106–107
  in *Lectures on the Vocation of the Scholar*, 102–103, 108–112, 115–117
  property contract and, 153–154
  in *The Republic of the Germans at the Beginning of the 22nd Century Under the Fifth Magistrate*, 61, 64
  of women, 64
educational philosophy, 3–4
educators. *See also* scholars; teachers
  in *Lectures on the Vocation of the Scholar*, 106–108
effect. *See wirkung*
effecting. *See wirken*
efficacy. *See wirksamkeit*
egoism, in *Lectures on the Vocation of the Scholar*, 119
egoistic stage, of humanity, 3
*eingreifen* (intervene), 225
*einsicht* (insight, understanding), 4, 7, 225
*einsprechen* (correspond to), 225
*eintreten* (to emerge), 225
eloquence
  in "Application of Eloquence," 15–16
  unmediated, 16
Encyclopedists, 41
end. *See zweck*
English, as language
  *Addresses to the German Nation* in, 1
  *Foundations of Natural Right* in, 1
Enlightenment, 4
ephorate theory, 5, 10–11
  civil contract and, 197
*erfassen* (to realize), 225
*erkenntnis* (cognition), 22, 39, 225

*erleuchtung* (illumination), 225
*erschaffen* (creating), 225
*erzieher* (person responsible for raising a child), 127n50
*erziehung* (education, upbringing), 127n47, 225
essence. *See wesen*
estate. *See stand*
eternal. *See ewig*
evil
  in *Lectures on the Vocation of the Scholar*, 120
  in *The Republic of the Germans at the Beginning of the 22nd Century Under the Fifth Magistrate*, 69–70
*ewig* (eternal), 225
existence. *See dasein*
experience
  in *Patriotic Dialogues*, 24, 26–27
  in *The Republic of the Germans at the Beginning of the 22nd Century Under the Fifth Magistrate*, 55

families, 221n236
Fichte, Immanuel Hermann, 51n23
Fichte, Johann Gottlieb
  authoritarian reading of, 5
  authoritarianism of, 9
  on civil contract, 9
  on civil rights, 10–11
  conceptual approach to, 1–2
  on constitutional rights, 10–11
  ephorate theory, 5, 10–11
  exile of, 3–4
  Hobbes and, 8
  on leisure, 10
  on nationalism, 5
  Pestalozzi as influence on, 11n7
  Philosophy of Right for, 7–11
  political philosophy of, 1
  state of nature for, 8
  on state power, 10–11
  University of Berlin and, 5–7
  University of Jena and, 1, 6–7

University of Königsberg and, 3–4
Fichte, Johann Gottlieb, works of. *See also Doctrine of Right* (1812); *Wissenschaftslehre*
  *Addresses to the German Nation*, 1, 3
  "Application of Eloquence," 1–3
  *The Basis of Right*, 10
  *Characteristics of the Present Age*, 3, 8
  *Closed Commercial State*, 8, 10
  conceptual approach to, 1–2
  *Contractual Basis of Government*, 9
  *Contribution to the Correction of the Public's Judgment on the French Revolution*, 2
  *Distinction Between Morality and Right*, 9
  *Economic Right*, 10
  *Foundations of Natural Right*, 1
  *Gesamtausgabe*, 4, 12n13
  *Lectures on the Vocation of the Scholar*, 1, 6, 89–125
  *On the Nature of the Scholar and Its Manifestations*, 6
  *Patriotism and Its Opposite*, 1
  *Property and Political Economy*, 9–10
  *The Republic of the Germans at the Beginning of the 22nd Century Under the Fifth Magistrate*, 1, 4, 55–88
First Conversation, in *Patriotic Dialogues*, 21–34
FNR. *See Foundations of Natural Right*
folly. *See verkehrtheit*
foolishness. *See also verkehrtheit*
  in *Lectures on the Vocation of the Scholar*, 124–125
force of right, 153
*forderung* (requirement), 225
form. *See bilden; gestalt*
formation. *See gestaltung*
formation of understanding. *See verstandesbildung*
formed. *See gestaltet*
Forster, Georg, 206n22
*Foundations of Natural Right* (FNR) (Fichte, J. G.)
  conceptual approach to, 1
  for English language readers, 1
  original right in, 8
  right as concept in, 7–8
freedom
  absolute assumption of, 220n213
  absolute inner, 210n81
  concept of, 208n68
  in concept of right, 134, 142
  in *Doctrine of Right* (1812), 130–131, 133
  forms of, 210n85
  in *Lectures on the Vocation of the Scholar*, 116, 118
  moral, 150
  original right and, 208n68
  property contract and, 138, 153, 181
  quantum of exclusive use of, 148
French Revolution, 214n138
  Fichte, J. G., on, 2, 8
functioning. *See wirken*

Gall, Franz Joseph, 31, 51n21
*gegensatz* (antithesis), 225
*gegenstand* (object), 225
*geistig* (spiritual), 225
generate. *See hervorbringen*
German, as language, *Patriotic Dialogues* in, 25
German Constitution
  civil contract in, 194–199
  goal of, 75–76
  in *The Republic of the Germans at the Beginning of the 22nd Century Under the Fifth Magistrate*, 66–67, 75–76

German Empire, Bonaparte military successes against, 2
Germany, as republic
  confederations in, 17n3
  constitution of, 4
  national identity in, 25, 45
  national pedagogy, 11n7
  religion in, 67–74, 76–84
  unification of, 73
*Gesamtausgabe* (Fichte, J. G.), 4, 12n13
*gesetzmäßig* (lawful), 225
*gesetzmäßigkeit* (lawfulness), 225
*gesicht* (idea), 7, 91, 225
  in *Lectures on the Vocation of the Scholar*, 90, 126n8
*gestalt* (form), 226
*gestaltet* (formed), 226
*gestaltung* (formation), 226
Gliwitzky, Hans, 51n23
goal. *See zweck*
God, in *Lectures on the Vocation of the Scholar*, 91–94
goodness, in *Patriotic Dialogues*, 21–22
goodwill, in *Lectures on the Vocation of the Scholar*, 96, 100
governance
  in *Patriotic Dialogues*, 21–22
  in *The Republic of the Germans at the Beginning of the 22nd Century Under the Fifth Magistrate*, 58, 62
government. *See staatsgewalt*
government administration. *See staatsverwaltung*
government administrators. *See staatsverwalter*
government agency. *See verwaltungsbehörde*
government officials. *See staatsbeamten*

governmental administrating agency. *See staatsverwaltende behörde*
*Groundwork of the Metaphysics of Morals* (Kant), 205n13
grundsatz (principle), 226

*handeln* (action), 226
Hegel, Georg Wilhelm Friedrich
  *Elements of the Philosophy of Right*, 7–8
  *Phenomenology of Spirit*, 10
  on recognition, 10
*hervorbringen* (generate, bring about), 226
higher education, in *The Republic of the Germans at the Beginning of the 22nd Century Under the Fifth Magistrate*, 56, 58, 67, 85n14
history, philosophy of, 3
Hobbes, Thomas, 131, 206n21
  Fichte, J. G., and, 8
Holy Roman Empire, 2
*How Gertrude Teachers Her Children* (Pestalozzi), 53n45
human race. *See menschengeschlecht*
human rights, 8
human welfare, 179
humanity. *See also menscheit*
  in *Addresses to the German Nation*, 3
  egoistic stage of, 3
  in *Lectures on the Vocation of the Scholar*, 116
  moral stage of, 3
  in *Patriotic Dialogues*, 23–24, 26
  purpose of, 23–24, 26
  sociability and, 84n2
humankind. *See menschengeschlecht*
Humboldt, Wilhelm von, 5

idea. *See also gesicht*

in *Lectures on the Vocation of the Scholar*, 108
idealism, subjective, 7
illumination. *See also erleuchtung*
 in *Lectures on the Vocation of the Scholar*, 105–106
image. *See bild*
immediate. *See unmittelbar*
independence, in *Patriotic Dialogues*, 22, 24
infinite. *See unendlich*
insight. *See einsicht*
instruct. *See belehren*
intellect. *See verstand*
intellectual education, in *Patriotic Dialogues*, 44, 46, 48–49
intervene. *See eingreifen*
intuition. *See also anschauung*
 in *Lectures on the Vocation of the Scholar*, 119
 in *Patriotic Dialogues*, 40–41, 45–49

Jakob, Ludwig Heinrich, 217n172
Jews, in *The Republic of the Germans at the Beginning of the 22nd Century Under the Fifth Magistrate*, 86n39

Kant, Immanuel
 *Critique of Pure Reason*, 31
 *Doctrine of Right*, 7–9
 *Groundwork of the Metaphysics of Morals*, 205n13
 *Metaphysics of Morals*, 9
 moral philosophy of, 8
 *Towards Perpetual Peace*, 131
 on truth, 36
 writing craft of, 37–38
knowledge, in *Lectures on the Vocation of the Scholar*, 89–94, 126n4
*kollegium* (assembly), 226
*kultur* (culture), 6

*kulturstaat* (cultured state), 226

labor, property contracts and, 149–150, 181
language, languages and, in *Patriotic Dialogues*, 40, 48
Lauth, Reinhard, 51n23
law. *See also specific topics*
 coercive, 190, 195–196, 201, 218n180
 conditional, 130
 criminal, 188–191, 219n204
 in *Doctrine of Right* (1812), 129–130
 moral, 142
 natural, 129–130
 practical, 130
lawful. *See gesetzmäßig*
lawfulness. *See gesetzmäßigkeit*
leadership, in *Patriotic Dialogues*, 27
*Lectures on the Vocation of the Scholar* (Fichte, J. G.), 1, 6
 action in, 97
 apprentices and apprenticeship in, 112, 114, 122
 artists in, 114–115
 divine imagery in, 93, 95
 education in, 102–103, 108–112, 115–117
 educators in, 106–108
 egoism in, 119
 enthusiasm in, 101, 104
 evil in, 120
 fine arts in, 109–110
 First Lecture, 89–97
 foolishness in, 124–125
 Fourth Lecture, 111–117
 frame of mind in, 98
 freedom in, 116, 118
 *gesicht* in, 90, 126n8
 God in, 91–94
 goodwill in, 96, 100

government administration in, 106
humanity in, 116
idea in, 108
illumination in, 105–106
implementability of education, 106–107
independent knowledge in, 94
inquiry in, 90
intuition in, 119
knowledge in, 89–94, 126n4
law of knowledge in, 92–93
negation in, 122–123
practical knowledge, 91
religion in, 98
religious mind in, 98
scholars in, 89, 94, 99, 104–106, 115–120
scientific world in, 104
second age of the world in, 109
Second Lecture in, 97–105
self-sufficiency in, 121
sensual world in, 98–99, 103–104, 109–110
spirituality and spiritual world in, 101, 117–118
supersensory in, 91–92, 95, 97–101, 106, 111–112, 115–119
teachers in, 120–121
Third Lecture, 105–111
truth in, 96
legal subject. *See rechtssubjekt*
legality. *See also* law
  morality as distinct from, 220n214
*lehre* (doctrine), 226
*lehrer* (classroom teacher), 127n50
Leibniz, Gottfried Wilhelm, 41
leisure, 164
*Leviathan* (Hobbes), 206n21
likeness. *See abbild*
Locke, John, 8, 41

*machen* (produce), 226

marriage, in *The Republic of the Germans at the Beginning of the 22nd Century Under the Fifth Magistrate,* 60
Marx, Karl, 6
Maximum of Intelligence, 30–31, 34
*menscheit* (humanity), 226
*menschengeschlecht* (humankind, human race), 226
metal money, 172–176, 215n164
metaphorical. *See bildlich*
*Metaphysics of Morals* (Kant), 9
model. *See vorbild*
model image. *See musterbild*
moral freedom, 150
moral law, in concept of right, 142
moral stage, of humanity, 3
morals, morality and
  in "Application of Eloquence," 16
  civil contract and, 185–187, 193, 195
  in concept of right, 136, 206n28
  families and, 221n236
  legality as distinct from, 220n214
  in *The Republic of the Germans at the Beginning of the 22nd Century Under the Fifth Magistrate,* 70, 72
  rightfulness and, 216n168
*Die Musen* (journal), 6
*musterbild* (model image, design), 226

*nachbild* (after-image), 226
nationalism. *See also* cosmopolitan nationalism
  Fichte, J. G., on, 5
Native North Americans, 32
natural rights, 8
  in *Doctrine of Right* (1812), 131–132, 217n172
nature. *See* doctrine of nature
negation, in *Lectures on the Vocation of the Scholar,* 122–123

nobility, in *The Republic of the Germans at the Beginning of the 22nd Century Under the Fifth Magistrate*, 72–74

object. *See gegenstand*
occupation. *See bestimmung*
*ohngefähr* (chance), 226
*On the Nature of the Scholar and Its Manifestations* (Fichte, J. G.), 6
*opus supererogativum*, 22
original right, 147, 208n68

paper money, 214n138
*Patriotic Dialogues*
  authorial devices, 31
  authority in, 24
  civic life in, 22
  cognition in, 22, 39
  collective German language in, 25
  cosmopolitanism in, 22–23
  depravity in, 38
  experience in, 24, 26–27
  First Conversation, 21–34
  German national identity in, 25, 45
  goodness in, 21–22
  governance in, 21–22
  heroism in, 35
  immediate life in, 40
  independence in, 22, 24
  intellectual education in, 44, 46, 48–49
  intuition in, 40–41, 45–49
  leadership in, 27
  literary structure of, 20
  Maximum of Intelligence in, 30–31, 34
  *opus supererogativum* in, 22
  paternalism in, 24
  patriotism as practice in, 21–22, 25, 27–28, 32, 34–35
  Pestalozzi in, 45–48
  as physical product, 28–29
  preamble, 19
  preface, 20–21, 50n5
  Prussian identity in, 25
  Prussian patriotism in, 25, 33, 35–36
  purpose of humanity in, 23–24, 26
  reason in, 35–36, 49
  religiosity in, 22
  role of language in, 40, 48
  science in, 24, 26–27, 31, 35–36, 38–43
  Second Conversation, 34–50
  self-communication in, 47–48
  self-reflection in, 36
  self-sufficiency in, 22
  self-understanding in, 36
  spiritual life in, 40
  teachers in, 41
  truth in, 43
  unity in, 29
  *Wissenschaftslehre* in, 35–36, 39–41
  writing in, 28–29
patriotism
  as practice, 21–22, 25, 27–28, 32, 34–35
  in Prussian Empire, 25, 33, 35–36
*Patriotism and Its Opposite* (Fichte, J. G.), 1
  cosmopolitan nationalism in, 3
pedagogy
  child-centered, 11n7
  German national, 11n7
perceive. *See auffassen*
perceptions. *See wahrnehmungen*
perpetual war, 205n7
person responsible for raising a child. *See erzieher*
personal right, 146–147, 208n68
perspective. *See ansicht*
Pestalozzi, Johann Heinrich
  *Book for Mothers*, 47–49
  child-centered pedagogy, 11n7
  educational philosophy of, 3–4
  Fichte, J. G., influenced by, 11n7

*How Gertrude Teachers Her Children,* 53n45
in *Patriotic Dialogues,* 45–48
"Random Thoughts in a Sleepless Night," 53n45
*Phenomenology of Spirit* (Hegel), 10
philosophy, philosophical systems and
in *Addresses to the German Nation,* 3–4
educational, 3–4
of history, 3
of Pestalozzi, 3–4
speculative, 5
in *Wissenschaftslehre,* 1
political economies, property contract and, 174
political philosophy, of Fichte, J. G., 1
Popular-Philosophers, 41
population. *See staam*
portrait. *See bildnis*
positive performance contract, 145
power
in concept of right, 139
executive, 196
state, 10–11
practical law, 130
preachers
in "Application of Eloquence," 16
in *The Republic of the Germans at the Beginning of the 22nd Century Under the Fifth Magistrate,* 58–59, 82
prehistory. *See vorwelt*
present. *See vorhanden*
*Preußischer Hausfreund* (journal), 3
produce. *See machen*
productive estates, 213n109
property contracts for, 156–158, 161
property, property rights and, 211n99. *See also* property contract

citizenship and, 222n246
in concept of right, 137
as exclusive right to action, 208n64
*Property and Political Economy* (Fichte, J. G.), 9–10
property contract
absolute property, 183
absolute right and, 148–149
affirmative expression of, 145
for agricultural industries, 179, 211n105, 212n107
analysis of, 147–184
application to state, 154–156
capital in, 171, 177–179, 214n140
for commercial estates, 162–163
concept of right and, 137–138, 148–149
deductions in, 156–158
education and, 153–154
for exclusive property, 158–159
force of right in, 153
foreign trade in, 180–183
form of state and, 153
foundations of, 148
freedom and, 138, 153, 181
fundamental measures in, 162–163
global wealth and, 180
inert money and, 176
interest elements in, 176–179
labor in, 149–150, 181
metal money and, 172–176, 215n164
money requirements in, 170–176
moral freedom and, 150
national wealth and, 165–170
original right in, 147
ownership rules in, 158
positive performance contract and, 145
product of work, 165–170
for productive estates, 156–158, 161, 213n109
proof for, 157

quantum of exclusive use of freedom in, 148
repayment conditions in, 174
state resources and, 155
taxation and, 168–170, 177–178
trade imbalances in, 170
undesignated property in, 182
value of work in, 165–170
prostitution, 55–56, 60
Protestant Christianity, 4
Protestantism, 78
Prussian Empire
national identity in, 25
in *Patriotic Dialogues*, 25, 33, 35–36
patriotism in, 25, 33, 35–36
"The Prussian Gallant," 51n21
public administration. *See staatsverwaltung*
public burial ceremonies, 80–84
punishment
civil contract and, 188–189, 192–193
in *The Republic of the Germans at the Beginning of the 22nd Century Under the Fifth Magistrate*, 59, 65–66

quantum of exclusive use of freedom, 148

*räte* (councils), 226
reason
in *Doctrine of Right* (1812), 131
in *Patriotic Dialogues*, 35–36, 49
*recht* (right)
human rights, 8
in literary works, 7–8
natural rights, 8
original right, 8
*rechtlich* (rightful), 226
*rechtlichkeit* (rightfulness, rightful status), 226
*rechtsgültigkeit* (rightful legality), 226

*rechtssubjekt* (legal subject, subject of right), 226
*rechtswidrig* (contrary to right, unjust), 226
recognition. *See anerkennung*
recognized. *See anerkannt*
reflection. *See besonnenheit*
religion, religiosity and
in *Lectures on the Vocation of the Scholar*, 98
in *Patriotic Dialogues*, 22
*The Republic of the Germans at the Beginning of the 22nd Century Under the Fifth Magistrate* (Fichte, J. G.), 1, 4
agriculture in, 63
apparel and attire in, 82–84
Catholics in, 67, 76–78
censorship in, 59–60, 64–65
Chivalry Studies, 71
Christianismus, 88n73
Christianity in, 67–68, 76–80
churches in, 79–80
citizens as farmers in, 57–58, 60
citizens as soldiers in, 57–58
citizenship requirements in, 62
cowardice in, 64–65
diplomacy and foreign relations in, 55, 75–76
divorce in, 55–56
education of women in, 64
egoism in, 70
elders in, 81–82
estates in, 57
evil in, 69–70
experience in, 55
German Constitution in, 66–67, 75–76
German provinces in, 63
governance structure in, 58, 62
governors in, 57–59
higher education in, 56, 58, 67, 85n14
Jews in, 86n39
jurists in, 56

marriage in, 60
ministers in, 58
morality in, 70, 72
nobility in, 72–74
notable persons in, 56–57
philology, 66
preachers in, 58–59, 82
prostitution in, 55–56, 60
Protestantism, 78
public burial ceremonies in, 80–84
punishment in, 59, 65–66
religion of Germans in, 67–74, 76–84
scholars in, 57
school systems in, 61
senate in, 57
tax system in, 62–63
teachers in, 61–62, 65
trade in, 56, 61
unification of Germany in, 73
universal Christian Church in, 77
urban citizens in, 59
urban environment in, 60
war in, 58, 85n15
women in, 55–56, 60, 64–65, 82
requirement. See *forderung*
right. See also concept of right; *recht*
  absolute, 148–149
  constitution of right, 136, 207n37
  cosmopolitan, 204
  force of right, 153
  morality and, 216n168
  natural, 8, 131–132, 217n172
  original right, 147, 208n68
  personal, 146–147, 208n68
Right of Nations, 199–204
rightful. See *rechtlich*
rightful legality. See *rechtsgültigkeit*
rightful status. See *rechtlichkeit*
rightfulness, 216n168. See also *rechtlichkeit*
Rousseau, Jean-Jacques, 6
  on general will, 8

scholars, in *Lectures on the Vocation of the Scholar*, 89, 94, 99, 104–106, 115–120
*schriftstellerei* (writing), 226
science, scientific principles and
  in "Application of Eloquence," 16
  in *Doctrine of Right* (1812), 129
  in *Lectures on the Vocation of the Scholar*, 104
  in *Patriotic Dialogues*, 24, 26–27, 31, 35–36, 38–43
  in *Wissenschaftslehre*, 5
*Science of Knowledge*. See *Wissenschaftslehre*
Second Conversation, in *Patriotic Dialogues*, 34–50
self-reflection, in *Patriotic Dialogues*, 36
self-sufficiency
  in *Lectures on the Vocation of the Scholar*, 121
  in *Patriotic Dialogues*, 22
sensual world, in *Lectures on the Vocation of the Scholar*, 98–99, 103–104, 109–110
"Some Lectures on the Vocation of the Scholar" (Fichte, J. G.), 6
speculative philosophy, 5
sphere of efficacy. See *wirkungssphäre*
Spinoza, Baruch, 39
spiritual. See *geistig*
spiritual life, in *Patriotic Dialogues*, 40
*staam* (descent, tribe, population, state), 226
*staatsbeamten* (government officials), 226
*staatsgewalt* (government, state power), 226
*staatsverwaltende behörde* (governmental administrating agency), 226

*staatsverwalter* (government administrators), 226
*staatsverwaltung* (public administration, government administration), 226
*stand* (estate), 226
state. *See staam*
state power. *See also staatsgewalt*
    Fichte, J. G., on, 10–11
stir. *See anregen*
*stoff* (substance), 226
subject of right. *See rechtssubjekt*
subjective idealism, in
    *Wissenschaftslehre*, 7
substance. *See stoff*
supersensible. *See übersinnlich*
supersensory. *See also übersinnlich*
    in *Lectures on the Vocation of the Scholar*, 91–92, 95, 97–101, 106, 111–112, 115–119

Tartars, 32
taxation, property contract and, 168–170, 177–178
teachers. *See also* education; scholars
    in *Lectures on the Vocation of the Scholar*, 120–121
    in *Patriotic Dialogues*, 41
    in *The Republic of the Germans at the Beginning of the 22nd Century Under the Fifth Magistrate*, 61–62, 65
to compose. *See bilden*
to cultivate. *See ausbilden*
to emerge. *See eintreten*
to excite. *See anregen*
to realize. *See erfassen*
to represent. *See darstellen*
*Towards Perpetual Peace* (Kant), 131
trade
    property contracts and, 170
    among states, 223n248
tribe. *See staam*

truth
    Kant on, 36
    in *Lectures on the Vocation of the Scholar*, 96
    in *Patriotic Dialogues*, 43

*übersinnlich* (supersensory, supersensible), 226
understanding. *See einsicht; verstand*
undesignated property, 182
*unendlich* (infinite), 226
unfold. *See aufgehen*
unfurl. *See aufgehen*
unity, in *Patriotic Dialogues*, 29
universal Christian Church, 77
University of Jena, 1, 6–7
University of Königsberg, 3–4
unjust. *See rechtswidrig*
unmediated eloquence, 16. *See also unmittelbar*
*unmittelbar* (immediate, unmediated), 226
*unrecht* (contrary to right, unrightful), 226
upbringing. *See erziehung*

*verfahren* (way of proceeding), 226
*verkehrtheit* (folly, foolishness), 226
*verstand* (intellect, understanding), 226
*verstandesbildung* (formation of understanding), 127n45
*verständnis* (comprehension), 226
*verwaltungsbehörde* (government agency), 226
view. *See angesicht*
viewpoint. *See ansicht*
vocation. *See bestimmung*
*The Vocation of the Scholar* (Fichte, J. G.), 1
*voraussetzung* (assumption), 226
*vorbild* (model), 226
*vorhanden* (present), 226
*vorwelt* (prehistory), 226

*wahrnehmungen* (perceptions), 226
war
  perpetual, 205n7
  in *The Republic of the Germans at the Beginning of the 22nd Century Under the Fifth Magistrate*, 58, 85n15
  right to, 223n252
way of proceeding. See *verfahren*
well-being, 186
*wesen* (essence), 226
*willkür* (arbitrary will), 226
*wirken* (functioning, effecting), 226
*wirksamkeit* (efficacy), 226
*wirkung* (effect), 226
*wirkungssphäre* (sphere of efficacy), 205n17, 226
*Wissenschaftslehre (Science of Knowledge)* (Fichte, J. G.), 52n28
  concept of right and, 141
  *Doctrine of Right* (1812) and, 129, 204n4
  in *Patriotic Dialogues*, 35–36, 39–40
  philosophical system in, 1
  scientific principles in, 5
  subjective idealism in, 7
women, in *The Republic of the Germans at the Beginning of the 22nd Century Under the Fifth Magistrate*, 55–56, 60, 64–65, 82
writing. See also *schriftstellerei*
  Kant and, 37–38
  in *Patriotic Dialogues*, 28–29

Zeune, Johann August, 50
*zweck* (end, goal), 226

www.ingramcontent.com/pod-product-compliance
Lightning Source LLC
Chambersburg PA
CBHW030759040526
R18238400001B/R182384PG44191CBX00001B/1